CONTENDING RHETORICS

CONTENDING RHETORICS

Writing in Academic Disciplines

GEORGE L. DILLON

INDIANA UNIVERSITY PRESS

Bloomington and Indianapolis

The paper used in this publication meets the minimum requirements of American
National Standard for Information Sciences—Permanence of Paper for Printed
Library Materials, ANSI Z39.48-1984.

Manufactured in the United States of America

Library of Congress Cataloging-in-Publication Data
∞™
Dillon, George L., date.
Contending rhetorics : writing in academic disciplines / George L.
Dillon.
p.   cm.
Includes bibliographical references and index.
ISBN 0-253-31743-6 (cloth)
1. English language—Rhetoric—Study and teaching.
2. Interdisciplinary approach in education.   I. Title.
PE1404.D54   1991
808'.042'07—dc20   90-25572

1 2 3 4 5   95 94 93 92 91

For My Teachers
Who Initiated Me into Academic Discourse

CONTENTS

PREFACE

This is a book for scholars and teachers, and perhaps even a few deans. It draws together discussions of writing within disciplines as diverse as history and biochemistry, attempting to find common issues and to cross-reference interesting ways of posing and responding to them. The last decade or so has been a period of unparalleled *glasnost* in the various knowledge-producing disciplines conducted in English; time was when all the disciplines insisted on the specialness of their discourses and maintained a facade of uniformity and consensus, and the resulting image of academic discourse was not unlike that of the Soviet Union before Gorbachev: a great gray uniformity in which individual variety and dispute were subordinated to the collective purpose of defending and extending hegemony. *Glasnost* with respect to academic discourse has taken as its slogan "it's all rhetoric," suggesting that the uses of language within academic walls are not different in kind from those of public and everyday life. Like all reversals in the grand play of same-and-different, this change has obscured some of what was insightful from the opposing perspective. The goal of this book is to sort out and assess much of what has been said about academic discourse in this recent period. This book itself is a piece of academic discourse and thus implicitly affirms the mode and the value of discoursing in it; more than that, however, the sorting out and assessing are guided by the desire to clarify how that discourse constructs not only knowledge but also value.

Such an undertaking is an extremely ambitious task both for writer and reader. It assumes the ability of both parties to follow and assess arguments and observations made about discourses in which one is not trained or expert, and it assumes an interest in doing same, as well as an interest, most broadly, in the workings of language—what might be called rhetoric or discourse analysis—neither of which constitute securely institutionalized disciplines or, Heaven help us, market niches. My publisher is to be commended for risking this venture, and that quite advisedly. For the writer, I have answered as best I can, assuming (postulating) a reader as brash and curious as myself.

A number of books have appeared while this book was in production that I would certainly have integrated into it so as to continue the discussion if such integration would not have resulted in further delays in publication. Among these are: Berel Lang, *The Anatomy of Philosophical Style: Literary Philosophy and the Philosophy of Literature* (Oxford, U.K.; Cambridge, Mass.: Basil Blackwell, 1990); *Reading Rorty: Critical Responses to Philosophy and the Mirror of Nature (and Beyond)*, ed. Alan R. Malachowski (Oxford, U.K.; Cambridge, Mass.: Basil Blackwell, 1990); Donald N. McCloskey, *If You're So*

Smart: The Narrative of Economic Expertise (Chicago and London: University of Chicago Press, 1990); and Greg Myers, *Writing Biology: Texts in the Social Construction of Scientific Knowledge* (Madison: University of Wisconsin Press, 1990).

Friends and colleagues have increased my confidence in The Reader and enhanced the quality of real readers' experiences of the book by their comments and queries. I should particularly like to acknowledge the help of Charles Altieri, Avon Crismore, Anne Doyle, Frederick Kirchhoff, and Joan Graham. Nancy Campbell did most of the legwork collecting reviews of the books discussed herein intelligently, efficiently, and cheerfully.

CONTENDING RHETORICS

INTRODUCTION
AFTER THE CARNIVAL

The spirit of carnival, according to Bakhtin, springs from the temporary suspension of hierarchies and is played out in promiscuous mingling, inversion, and collapse of oppositions and exclusions. In particular, the higher makes contact with the lower which it has repressed; the energy released comes from the violation of taboo. The carnivalesque spirit seems to have erupted in academic circles in the last decade, especially in circles actively engaged in the regulation of discourses and disciplines: editors, conference organizers, writing teachers, referees, and reviewers. The traditionally firm lines between science and literature, reason and rhetoric, have been challenged and abolished with a resulting flow from higher into lower. Professors of sociology and philosophy and the sciences natural and social have embraced the slippery signifier with its uncanny power, proclaiming "it's all rhetoric." They have begun reading Aristotle, Burke, and Perelman, and/or Kuhn, Foucault, and Derrida. They have invited literary theorists and rhetoricians to their conferences and solicited their insights into the "writtenness" of their disciplinary discourses. Here for example is an ethnographer's celebration of the emerging new era of rhetoric. It is taken from James Clifford's preface to a collection of papers given at a recent conference on writtenness of anthropological discourse: "the return of rhetoric to an important place in many fields of study (it had for millennia been at the core of Western education) has made possible a detailed anatomy of conventional expressive modes. Allied with semiotics and discourse analysis, the new rhetoric is concerned with what Burke called 'strategies for the encompassing of situations.' . . . It is less about how to speak well than about how to speak at all, and to act meaningfully, in the world of public cultural symbols."[1] That is a tall order for rhetoric, new or otherwise enriched by alliances with semiotics and discourse analysis, though it is very similar to the literary theorist Terry Eagleton's programmatic call for the replacement of literary theory by rhetoric.[2] In Eagleton's program, however, rhetoric is to be enriched with insights from psychoanalysis and deconstruction. Deconstruction does promote the dissolution of genre distinctions; Jürgen Habermas summarizes the consequences of Derrida's theorizing in this fashion:

> What remains is self-inscribing writing as the medium in which each text is woven together with everything else. Even before it makes its appearance, every text and every particular genre has already lost its autonomy to an all-devouring context and an uncontrollable happening of spontaneous text production. This is the ground of the primacy of rhetoric, which is concerned with the qualities of texts

1

in general, over logic, as a system of rules to which only certain types of discourse are subjected in an exclusive manner—those bound to argumentation.[3]

One might note that a minor casualty of this general merging is the distinction between rhetoric and literary criticism; as Habermas notes, the new criticism of texts-in-general practiced by deconstructionists is modeled on and owes most to literary criticism, and, he also notes, when applied to philosophical texts, this criticism concentrates on the way the writing subverts the argument of the text: "The procedure of deconstruction deploys this generalized criticism to bring to light the suppressed surpluses of rhetorical meaning in philosophical and scientific texts—against their manifest sense" (p. 191). Thus the "primacy" of rhetoric means that literary-critical analysis provides a deeper account of what is going on in a philosophical or scientific text than a mere analysis of its argumentation.

There is thus a certain amount of confusion surrounding the repeated polemical and by now ritual slaying of positivism, foundationalism, correspondence theories of truth, and Methodology—and the carnivalesque dancing upon their graves—confusion, for one thing, about where the new insights into language are to be found, and, for another, what new distinctions and oppositions are likely to emerge after the heady spirit of carnival has passed, especially if we are to avoid a nasty hangover of cynicism, passively contemplating the workings of unlegitimated power. The conception of an enlarged study of discursivity in general is an attractive one, arising as it does from the awareness that academic and scientific discourse is woven out of human actions and is as rooted in human desire as a love letter or a legal complaint, but there are profound differences that cannot simply be swept away with a wave of the hand.

One quick finding from a survey of rhetorical theories is that reason and rhetoric have long been a doublet, and an antagonistic one at that, dividing the world of discourses between them, each regarding the other with hostility and suspicion. The New Rhetoric that has emerged in the twentieth century is characterized by attempts to reduce the domain and prestige of Reason (generally in some positivist, objectivist, or physical/mathematical scientistic form) and to claim for itself the entire domain of Aristotle's dialectic—reasoning about the probable—leaving to Reason (or Rationality) only the apodictic reasoning about the demonstrable. But the sense of difference, though deferred, cannot finally be denied: surely there are major differences, one wants to say, between deliberating upon the location of peptides in the DNA molecule and deliberating upon the location of a nuclear waste dump in one's state—and between deliberating upon a law guaranteeing the rights of minorities or individual privacy and deliberating upon the meaning of a poem by Wordsworth. It is all very well to talk about the "conversations" of scientists and scholars, but surely there are differences between such conversations and those of city councils or wrangling spouses that need to be described.

One reason they need to be described is that learning these differences is a traditional purpose of schooling. The reason/rhetoric carnival poses an acute embarrassment for educators who account for what they teach in traditional terms of making and evaluating arguments critically, marshaling evidence, and drawing logical, well-founded conclusions, eschewing emotional and personal appeals and other illegitimate, manipulative maneuvers. Although teachers of writing housed in English and literature may be gratified that their special lore is receiving new prestige as vital to all academic discourse and not just humanist belles lettres, they may find themselves hard-pressed for well-grounded accounts of what they teach and why. In fact, the journals of college writing teachers reflect not just acute embarrassment, but a genuine and deep crisis of values: an uncertainty that begins with what norms of discourse, academic or otherwise, should be taught and extends to questioning whether the inculcation of any norms whatsoever is a socially legitimate activity. Pursuing such questions, one may theorize, as Michael Ryan does, about plural voices and discursive groups replacing a unitary conception of political discourse, but such openness to plurality does not help the teacher trying to give general guidance to twenty or twenty-five potentially plural "centers" in a writing class.[4]

Even those who have issued a clear call for teaching academic discourse have exposed vast areas of ignorance and uncertainty. Elaine Maimon's "Maps and Genres: Exploring Connections in the Arts and Sciences," for example, takes a strong stand on a very general level, calling for English teachers to explore and map the "genres" and conventions of writing in other disciplines, so that they can initiate students, and themselves, into the academic discourse community generally and various disciplines within it.[5] Maimon conceives of disciplinary discourse principally in terms of forms (which pose "constraints") along with some differences of evidence and types of argument; in addition, all academic discourse is characterized by certain common modes of behavior such as formal acknowledgment of assistance and certain values ("intellectual honesty and free exchange of ideas") associated with them. Her basic metaphor is thus the exploration and mapping of discursive space, populated by helpful natives, and filled mainly with rules clustered around genres. Had she considered instead the equally common metaphor of disciplines as cultures, however, she might have been a bit less sanguine about the ease with which her English teachers could "become conversant" in other disciplines, much less penetrate to the tacit knowledge of participants, package it, and convey it to students in a required composition course. Further, the following chapters will argue that the discursive terrain is neither neutral nor inert; rather, like cultures, the disciplines embody practices and values that conflict, not only with other disciplines, but within the disciplines themselves. What Maimon's program and others of similar inspiration reveal is how little "English" teachers have in the way of discursive theory or practical understanding of other disciplines. It is true that academic disciplines all produce written texts that purport to increment public knowledge, but it is also true that they have serious doubts about other disciplines and about some of the work done in their own, doubts that have been articulated through the traditional oppositions of reason and rhetoric. I don't mean to dismiss the program of teaching academic discourse to college students—indeed, I believe it to be proper and desirable—but rather to orient and equip it with a more informed and critical understanding so as to get beyond well-meaning platitudes of "the colleagueship we cherish" and "liberal education." We will return to the teaching of academic discourse in the final chapter, after we have a better sense of what is involved.

The metaphor of academic discourse as a discursive space, as territory describable in terms of dimensions or parameters of variation ("continua," "spectrum") recurs in the quasi-inductive studies of Charles Bazerman and Susan Peck MacDonald, each of which attempts to differentiate the discourses of natural science, social science, and the humanities by examining sample articles from disciplines in each of the broad categories.[6] Each study acknowledges the limitations of drawing broad generalizations about differences in discursive modes from analyses of a few articles deemed to be typical, and each calls for more close examinations of examples to enrich the inductive data base. It is by no means clear, however, that such a research program will produce the hoped-for "map" in the near future. MacDonald's essay, contrasting problem definition in the natural and social sciences from that in the humanities (as reflected in the articles in the January 1986 *PMLA*), was greeted by several responses criticizing the typicality of her examples, the statement of her parameters (e.g., degree of communality, publicness of problems), the accuracy of her readings, the very notion of continua, and a number of other points—along with considerable sympathy for her underlying motive of calling to English teachers' attention the particularity (or parochialism) of a view of academic discourse based on that of their own discipline. These articles are quite successful in suggesting and illustrating major differences of discursive approach and argumentative strategy, though these differences were hardly discovered by purely inductive sampling and analysis; rather, they owe a good bit to existing philosophy and sociology of science, and it is not exactly clear how further analysis and comparison of articles would improve the sketch of broad differences in "faculties" or "colleges," or indeed what the interest of such an improved sketch would be. Bazerman's subsequent work has moved away from such an inductive finding of discursive principles in the direction of historical analyses of explicit disciplinary "style sheets" and the formation of the conventions of the experimental report.[7]

The "terra incognita" metaphor for disciplinary discourse is not in most respects a very accurate one, and it is considerably less so than when Maimon wrote some seven years ago. The reason/rhetoric carnival is really a symptom of ferment and a desire once again to raise fundamental questions by challenging answers that were axiomatic for the last generation or two of scholars. Just this current ferment and debate alone make Maimon's program more difficult to execute. Our procedure will be to review the discussions that set up the problematic, to examine in detail and as it were in slow motion the terms which circulate in theoretical oppositions and polemical declarations—rationality/rhetoric, norms/practices, impersonality/subjectivity, demonstrative proof/personal authority, and several others. Claims within specific fields ("the rhetoric of" economics, sociology, science, social problems, and the like) tend to be couched polemically, scoring points off of rather broadly sketched targets and treating *reason* and *rhetoric* as commonsense terms which require at most one or two lines of definition, rather than complex terms functioning in dense and rich traditions of academic theorizing and reflection. These traditions, to be sure, straddle or overlap current disciplinary boundaries (especially philosophy, sociology, speech and communication, education, and "English") and are differently manifested in different national cultures (Hegel being regarded as a social theorist, for example, in certain traditions). And, too, the terms are so basic to general academic reflection and self-understanding—so much a part of the common surrounded by the individual fields—that there is an understandable reluctance to see them fenced in as the special property of any specific disciplinary tradition. Nonetheless, if we want to assess how things stand and how we should proceed in practicing and propagating the academic culture, we need to draw these particular, polemical sketches together as episodes which have occurred in common tradition of reflection. Thus, while not assuming the identity of all disciplinary discourses ("they're all rhetoric"), we can attempt to cross-reference and integrate *accounts of* disciplinary endeavors within a tradition of academic theorizing and reflection. The first two chapters, called "Foundations," draw together some of the basic terms and issues from several traditions of reflection, notably philosophy, sociology, and education. We will essentially be pursuing the question, what makes academic discourses academic (or "pure" or scientific in the broad sense). In the second part, we will turn toward more recent studies of how discourse works in particular fields, all of which apply and criticize parts of the tradition. Here we will encounter a diversity of views partly reflecting differences in the purposes of the disciplines and partly the diversity of the individual analyst's conceptions of rhetoric.

Our account, or account of accounts, will therefore be more academic than polemical, more oriented toward drawing distinctions and pursuing implications than kicking butts, tipping the boat to the other side, or making a clean and thorough break with the past. As a first pass at sketching this orientation, especially its passion for distinctions, we can note that "it's all rhetoric" arguments have generally proceeded along no less than seven lines yielding widely disparate results:

(1) all academic disciplines present probable arguments, not demonstrations (by enthymemes, in one sense, not syllogisms). As noted above, this line has been pressed for over thirty years, though one still finds articles announcing it as news, especially in regard to science and the toughest case—mathematics. It sets the stage for the other lines of argument, and for the purposes of this study, it will be treated as axiomatic.

(2) disciplinary discourse is personal, not impersonal, engaging both writer's and reader's prejudices, attitudes, interests, and desires, even if it says it doesn't.

(3) disciplinary discourse is no different from other kinds of argument; it relies on common topics not (or as well as) topics special to the discipline (their special "logics" and proofs). By common topics, we mean the kinds of argumen-

tative tactics sketched by Aristotle in his *Rhetoric*: appeals to authority, the credibility of the writer, the desires and interests of the audience, and so on.

(4) academicians are commonsense or practical reasoners; "scientific theorizing" is rarely attempted and never fully attained. A related articulation is that scientific reasoning is *informal* and cannot be rendered formally.

(5) disciplinary discourse is socially constructed in particular communities which negotiate what counts as knowledge in flexible and changing ways according to the passions and interests, the position and influence, of its members.

(6) all academic discourse is covertly technological (there are no pure disciplines); the problems they identify, the resources they attract, the significance of their findings all are assessed in relation to application and utility and hence constrained by practical deliberation on personal and social well-being, the beginning of which is National Security.

(7) disciplines are founded upon contradictions; their discourses inevitably patch over these conceptual abysses and hence are "written" in the deconstructionist sense.

In subsequent chapters, we will see these lines of argument developed in detail as well as some of the resistances they have encountered. The general principle of deferred distinction could be illustrated for each of them: if it's all argument, then there must be different types of argument, some more reasonable than others; if all accounts are fictions, then why are some taken more seriously than others? If all disciplines are impure, is solar physics constrained by policy implications in the same way criminology or epidemiology are? And so on. Nonetheless, displayed in this list, these theses seem mutually reinforcing and collectively sufficient to make one want to substitute *persuasive* for *true* and *believe* for *know* whenever they occur. To regain a critical stance, we return briefly to Habermas's article which outlines a position resisting most of these points.

Habermas presents a general map of discursive space or practices which preserves some of the distinctions of disciplines and truth claims by restricting the object of literary criticism to literature, where literature is defined as language used so as to foreground its reflexive or world-disclosing force. At the opposite end of the spectrum is language used to solve problems of knowledge and coordinated action—the special expert discourses of science, law, and morality. Lying between them is the "normal language of ordinary practice [normalsprachlichen Alltagspraxis]," in which both functions are commingled; one might represent these relations in a diagram:

language oriented

toward problem solving: toward itself:

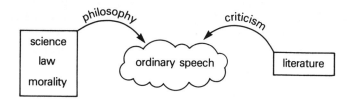

Only at the extreme of literature do the characteristics of language as pure textuality come to the fore:

> The rhetorical element occurs in its *pure form* only in the self-referentiality of the poetic expression, that is, in the language of fiction specialized for world-disclosure. Even the normal language of everyday life [normale sprache des Alltags] is ineradicably rhetorical; but within the matrix of different linguistic functions, the rhetorical elements recede here. The world-disclosive linguistic framework is almost at a standstill in the routines of everyday practice. The same holds true of the specialized languages of science and technology, law and morality, economics, political science, etc. They, too, live off of the illuminating power of metaphorical tropes; but the rhetorical elements, which are by no means expunged, are tamed, as it were, and enlisted for the special purposes of problem-solving. (p. 209)

Thus Habermas rejects what one might call the Bacon-Sprat-Royal Society equations of scientific = literal, poetic = figurative, and concedes that one might well undertake the study of what John S. Nelson calls the poetics and the tropics of inquiry, but insists on the fundamentally different functions and communicative weights borne by these aspects of language in the different domains.[8] Within this scheme, Habermas conceives of philosophy and literary criticism as mediating discourses bridging the polar extremes into ordinary discourse. As such, they are committed to being mixed discursive modes, using on the one hand the specialized discursive mode but rendering the contents accessible to non-specialists in the mode of everyday discourse. Inevitably, then, they must convey some of their meanings indirectly, which is to say improperly/ rhetorically, and in that sense their language resembles that of literature, though their purposes are different since they are both forms of argumentation (which literature is not). (*Rhetorical* is being used here in the sense of metaphoric or displaced—language that cannot ground itself as literal or proper.) Further, the relatively specialized language of literary criticism is appropriate for its purpose (elucidating literature) but not for doing philosophy, and vice-versa (i.e., treating literature as if it were putting forth theories of how the world is). Thus

Habermas is willing to grant a general quality of rhetoricity to discourses in all domains, though it is damped down, or ignored, or indeed suppressed in the domains of problem solving and everyday discourse by conventions serving the overarching aims of language use in those domains. One of the main purposes of the legal discourse, for example, is to render decisive verdicts in all cases that arise, and, as Walter Benn Michaels notes, a judge who commenced to hold forth about the shimmering ambiguities of a particular passage of law would arouse alarm and consternation in the court.[9] "The normal language of everyday practice" is not the problematic concept of "ordinary" or "literal" language criticized by many textualists: it does not constitute an unmarked case or baseline of literal or uncontorted usage, nor is it a pure type of anything, except insofar as it is the medium for what we will later call, following Alfred Schütz and Harold Garfinkel, everyday theorizing (or practical reasoning). In addition, there is a second, special kind of rhetoricity in the discourses of literary criticism and philosophy arising from their bridging of domains.

There are of course many arguable points to this sketch. I introduce it here principally to show how approaches to language as argumentation and communicative action might coexist alongside of approaches which highlight unstable and plurivocal meanings without either claiming to have grasped the essence of textuality in general. Indeed, within a theoretical framework such as Habermas's, which distinguishes discourses fundamentally in terms of their purposes, there does not seem to be any place for an overarching criticism (or rhetoric) that would grasp the essence of textuality as such. The guiding purpose in each discursive mode imposes on language its mode of operation (via norms and conventions special to that mode). And one might note that, for Habermas, this differentiation is not based on the intentions of centered subjects, but on socially established norms and practices. Habermas is far from lamenting the fragmentation of knowledge into expert cultures. Indeed, he argues that the specialization and relative autonomy of expert cultures with their own special articulations of validity (their own logics) safeguard these norms of validity from reduction to the presently useful and politically expedient. There is great value and the basis for critique of practices in this impractical excess generated in the disciplines (and in literature), but the excess may also remain esoteric without the bridging work of philosophy and literary criticism.

Habermas's defense of disciplinary boundaries points to one of the fundamental stumbling blocks lying in the path of a general theory of discursivity merging the deconstructive view of textuality and traditional rhetoric. There is in traditional rhetoric a strong sense that context is determinative—that speaker, audience, occasion, and purpose, when known and reflected upon, restrict and stabilize the many possible interpretations one might give of a sentence or a text. To understand how the language of a particular text works, that is, we must understand how it is accommodated to the audience, occasion, and purpose at hand. The rather abstract schemes of words, for example, can be fleshed in as gestures in particular performances. Rhetorical criticism practiced "thick description" long before it was publicized in ethnography, and it has welcomed the similar recent emphasis in linguistic pragmatics and discourse analysis on contextual determination of form and meaning. But a deconstructionist is likely to object that such filling in of context is an attempt to restore "presence" to the text—to deny, that is, its textuality in so far as the text itself projects and constitutes (or "constructs") the effective definitions of writer and audience, occasion and purpose.[10] The audience, occasion, and purpose are never merely "at hand"—texts frequently must conjure up an occasion for themselves, announce an ostensible purpose, and cast a role for the reader to play, all while crafting a persuasive persona for themselves. A strongly deconstructionist sense of textuality, however, suggests a kind of absolute freedom for writers which ignores historical and material constraints on them as actors and writers. Any particular writer can only say and be heard saying certain things and not others at a given historical moment. We will see this tension underlying many of the discussions of disciplinary language considered in the following chapters.

A number of rhetorical theorists have also queried the proposed expansion and enhancement of rhetoric to the status of a general study of discursivity or textuality. Michael Leff notes that rhetoric has always been centered on deliberation of public or civic affairs,[11] and to extend and generalize its domain to academic, expert discourse via the notion that it too attempts to persuade will obliterate many crucial distinctions. Academic and public discourse "differ typically in complexity of reasoning, use of evidence, frequency and types of images, syntactic constructions, vocabulary, assumptions about the audience's knowledge, and almost every other category relevant to classification types of rhetoric" (p. 34). He concludes, "Rhetorical models for technical fields and for the public sphere do not correspond, and attempts to map one directly onto the other are bound to produce considerable distortion" (p. 34). A rather similar argument is put forth by Michael Calvin McGee and John R. Lyne that the domains of technical and social reason are separate and irreducible (governed respectively by the codes of antirhetoric and rhetoric), but also in need of a bridging discourse (or dialectical synthesis) directed toward "managing the inevitable integration of power/knowledge within discourses that give life direction" (p. 388).[12] They are thinking, for example, of expertise as arising in the expert domains on the one hand and grounded in their domain-specific modes of proof, but as functioning in a quite different way when the knowledge so developed is introduced into the public arena via testimony, advice, and reportage. Expert testimony is understood and evaluated differently by juries of laymen and by fellow experts, and this important distinction would be lost if one simply abolished the antirhetoric of the disciplines and merged the juries of one's professional peers with one's civic ones. (For these theorists, the public or civic debate would seem to fall within Habermas's domain of everyday discourse, but the rhetoric of inquiry would not have the mainly interpretive function of philosophy in his scheme.) Note that McGee and Lyne's concept of technical reason is a narrowing of Habermas's understanding of expert discourses in that it does not include within itself any potential for critique. Expertise is a hybrid: knowledge applied to specific practical problems.

Rhetorical theorists are themselves divided, however, on what degree of centrality or primacy to give to "deliberation upon public (civic) matters." The rhetoric-as-epistemic school, for example, carries on the tendency of Burke and Perelman and Olbrechts-Tyteca to annex all non-demonstrative reasoning to rhetoric. Richard Cherwitz and James Hikins, for example, define rhetoric as "the art of describing reality through language."[13] This is even broader than Burke's "the use of words by human agents to form attitudes or induce actions," mainly because they choose not to tie rhetoric to either the intent or the effect of persuading—though they hold all such descriptions of reality as "potentially persuasive."[14] (For them, the fundamental contrast is with fiction, which does not purport to describe reality.) Similarly, Cyril Knoblauch defines rhetoric "boldly" as "the *process* of using language to organize experience and communicate it to others"[15] and his conception is apparently even broader than Cherwitz and Hikins's in that it treats all accounts as interpretations and all interpretations as fictions. These definitions seek to include within rhetoric the symbolic or poetic functions of language (what is called the "literary" aspect of language by other writers), and the interpersonal orientation toward "gaining adherence" (Perelman and Olbrechts-Tyteca) fades away as a distinguishing criterion of rhetoric. The way thus lies clear to joining hands with the textualists in defining rhetoric as the study of discursivity in general.

The focus of our inquiry, however, is away from discursivity in general and toward the workings of language at particular disciplinary sites, where fortunately a great deal of work has been done in the last decade. In the section on Applications, we will be comparing and criticizing a number of these particular studies with a view toward extracting at least a manual of techniques and possibilities that could be applied elsewhere. In a sense, we will be doing the rhetoric of "rhetorics of."

There are a number of questions that any inquiry such as the one being sketched could anticipate; I will pose and answer a few of them, shifting into overt dialogue.

The scheme is now clear enough, but isn't this a job for philosophers? Doesn't talking about knowledge claims rather than knowledge just repackage the problems of epistemology and philosophy of science so that you can call it discourse analysis or rhetoric? Haven't Feuerabend and Kuhn, Toulmin and Laudan, addressed most of these questions? And, looking a little farther back, Popper and Lakatos and Polanyi? Are we going to have to go over all that ground again?

They have indeed identified a number of the main questions about scientific knowledge (e.g., how consensus is formed, how it is progressive, what relation methodology has to the conduct and evaluation of science) and their work does provide a background for the closer-in studies of particular disciplines that have subsequently been done. Methodological reflections have at least two distinct purposes, one, as an apology for the discipline, and two, as a practical guide to research. Philosophers generally concentrate on the first, but our concern is more with the second, and hence with academic discourses as situated practices. By the time they finish this book, readers will not know much more about the grounds of knowing, scientific or otherwise, than they did at the outset, but they will know a good bit more about how individual writers have attempted to ground their endeavors. Grounding, that is, will be viewed as a practical need calling forth various strategies, not a philosophical problem. Philosophers are at heart logicians, concerned with what makes arguments valid or invalid; here we will be concerned with what makes them persuasive, and with the way they are scrutinized and responded to—with rhetoric and dialectic, respectively.

Well then, if your focus is on concrete practices and the culture of communities, isn't this a job for the practitioners themselves? How can you, an outsider, seriously propose to describe how it works in a discipline in which you have not been trained, a game in which you are not a player? And a related question: why do you concentrate on the natural and social sciences, rather than on humanities like History or English?

The crucial question here is how much practical knowledge and experience in a discipline do you have to have to do rhetorical analysis and critique? This is indeed a serious problem and a major theme in many of the works to be discussed, but I think it is at the outset an open question how esoteric disciplinary discourse is, especially when we are assisted by the cooperation and accounts of insiders. Another cause for some hope is that disciplines may display a face of uniformity, but they also are often riven by controversies over their basic purposes and proper methods; participants in a controversy often appeal to outsiders, or to the generalist in their antagonists, for support. Categorical positions on this matter, as we shall see in chapter three, generate dilemmas, and it may well be that some aspects of academic discourse are more penetrable and apparent to outsiders than others.

As to the second question, the sciences are the best place to field and test claims that it's all rhetoric, since these are the places where reason, method, and special norms have traditionally been said to rule. The rhetoric claim creates less scandal and resistance in the humanities, perhaps too little. As far as the argumentative logic goes, if the claims succeed for the sciences, then, a fortiori, they succeed in the humanities as well. One would scarcely expect to see people in History or English Literature claiming to be the only true scientists left around. And, by the curious twists of abduction, if the claims fail for science, there may be something wrong with them when applied in the humanities as well. When we do examine rhetorics of History later on in the book, it will begin to seem that the reason/rhetoric doublet has a life of its own, irrespective of the discipline.

So you admit you may be missing some important pieces of the puzzle. That's good, but isn't this project still an insidious attempt to recapture control of local practices of rhetorical analysis and place them under the disciplinary guidance of Rhetoric, so that you can write manuals and teach courses to people in how to write, and how they should write, in their disciplines?

Some of the most vigorous and illuminating analyses of writing I have read are contained in the works to be discussed, and they are analyses that neither I nor anyone trained only in Rhetoric could make. Of course I want to focus attention on them and the issues they raise, and to establish a kind of clearing house for the rhetoric of academic disciplines which provides as one of its services a critical assessment of strengths, limitations, and promising directions. The sociologist Joseph Gusfield, whose "Comedy and Pathos in Drinking-Driving Research" was a seminal work for recent "rhetorics of," was asked why he had used a lot of Kenneth Burke but not Perelman and Olbrechts-Tyteca. He replied that he happened to know of the former, but not the latter, thanked his questioner, and proceeded to read, and use, them in later work. Works on the rhetoric or literary art of disciplines straddle disciplinary boundaries; they are somewhat peripheral in their disciplines, but central, I want to show, to Rhetoric, and, just as the philosophy of science is a clearinghouse for the methodological reflections of disciplines, so Rhetoric ought to be for their rhetorical reflections.

Since people these days distrust impersonality and look for the interests and investments animating any discourse, would you please candidly declare your own? I'm not sure people these days have the time or inclination they used to to play academic "let's pretend it comes to mind to discourse upon reason and rhetoric."

As for candor, there are of course no absolute guarantees, and there is pleasure to be had in a little authorial cat-and-mouse, but I will make a stab, two stabs, at an answer. First, an authorial one. Some years ago I wrote a book, *Constructing Texts*, which dealt with a rationale for the teaching of "composition" in college, but which did not examine academic writing very closely or critically in its social and institutional ramifications. Work done during the last ten years, on which this book is largely based, now makes it possible to extend and deepen that reflection, though I will not spell the implications out until the last chapter. In a subsequent book, *Rhetoric as Social Imagination*, I did begin to explore reading and writing as social acts, but the type of writing I examined was the popular genre of advice writing, rather than that designed to augment and advance learning. So in a sense I am returning to the fold, in that academic teaching and analysis of writing is more naturally directed toward academic books and articles than those giving "advice." The fold, yes, but not necessarily the ivory tower, since one of the major questions is of what substance the tower is made.

Second, a pseudo-impersonal one. One occasionally finds oneself in the midst of conflicts that, unexpectedly, prove unresolvable by reason or argument, situations in James Boyd White's words (lifted from the *Iliad*) when words lose their meaning. Whether this is a common or especially urgent contemporary experience I am not sure, but theorizing about reason and the power of language to persuade is very active, suggesting that these are no longer things that we can take for granted, like our ears—or our balance. They have become troubled, and so it comes to mind to discourse upon them.

Perhaps the biggest obstacle that must be overcome at the outset is the very common, prejudicial stereotype of academic discourse as some great, gray juggernaut or text-generating machine that goes on cranking out ever-increasing amounts of copy (scholarly "work"). Part of the appeal of the textualist claim that it's all rhetoric (or textuality, or even poetry) is that this view glamorizes the ordinary scholar's pedestrian endeavors, suggesting that we can appropriately train upon them the same alert receptivity and excited ingenuity that we direct to literary art. Entirely compatible with the great gray machine view of ordinary academic discourse is the assumption of radical and interdisciplinary studies that the major frontiers of innovation and creativity are at the margins of disciplines or in critical and insurrectionary practices that challenge the establishment, especially its assumptions and procedures for arriving at consensus. Linda Brodkey, in *Academic Discourse as Social Practice* (Philadelphia: Temple University Press, 1987), describes a prolonged struggle to collaborate on a discussion of feminist reading between a liberal male professor and a radical female assistant professor, during which the latter systematically refuses the former's offers to reconcile the differences in their readings of a story on the basis of common assumptions about what makes a good reading. Her efforts to refuse compromise or even a common definition of their enterprise raised serious personal tensions between these colleagues and significant intellectual questions about how a radical rhetoric challenging the fundamental assumptions of a normal disciplinary rhetoric can exist within the discipline itself.

However, while it may appear from the vantage point of a radical, deliberately external perspective that normal disciplinary discourse is one monolithic component of a great gray machine, recent, closer looks at the "normal" practice of disciplines show anything but uniformity and consensus about the rules of the game, and this diversity does not present a picture of happy pluralism, but of competition and contention. Also, prevailing practices have been subjected to critique, and questions have been raised of substance, detail, and value. These studies and reflections are the primary focus of this inquiry. The assumption, which at this point I can only expect the reader to take as a promise, is that "normal" discourse is a much more complex and interesting subject than the stereotype would lead us to believe. At the same time, we will in effect concede that the "it's all rhetoric" claim has shifted the burden of proof onto the disciplines; it is up to them, or to us, to show that there are qualities special to disciplinary discourse that distinguish it from other kinds.

Foundations

The first chapter will take up the term *rationality* and its complex relations to *reasonableness* and *rhetoric*—the different definitions of it that have been employed in recent years, including those distinguishing between popular and intellectual culture, and especially the theories of Habermas, who recasts the traditional instrumental definitions of rationality in terms of human dignity and freedom, shifting it from cognitive to ethical grounds. Discussions of rationality tend to move between strong accounts of impersonal, objective methodology and qualifications of such accounts by personal and professional judgment, practical purposes, and discursive negotiation. This chapter will introduce the distinction of everyday/scientific theorizing, which will surface repeatedly in subsequent chapters.

The second chapter will focus on the mode of rationality and norms of discourse particular to knowledge-producing discourse— that is, the expert cultures oriented toward advancing our knowledge of the world, namely, scientific-academic discourse. Here, as in the previous chapter, we observe an interplay of cognitive and ethical considerations and an alternation between norms as governing the actions of scientists and scholars and norms as a decorum of public discourse. The main foci will be the sketches by David Olson of code of Text(uality), by Alvin Gouldner of the Culture of Critical Discourse, and by Robert Merton of the ethos of Science. Gouldner describes the "CCD" as following two dialectically opposed impulses—an impulse toward creating self-grounded discourses and one toward increasing critical self-consciousness.

These two chapters constitute the foundations for the more specific inquiries discussed in chapters three and four, which focus on discursive practices in particular disciplines, sometimes even single laboratories or controversies. Chapter three takes up some of the more innovative studies which were conducted under the general program of social constructionism: Joseph Gusfield's *The Culture of Public Problems*, Bruno Latour and Steve Woolgar's *Laboratory Life*, and Nigel Gilbert and Michael Mulkay's *Opening Pandora's Box*. "Social construction" views scientific knowledge as that which is accepted as such by the expert community. It then proceeds to examine the actions and discourse of scientists as they are oriented toward gaining this acceptance (and denying it to others), employing an outsider or stranger stance as observers trying to make sense of what the natives say and do, to grasp the implicit norms that guide their activities. This approach almost inevitably leads to critical reflection about the claims of the analysts themselves and to the search for ways of writing that do not embody the "windowpane" assumptions that traditional scientific writing (mistakenly) invites. Thus, analyzing the scientists' uses of rhetorical appeals, they (insofar as they are scientists) are led to examine their own rhetorics, and to attempt new styles of self-conscious reflective rhetoric for the sciences.

The fourth chapter takes up analyses of scientific writing as rhetorical, this time not "in the making" but as "made"—a more traditional way of approaching discourse. Here again we will examine books on the rhetoric of sciences, this time social: economics (Donald McCloskey), sociology (Ricca Edmondson), and anthropology (Clifford Geertz). These books, however, are written from the insider's perspective, and are not only descriptive, but normative for writing in their disciplines. These studies allow us to focus on the question of the ways in which the general purpose of producing knowledge is specialized in each discipline, along with the kinds of arguments and strategies appropriate for producing it. Both of these chapters will draw heavily on the reviews and citations of the books, so that we develop our understanding and evaluation of them in relation to their reception within their own special disciplinary contexts. No serious, non-trivial academic argument is ever accepted with universal assent and gratitude, and these books are no exception. This procedure has the effect of highlighting controversial aspects of the books, and gives many illustrations of one salient trait of disciplinary discourse, namely, that it is dialectical.

The fifth chapter will then turn to the discipline of history, which is traditionally poised between the social sciences and the humanities, partly because analyses of its rhetoric by J. H. Hexter, Hayden White, and Dominick LaCapra interestingly parallel the writings of the interpretive social scientists, but partly as well to see how science functions as the foil of rhetoric even in this discipline not noted for its aspirations to science. A central issue for all of these writers is how History can be regarded as a knowledge-producing discipline without being a science.

The final part—Implications—pans back from individual disciplines to treatments of academic discourse generally. The sixth chapter considers the ways that academic discourse has been symbolized, focusing on the notions of argument, conversation, and dialectic as developed by the social psychologist Michael Billig, the philosopher Richard Rorty, and writers in the tradition of rhetorical theory. The crucial, recurrent issue in this discussion is the orientation toward consensus and agreement and the mechanism by which it comes about. We then turn to the way academic discourse has been conceived by writers in the field of composition studies and to arguments that it should be the object of writing instruction in college. The conclusion concludes with as much consensus as can be had about current ways of conducting academic discourse.

I
Foundations

I

REASON, RATIONALITY, AND RHETORIC

One salient attribute of academic discourse, at least in its image of itself, is rationality, a term often associated with logic and regarded as a feature of argumentative structure. This view of academic discourse as somehow epitomizing rationality is of course both asset and liability; the academically successful are treated with deference and held in considerable awe even as they are regarded as impractical types dwelling in ivory towers far removed from the practical concerns of real life. To say a question is academic is to say it is without practical consequences. This division of prestige and value doubtless descends from the medieval distinction of contemplative and active lives and was reinforced by classical and Renaissance notions of the rational soul as the highest and most intrinsically human faculty of our natures; rhetoric appeals to faculties humans share with the animals—imagination and the passions—and conflicts between it and logic/reason are possible at every turn. As Bacon articulates the Renaissance humanist vision of the well integrated psyche: "Rhetoric is subservient to the imagination, as logic is to the understanding; and the duty and office of rhetoric . . . is no other than to apply and recommend the dictates of reason to imagination, in order to excite the appetite and will."

Renaissance faculty psychology, of course, is long dead. Opposition to it was a foundational move made by all schools of psychology in the twentieth century. Similarly, modern philosophers treat rationality as an attribute of actions, and there is widespread agreement that discourse must be understood as a type of action as well. One can easily see from this very general perspective how rationality would collapse into rhetoric, and "it's all rhetoric," far from being controversial, would simply be a belated recognition that this whole conceptual reorientation has occurred. Thus, curiously enough, the first step in clarifying the scope of rhetoric and its relation to the academic disciplines is to examine theories of rationality and the closely related term reason.

The near synonyms *reasonable* and *rational* seem on the face of it to differ mainly along connotative lines, with *rational* sounding more theoretical and rigid than *reasonable*. Within the philosophical and rhetorical traditions we will be examining in the chapter, a distinction is in fact sometimes drawn between them, or between different rationalities, but we begin with a common-sense understanding of rationality which makes no such distinction, developing it fairly quickly into what is probably the most common concept of rational action, at least in English-speaking countries, namely, the cognitive-instrumental or means-end one. It is perhaps best viewed as a point of departure which can be elaborated into various specific theories and constructs such as those of scientific and mundane rationality and the *homo economicus* of neo-Classical microeconomics.[1] The cognitive-instrumental view predicates rationality of the cognitive processes and decisions of individuals. It is, as it were, a psychological rather than a social concept, and it is applied to choices and actions rather than to discourse, though it can be viewed as having implications for groups via such principles and procedures as the Cooperative Principle spelled out by H. Paul Grice, the methodological canons of academic disciplines, and the different "attitudes" of scientific and everyday understanding discussed by Alfred Schütz and Harold Garfinkel. The first three sections will sketch and develop these perspectives.

In the fourth section, however, we will introduce an alternative conception of rationality that does make it an attribute specifically of discursive norms and practices, namely the theory of communicative rationality developed by Jürgen Habermas. Habermas criticizes the cognitive-instrumental view, with its focus on efficient pursuit of ends and the maximizing of same for groups (what he calls strategic action), and argues for rational discourse as the fulfillment of the human capacity for speech and as ethically superior to other modes of inducing cooperation, which boil down to force or fraud. It is not in efficient action, but in argumentation in the service of communicative action that rationality achieves fullest realization.

1. Cognitive-Instrumental Rationality

It is convenient to begin with a rather basic, commonsense notion of rationality shared, with various elaborations, by many philosophers and sociologists as well as laypeople. It presupposes that the actions of individuals are directed toward goals, and defines the rationality of actions in pursuit of those goals in terms of instrumental effectiveness: someone believes, says, or does something which, according to his or her beliefs, is most likely to attain the goal. The beliefs that support the particular choice are the reasons for it, and when a person selects and acts on the best reasons (according to his or her lights), he or she is commonly said to be acting rationally. The reasons one might give for one's actions, or hypothesize for another's actions, are not generally understood as motives (about which much might always remain mysterious), but as warrants for believing, saying, or doing something— grounds one might give in an account of why one acted as one did. Such accounts are not always retrospective—they may be given ahead of time—but they are constructed out of a vocabulary of commonsense reasoning in a way that makes (common) sense of what is believed, done, or contemplated. It is widely recognized that people may heighten the rationality of their actions in their accounts, but rational accounts are often taken as an unmarked baseline: people are assumed to act rationally unless there is some reason to think otherwise (including inability to give an account that seems plausible according to their own beliefs).[2]

This simple view of rational choice of actions in pursuit of goals is a baseline in another sense as well, namely in contrast to other grounds of action such as habit, obedience to authority, submission to external or internal compulsion, ritual, manipulation, indifference, or sheer folly. Submission to compulsion may be rational, of course, in that it may arise from an overriding goal of avoiding punishment, but in that case, the action taken is not a result of freely selecting the best means to attain a goal. So there is an image of freedom from constraint implicit in this view of rationality. And this view also furnishes a contrast with "rhetoric" in that one convinces another of a belief or course of action either on grounds of best reasons, or on some of the other grounds (authority, tradition, desire, etc.); the latter mode is sometimes called persuasion.

The account I have given (borrowed from W. H. Newton-Smith's *The Rationality of Science*) reckons rationality relative to the beliefs of the actor, the assumption being that in order to understand the rationality of another's actions, we may have to enter into a lifeworld of beliefs and values different from our own, and similarly, to convince him or her. Thus the very act of assessing the rationality of another's action or belief presupposes the possibility of understanding it in terms of his or her reasons, though the sense of best reasons may differ from our own. This possibility has been extensively explored in relation to cross-cultural communication and in relation to the actions of scientists and other actors separated from us across an expanse of time, or by beliefs about nature different from those currently prevailing ("paradigms"). This assumption of the non-universality of best reasons reverses the long-standing traditional one that reason is one and that common ground can be found from which we can convince another to think or do as we do. But to repeat, within this view, rationality is an attribute not of beliefs or of goals, but of the selection of means relative to beliefs and goals. Newton-Smith calls this view the minirat version of the cognitive-instrumental rationality; Chaim Perelman calls it prudence, which for him translates Aristotle's term *phronesis*.[3]

Not all philosophers or social theorists would accept this relativism, at least not for all purposes. Consider first the philosophers of science. Newton-Smith argues that we can decide whether scientists of the past acted rationally (minirat) according to their own lights, but we can and should also explain how their actions contributed to the progress of science in constructing better models of the world. He believes that modern science, with its scientific method, does successfully improve the verisimilitude of its models, and argues that we can evaluate the reasons that proved productive and unproductive in the past in the light of currently employed beliefs and methods. If indeed modern beliefs and methods are successful, then previously successful science should have been conducted under principles that approximate the modern ones. This is an interesting and carefully articulated position that does not claim absolute privilege for the current understanding of best scientific reasons and procedures, but does exploit the claim of science to produce not just consistent, well-warranted models given the context but a cumulative body of ever more accurate models which have a fair claim to be called knowledge (though not the final truth).

Because the minirat view places assessment of rationality so centrally within the beliefs, values, and intentions of individual actors, it raises questions about how anyone, say a social scientist, could claim to discern rationalities in social systems unglimpsed by individual actors, or even to augment the accounts individuals would give. In a famous passage in his monumental work *The Structure of Social Action* (1937), Talcott Parsons defines rationality as follows: "Action is rational in so far as it pursues ends possible within the conditions of the situation, and by the means which, among those available to the actor, are intrinsically best adapted to the end for reasons understandable and verifiable by positive empirical science."[4] Parsons makes two claims here that have proved highly contestable: on the one hand, he claims that the sociologist's understanding of rationality is not different in kind from that employed by ordinary people, but on the other, he seizes a superior vantage point for the sociologist, from which he can assess the relative rationality of individual's actions. We will examine the arguments against this view in the third section.

Though the cognitive-instrumental (or means-ends) model is a theory of action, it is clearly at base one of individual action, and a social theory which begins with it has to account for what is sometimes called "the coordination problem."[5] If we begin with an image of individuals pursuing success in attaining their goals, we must take account of their need to secure the assistance of others pursuing their own individual goals. In practice, we need information and assistance from others to attain even the most modest and mundane of ends, and obviously (though not necessarily, on this view) we converse and communicate with them to coordinate our knowledge and intentions. "Conversation" in the sense of H. Paul Grice thus emerges as a cooperative (or coordinated) social activity governed by certain norms that maintain its efficiency as a means. These norms are the famous Maxims of Quantity (say as much as is relevant), Quantity (say only that for which you have good warrants), Relation (say only what is relevant), and Manner (say it clearly and briefly), all of which taken together constitute the Cooperative Principle: "Make your conversational contribution such as is required, at the stage at which it occurs, by the accepted purpose of the talk exchange in which you are engaged."[6] Mutual interest should induce people to follow the Maxims. That is, Grice suggests that the adherence to the basic principle of cooperation should derive from everyone's desire to conduct efficient and businesslike ("profitable" is his word) exchanges with other people—in short, that conversation function as a means of practical action such as exchanging information and influencing the actions of others. In addition, speakers have an interest in maintaining their own "credibility" (as Trevor Pateman remarks). Note that *reason* has a tendency on this account to reduce to efficiency, least effort, or 'cheapness' as in Asa Kasher's discussion.[7] Kasher argues that Grice's account of communicative rationality can be derived from means-ends rationality as such ("Given a desired end, one is to choose that action which most effectively, and at least cost, attains that end, *ceteris paribus*," p. 32)—there is nothing specific to using language involved. (Grice almost invites this observation, noting that there are nonverbal equivalents of the Cooperative Principle). Grice argues specifically that speaking cooperatively is not a contract-like convention that we agree to but should be regarded as inherent in what it means to act reasonably. (We should note that this argument is only as strong as the value placed on efficient exchange of information as a goal: all cultures in some circumstances allow or require considerations of politeness or other interactional norms to override business-like efficiency.[8] As a result, Mary Louise Pratt notes, a great deal of verbal interaction is not straightforwardly rational, according to Grice's model.[9]) For the present purpose, it is sufficient to see how we might justify labeling as irrational such conversational practices as wandering off the point, speaking enigmatically, prolixly, or with pedantic overspecification—that is, how the cognitive-instrumental view of rationality gives rise to certain discursive norms that individuals would undertake to further their ends. However, when rationality becomes a predicate applicable to means, it does not apply to ends, the purposes an individual or group choose to pursue, except insofar as they can be treated as means to further ends. The cognitive-instrumental view of rationality is thus compatible with ethical relativism. It is the rationality of the technocrat.

2. Scientific Rationality

Grice clearly intended his model of conversation and its rationality to be very comprehensive; in fact, he indicated a desire to broaden it to include persuasion to action. This generality partly accounts for the strong interest in his model on the part of linguists seeking general principles of pragmatics and categories for discourse analysis. Returning to the definition of rationality, we can see that it has even greater generality. One might inquire whether and in what ways the concept might be specified by the particular goals individuals choose to pursue. We would move in that case from the initial commonsense or "folk" understanding of goals and warrants to the special and institutionalized goals and reasonings of science or literary criticism, judicial or psychotherapeutic discourse, etc. The nonspecialist, after all, does not always grasp why the language of a particular document is the best means to attain a legal goal, or why a critic says what she does about a poem or painting—or, for that matter, why a scientist chooses a particular theory or problem to work on. This is the strategy of Paul Newton-Smith: he begins with the general schematic definition of rationality described in the previous section, and then defines scientific rationality as that which emerges when pursuing scientific goals. It is worthwhile to survey and elaborate his sketch a bit to see what might be meant by particularizing rationality, especially since science is generally regarded as the epitome of rational endeavors. To claim that a certain body of statements constitutes knowledge of the world is to claim that the scientist believes that body of statements for good reasons and that those reasons should be good for everybody; they are not in any important way relative to the assumptions and beliefs of the particular scientists.

Newton-Smith does not say outright what a scientific goal is, partly I suspect because it is a controversial point. Broadly (and noncontentiously) there is agreement that science seeks knowledge of the world and seeks it for its own sake (so the science in question is "pure"); this is necessary so that the pursuit of clarification and understanding not be terminated by some practical end (i.e., one never stops with "good enough to get the job done"). And too there is agreement that this knowledge is pursued by constructing models and theories of the phenomena and choosing the best one. Science thus needs principles for comparing theories—its methodology—and if these principles could be exhaustively listed and their application precisely specified for all cases, then science would have many of the properties of demonstrative (apodictic) reasoning, most notably freedom from subjective factors of judgment and intuition. And such principles would account for the extraordinary rapidity and completeness with which consensus on a theory emerges in the scientific community. (It would not account for controversy and dissensus, of course, which are also facts of scientific life). Although philosophers of science currently agree that there is no such thing as scientific method in this strong sense, belief in something like it did prevail for decades; it is sometimes referred to, as by Michael Mulkay, as the "standard theory."[10] When people assail Scientific Method (part of the "it's all rhetoric" campaign), this strong characterization is usually what they have in mind. Sociologists of science have frequently pointed out that it was believed even within their own discipline, so that sociological inquiry was only warranted when the system broke down—i.e., in cases of controversy, mistaken rejection or adoption of a theory, and so on, or in regard to institutional functioning. But if scientists necessarily employ their professional judgment and intuition in applying the criteria of selection, then the processes of forming consensus are as much the proper object of sociological inquiry as controversy and dissensus, and scientific arguments are not demonstrative. Professional judgment does not simply replace scientific method, however, for professional judgment itself presumably is guided by a sense of "good-making" criteria for theories (or cognitive/technical norms, in Michael Mulkay and Gernod Boehme's terms[11]) the sense of which is shared by scientists, but it does mean that the criteria cannot be fully written out along with a manual for their application. Scientists in this regard are in the same boat as everyone else: they are fallible and will make mistakes.

A somewhat different perspective on scientific rationality arises from one very common definition of the goal of science as "adding to the body of certified knowledge" (or public knowledge, as Ziman calls it).[12] If one thinks of the sciences as discursive practices which, among other things, certify certain findings and theories as knowledge, then they must be protected from contamination by frauds, quacks, and impostors, and scientific method is often cited as the grounds for ruling certain work as out of bounds, thereby protecting the orderliness and purity of the discipline. The orderliness of scientific work was a major concern of Michael Polanyi's, who took the notion of discursive space very literally—the journals would quickly be diluted or crammed with wretched excuses for science, he argued, if the stuff was not excluded. But, Polanyi argues, it is not scientific criteria uniformly and impersonally applied which do this but structures of authority made up of referees, editors, and reviewers who exercise their professional judgment about theories and reported findings. The overall value placed on a piece of science, Polanyi says, arises from three sources of value: scientific merit, plausibility, and originality. Scientific merit per se he divides into three factors (accuracy, systematic importance, and interest of its subject-matter).[13] Clearly even the factors of scientific merit draw on the subjective judgment and intuition of the assessor, and those of plausibility and originality do even more heavily. Further, Polanyi observes, assessment of these factors is weighted heavily in favor of conformity to the prevailing consensus. Plausibility is a particularly complex criterion which can be used to reject or ignore findings which may never be formally invalidated; it will be applied more lightly when the relatively implausible claims are made by an established scientist of good reputation (indeed, it is sometimes said one reason for acquiring a reputation is to be able to get one's less plausible ideas a hearing); and it will result in some genuine discoveries and valid theories being ignored, or their recognition delayed for an indefinite period, often quite long. Nonetheless, Polanyi strongly endorses the criterion of plausibility, regarding it as the first line of defense against adulteration of scientific discourse by cranks, frauds, dabblers, and bunglers. His plea for discipline in the ranks is made particularly forceful by his having suffered at the hands of the system.[14]

Even though fair and orderly evaluation, according to Polanyi, does not require or in fact employ a complete and explicit list of criteria and an algorithm for applying them, it does imply the existence of a consensus concerning good-making criteria, and would seem vulnerable to the Kuhnian argument that it characterizes only normal science, and that the rupture associated with paradigm shift would still result in unaccountable shifts in the consensus.[15] Editors and referees would at such moments have to close their eyes, grit their teeth, and either jump on the bandwagon, obstruct its path, or throw up their hands and announce a temporary inability to choose between competing theories based in different paradigms. A great deal of recent work in the philosophy of science, however, has argued that "paradigms" in the Kuhnian sense are not so all-encompassing (or holistic) as Kuhn at one time claimed.[16] The interested reader may examine the references in the note for more extensive discussion.

Clearly the critique of the standard account of scientific rationality opens up large areas for inquiry by sociologists of science and for rhetoricians: the actual grounds, norms, and processes by which scientific consensus is negotiated, and persuasion effected, can be investigated using many of the same assumptions and techniques one would apply in studying other discursive communities and practices. We will pursue these questions further in the next chapters. We can summarize what we have learned from the critique of the standard account of science by saying that science is a specialized form of social action, but not a privileged one—privileged in the sense that it escapes the subjectivity of individual actors judging best reasons, and in the sense that it produces compelling demonstrations based on criteria that are fixed, shared, and uniformly applied by all scientists.

3. Two Rationalities?

As we have seen, Talcott Parsons claimed that the rationality of social actions can be understood in terms of means-ends reasoning by actors which is more or less mirrored by the sociologist's attempt to understand the actions. This conception was vigorously criticized by Alfred Schütz in a series of papers beginning with "The Problem of Rationality in the Social World" in 1943; this critique was renewed and extended by Harold Garfinkel in his *Studies in Ethnomethodology* and has become a fundamental argument in ethnomethodology.[17] Schütz sharply contrasted the attitude of scientific theorist with that of the practical reasoning actor engaged in the tasks of everyday life, arguing essentially that the goals of scientific theorizing differ so radically from those of the practical actor as to produce two sharply contrasting "rationalities." It follows that the attitude of scientific theorizing is bound to misunderstand the processes of everyday action and indeed exaggerate the irrationality of individual actions and the disorganization of social interactions. It is important to analyze this argument fairly closely, for a critique of the scope of scientific theorizing provides the basis for a critique of discursive norms and practices promoted to facilitate such theorizing.

Following Schütz, Garfinkel lists fourteen ways of behaving that lead people to evaluate actions and actors as more or less rational. Ten of these apply both to the activities of everyday life and to scientific theorizing (categorizing and comparing, accepting tolerable error, search for means, analysis of alternatives and consequences, strategy, concern for timing, predictability, rules of procedure, choice, and grounds of choice). The last four, however, are characteristic only of scientific theorizing (compatibility of ends-means relationships with principles of formal logic, concern for semantic clarity and distinctness, clarity and distinctness for its own sake, and compatibility of the definition of the situation with scientific knowledge). It would seem fairly clear why the last four have value only relative to the goal of constructing general models of the world for their own sake. The two attitudes of practical and scientific theorizing are brought more sharply into focus by six contrasting presuppositions which they make concerning such matters as apparent facts (take them at face value vs.

apply methodological doubt), applicability of personal knowledge and commonsense (much vs. none), perspective on time, expected limits of disclosure
(some things are private vs. all relevant motives and interests are in principle
public), and scheme of communication (relying on implicit knowledge shared
with particular others vs. anonymously addressing all competent investigators).
Garfinkel's sketch of the scientific side of the contrasts makes it clear how the
attitude would appear slightly crazed if applied in contexts calling for everyday
practical action. Here for example is his characterization of the scientific scheme
of communication:

> The "relevant other persons" for the scientific theorizer are universalized "Any-
> men." They are, in the ideal, disembodied manuals of proper procedures for
> deciding sensibility, objectivity and warrant. Specific colleagues are at best for-
> giveable [*sic*] instances of such highly abstract "competent investigators." The
> scientific theorizer is obligated to know only what he has decided to lend
> credence to. It is his mere option to trust the findings of colleagues on the
> grounds of membership in a professional or any other society. If he witholds [*sic*]
> credence, he is permitted to justify this by invoking as grounds his impersonal
> subscription to a community of "competent investigators" who are anonymous
> with respect to collectivity membership and whose actions conform to norms of
> the manual of procedures. By such actions he may risk criticism for unreasonable
> rigor. But such actions in daily life would risk a change in status to criminality,
> sickness, or incompetence. (p. 275)

Sometimes it seems Garfinkel is parodying academic/scientific conventions or
poking fun at intellectuals' chronic inclination to scrutinize and articulate
matters usually taken for granted. It is not clear whether Schütz and Garfinkel
think the scientific attitude has any proper domain of application (natural
science?), but their main point is clearly to argue its inapplicability to the
human sciences, which, they maintain, must understand social (read: everyday)
action from within its own principles. Schütz later made his peace with scientific model building in social science, though the homunculi of social models,
he points out, are extremely simplified constructs.[18] Garfinkel's remarks remain somewhat cryptic, however, and have left an enduring uncertainty as to the
exact relation of social theorizing to commonsense reasoning that we could call
Garfinkel's legacy. We will take up some of the responses to this legacy in
chapter five.

As developed by ethnomethodology as a working strategy for ethnographers,
the Schütz-Garfinkel preference for everyday understanding means that to
understand how truck drivers interpret and make sense of their lives, one
should take some rides in the cab and learn to think and talk like a truck driver,
and above all, use no terms and draw no conclusions that your truck driver
would not agree are appropriate and correct. In short, the ethnographer should
not assume that there is only one kind of smart, and that is the kind embodied
in scientific theorizing. We cannot expect these programmatic essays to answer
all the questions that might arise about this perspective, such as how many

rationalities there might be and how they might be compared, as well as other questions about the exact stance of ethnographer as knowing subject raised by Habermas.[19] It is sufficient for our purposes to note their attempt to pluralize the notion of rationality even within what is generally regarded as one culture, and to note that they do not criticize the notion of means-ends rationality as such—in fact, they employ it—but only the analysis of it (in everyday contexts) according to the scientific canons of systematic doubt, completely explicit articulation, full disclosure, logical consistency, compatibility with other scientific beliefs, and freedom from concerns with practicality and application. They thus pose a question of whether and to what degree the canons of academic discourse are appropriately applied for purposes other than scientific theorizing. As we will see in the next chapter, the theory of Text developed by David Olson lies wide open to this question.

Further, the two rationalities may be not only antithetical but actually antagonistic, as when experts in the scientific discourse give testimony or advice concerning public problems such as crime, health, abuse of substances or persons, impact on the environment, liability, and the like. The procedures of science characteristically place in question assumptions that practical discourse must make in order to decide on a course of action—about causality, for instance—and this questioning may seem at best trifling or hair splitting to the practically minded and at worst paralyzing and subversive of all well-intentioned effort to alleviate human disease, misery, and suffering. Joseph Gusfield writes of the "ironizing" effect inherent in sociologists discoursing upon the "social construction" of a particular piece of practical reality and of accusations of irresponsibility leveled at him as an expert in "drinking-driving."[20] Scientific theorizing requires an attitude of provisionality and systematic doubt to remain self-critical and open to innovation, and this attitude is at odds with the need for certainty and conviction to ground and motivate intervention in people's lives and practices. On the other hand, expert opinion may be accepted not according to the standards of proof and support cultivated in its own domain but according to the prestige and apparent probity and good will of the expert witness. As McGee and Lyne remark, "Ironically, experts who try to inform with reason wind up *being yielded to* in an act of obeisance to power reserved in former ages for kings, priests, magicians, and wizards. As a rule, decision-makers who yield neither understand nor care about the rational procedure underlying expert advice; for them, the only proof is in the eating; and except on the most vital questions, there is always time to hang an errant expert out to dry."[21] Clearly, experts who advise or testify put their knowledge into play in a game they do not control, and in which they are not expert. Indeed, there is now arising a new expertise in the rhetoric of expert testimony![22] (This is not to deny the often observed trend in modern or postmodern cultures toward the formation of policy elites which parlay expertise and information into power to act without submitting the actions to any effective public deliberation.) These are a couple of ways of thinking about the "displacement" of expert discourses which carry the discussion beyond the notion of impropriety or metaphoricity touched on in the introduction.

Although neither Schütz nor Garfinkel mentions it, their distinction of two rationalities—practical and scientific—is remarkably similar to that between *episteme* and *phronesis* drawn by Aristotle in the *Nichomachean Ethics* (1139ff.) and revived by Hans Georg Gadamer.[23] Aristotle distinguishes between demonstrative knowledge of the unchanging (e.g., mathematics)—episteme—and calculative savvy (practical wisdom) in dealing with the changing world of actions and events—phronesis—which involves applying informed and far-reaching grasp of the good in general to particular situations by means-end reasoning. It may even be said to be possessed, Aristotle says, by some of the lower animals "viz., those that are found to have a power of foresight with regard to their own life" (1141a[24]). It is in short the faculty of good judgment in practical matters and it appears, for example, in good managers of households or states. It is only acquired by experience, Aristotle stresses, which is why young men may exhibit prowess in the episteme of mathematics but lack the developed power of phronesis. Hence it cannot be taught, as can even the know-how (techne) of the craftsman, but is distinct from intuitive reason, which cannot be taught, but is the grasp of the unchanging first principles of philosophy and mathematics. Finally, Aristotle defines philosophic wisdom as a combination of intuitive wisdom and scientific understanding, noting that philosophers such as Anaxagoras and Thales are said to have philosophic but not practical wisdom when we see them ignorant of what is to their own advantage and in possession of knowledge with no application to attaining human goods (1141b). Despite its concreteness and particularity, phronesis is a faculty for knowing the truth, insofar as it grasps rational principles; it is not just the happy fortune of being in possession of right opinions, but the capacity to form them.

There are of course many differences between modern assumptions and Aristotle's axiomatic distinction of the two realms (the eternal, unchanging and the contingent, changing). The rather similar distinction drawn by Schütz and Garfinkel is based on the "for-itself" goal of scientific knowledge vs. the "for the purposes at hand" of practical reasoning (and not the demonstrativeness vs. probability of its conclusions), but it is nonetheless quite striking as a reinscription of the ancient doublet episteme/phronesis. The parallel is not quite so tidy, however, for what Aristotle meant by phronesis is a highly controversial topic in current scholarship: the core of the controversy is whether Aristotle meant to define phronesis purely in terms of means-ends effectiveness, or whether he later introduces an enriched definition in terms of wise selection of ends which might better be called by some other name, such as practical reason. Chaim Perelman assumes that phronesis/prudence must be supplemented by practical reason, but Richard Sorabji and David Wiggins have argued that Aristotle intends no such distinction and that the enriched conception is what he had in mind all along.[25] This debate thus follows the lines of the minirat/maxirat distinction, since if one's practical wisdom (= phronesis) involves a grasp of the good in general terms, then one can assess the reasonableness of an actor's actions without relativizing the assessment to the actor's lifeworld. Whether we take the cognitive path of Schütz and Garfinkel, distinguishing between kinds of theorizing, or the ethical one of Aristotle, we arrive at a distinction between the rational and the reasonable, where the reasonable attitude is much more sensitive to the particular needs, interests, and constraints arising in concrete situations, and the rational (= scientific) attitude carried into the realm of practical action creates some sort of monster with impossible expectations for himself and others.[26]

Georgia Warnke observes that Gadamer tends to generalize from the situation of ethical action to make concrete contextual constraints determinative of all understanding, so that even science itself can be seen "as tied to a technical form of know-how, the purpose of which is not to set the agenda for reason in general but to facilitate social aims and purposes."[27] The trouble with this conception, Habermas suggests, is that it places science at the mercy of existing structures and practices of power, effectively nullifying the capacity of scientific theorizing to mount a critique of existing conceptions and practices. Paradoxically, it is the very impracticality and integrity of scientific rationalities that make them ultimately most serviceable for civic reflection and deliberation. Hence he argues against the reduction of the expert cultures to the status of technologies, or the abandonment of scientific theorizing, on the grounds that it is a self-serving self-deception.

4. Habermas's Theory of Communicative Rationality

Despite the wide range of its employment and virtually axiomatic status, the cognitive-instrumental theory, Jürgen Habermas argues, is fundamentally faulty as a characterization of human rationality. For one thing, it has a very weakly developed ethical component. It has little to say about why people should act rationally—why it is good to be rational—beyond saying that we all have an interest in the efficient conduct of business. For another thing, it is a theory in which human speech and argumentation have only a secondary, instrumental role and only speech with cognitive and instrumental aims at that. That is to say, when one's speaking is in pursuit of knowledge or to influence the actions of others, then its rationality can be assessed in terms of its success in furthering those aims. But there are several other kinds of speaking such as discussing one's actions in the light of cultural and ethical norms, criticizing a work of art, or disclosing one's feelings, the rationality of which is not so easily assessed in terms of successful pursuit of a goal.

Habermas seeks to develop a theory of social action in which communicating with language is essential, not ancillary and instrumental, and in which the highest (and normative) form of rationality is achieved. The core of Habermas's reconceptualization of rationality is to take the attainment of rationally motivated consensus as the key phenomenon to be explained and indeed the chief value and purpose of human speech. (The term *speech* will be used to include written discourse as well; the term *language* is too abstract.) Habermas's theory is not without obscurities and difficulties. It has aroused vigorous opposition, and even those sympathetic to its aims find weaknesses in it, but its scope and originality make close examination of it crucial for our purposes. We will concentrate on the theory presented in *The Theory of Communicative Action* although there are some indications of substantial revisions yet to come.

Those familiar with Habermas's thinking about communicative rationality only from his essay "What Is Universal Pragmatics?" (translated in 1978; hereafter "UP") might well conclude that his theory is just a variant of Grice's.[28] One can read this essay as arguing that for illocutionary acts to work, the parties must implicitly be committed to telling the truth, speaking comprehensibly, with trustworthiness, according to norms of right and appropriate action; one then can see something of a deduction of these norms and the basis for a mild exhortation that we should observe them. It would seem to be, like Grice's, a deduction based on utility, or on the structural (or logical) presuppositions of speech acts. This appears to be what Donald McCloskey, for example, extracts from Habermas's earlier writings as the rules that should regulate academic discourse ("conversation" he calls it, following Michael Oakeshott and Richard Rorty).[29]

Habermas's subsequent work, however, most notably *The Theory of Communicative Action* (hereafter *TCA*), expands and elaborates the notion of communicative action as oriented toward reaching an understanding. It does so by emphasizing repeatedly the sociality implicit in the process and its ethical force as an ideal of unconstrained consensus. Thus there is a shift of emphasis away from notions of communicative competence and the structural presupposition of speech acts toward the social theory of consensus formation, and it is frustrating and ultimately unsatisfying to read *TCA* through the lens of "Universal Pragmatics" (as Jonathan Culler seems to do).[30] The passages of *TCA* setting forth this more social approach are generally dense and unrelentingly abstract, but are the basis of his argument and should be quoted in full. In the first passage, he is contrasting his approach with the cognitive-instrumental one already discussed:

> On the other hand, if we start from the communicative employment of propositional knowledge in assertions, we make a prior decision for a wider concept of rationality connected with ancient conceptions of *logos*. This concept of *communicative rationality* carries with it connotations based ultimately on the central experience of the unconstrained, unifying, consensus bringing force of argumentative speech, in which different participants overcome their merely subjective views and, owing to the mutuality of rationally motivated conviction, assure themselves of both the unity of the objective world and the intersubjectivity of their lifeworld.[31]

It is a little off the mark, I think, to claim, as Robert Hollinger does, that this account presupposes an abstract, preexisting Reason that gives "one right answer" to every question.[32] Rather, it is implicit in and enacted in the process of coming to an understanding, and there is no guarantee that the particular consensus reached is in fact the truth of the matter, only that it is the best approximation produced by the concerted efforts of the participants. Perhaps the most surprising term here is *argumentative speech*, which clearly signals a focusing in on a particular type of speaking in which the social nature of rationality is foregrounded. After a discussion of different types of communicating, Habermas summarizes:

> we can say that actions regulated by norms, expressive self-presentations, and also evaluative expressions, supplement constative speech acts in constituting a communicative practice which, against the background of a lifeworld, is oriented to achieving, sustaining, and renewing consensus—and indeed a consensus that rests on the intersubjective recognition of criticizable validity claims. (p. 17)

It is now clear how far beyond cognitive-instrumental discourse Habermas wishes to extend the concept of rationality (and communicative action). Moreover, there are certain types of cognitive-instrumental talk that are excluded from communicative action, such as instances in which one is merely pursuing her own purposes without seeking the reasoned assent of the other—e.g., giving instructions, giving play-by-play description of a ball game, giving orders from a position of institutional authority. Habermas emphasizes repeatedly that in practice one does not have to produce and justify the implicit validity claims— typically, in fact, one does not, and is able to rely on an already established and operating consensus; it is the readiness to produce them, and entertain them (on the hearer's part) that provides the basis of rationally grounded consensus (as opposed, he later says, to a diffuse good feeling or likemindedness—p. 287). The mention of a common lifeworld functioning as a background is an important qualification often overlooked by Habermas's critics: he does not assume everyone is in possession of the same ultimate set of reasons and best reasons.

In a later passage, Habermas distinguishes once again between instrumental actions oriented toward the speaker's success and true communicative action:

> By contrast, I shall speak of *communicative* action whenever the actions of the agents involved are coordinated not through egocentric calculations of success but through acts of reaching understanding. In communicative action participants are not primarily oriented to their own individual successes; they pursue their individual goals under the condition that they can harmonize their plans of action on the basis of common situation definitions. (p. 286)

Habermas recognizes that such harmonizing cannot always be achieved; he argues, however, that one is only engaged in communicative action so long as that condition is assumed by all parties. Hence bargaining and negotiation are *not* instances of communicative action, but rather of harmonizing "non-generalizable interests on the basis of balanced positions of power" (p. 35). (It is interesting to note, however, that the core of the Harvard Negotiation Project's advice on negotiating agreement is to argue in terms of principles, not positions, and use "objective criteria.") He insists that competent speakers know when they are engaged in communicative, as opposed to strategic, action, and they know when they have failed. Reaching understanding, he concludes, is not an incidental employment of language: "Reaching understanding is the inherent telos of human speech" (p. 287: Verständigung wohnt als Telos der menschlichen Sprache inne"—TKH, p. 387)—a statement he proceeds to provide arguments for. This line is one that Hubert Dreyfus and Paul Rabinow object to in their defense of Foucault against Habermas. They offer a slightly different translation ("understanding is the inner *telos* of language") and read it as privileging the communicative use of language.[33] But that is not what *Verständigung* means here, as seems evident from the preceding sentence: "Könnten wir nicht auf das Modell der Rede Bezug nehmen, wären wir nicht imstande, auch nur in einem ersten Schritt zu analysieren, was es heißt, daß sich zwei Subjekte miteinander verständigen."—TKH, p. 387; ("If we were not in a position to refer to the model of speech, we could not even begin to analyze what it means for two subjects to come to an understanding with each other." TCA—p. 287). McCarthy's translation of *menschlichen Sprache* as "human speech" rather than "language" seems exactly on the mark: Habermas is viewing speech as something people do with each other. That is, Dreyfus and Rabinow apparently have in mind such functions of language as symbolizing experience which might have a fair claim to bid for the inherent telos of *language*, but such functions would not so immediately come to mind if we think of "menschlichen Sprache" as "argumentation." Note that on his view, coordination of actions might be achieved by grunts and gestures (as Grice at one point contemplates), but it would not be a reaching of understanding— it is only the latter that is inconceivable without speech.

Attempting to ground the telos claim, Habermas has recourse to an analogy drawn from speech act theory which has occasioned much confusion and consternation. Distinguishing between strategic and communicative action (and arguing the primacy of the latter), he invokes Austin's distinction of illocutionary and perlocutionary acts as drawn along the same lines. This understanding of the relation between illocutionary and perlocutionary aspects of a speech act would strike most of the (English speaking) interpreters of Austin as decidedly deviant. It amounts to identifying perlocutionary with ulterior motive—an unacknowledged and therefore manipulative intention for saying something. For once, Habermas gives examples and they are unequivocal in import:

> the speaker can pursue perlocutionary aims only when he deceives his partner concerning the fact that he is acting strategically—when, for example, he gives the command to attack in order to get his troops to rush into a trap, or when he proposes a bet of $3000 in order to embarrass others, or when he tells a story late in the evening in order to delay a guest's departure. It is certainly true that in communicative action unintended consequences may appear at any time; but as soon as there is a danger that these will be attributed to the speaker as intended results, the latter finds it necessary to offer explanations and denials, and if need

> be, apologies, in order to dispel the false impression that these side effects are
> perlocutionary effects. Otherwise, he has to expect that the other participants
> will feel deceived and adopt a strategic attitude in turn, steering away from action
> oriented toward reaching understanding [verständigungsorientiertem Handeln].
> (pp. 294–95)

Habermas's discussion comes close to suggesting that the orientation toward
reaching understanding must be disinterested, but sympathetic commentators
conclude that this cannot be Habermas's intention. David Ingram argues that
reaching an understanding may be a personal goal of a speaker (or, better, a
voluntarily adopted limitation to the means employed in pursuit of that goal).[34]
One point that Habermas does want to stress in this discussion is that in action
oriented toward understanding, all one's intention cards should be on the table,
and the expectation that this is so creates possibilities for manipulation and
deceit. The passage becomes quite reasonable and sound when carried in this
direction, but it doesn't then provide much grounding for the telos claim, and
thus the telos claim, though interesting and plausible, has the status of an
ungrounded axiom in Habermas's theory.[35]

Dreyfus and Rabinow strongly object to this passage and to the implications
that arguments are decidable on the basis of general, abstract, and public
grounds. Assuming a Kuhnian/Foucaultian perspective that discourses of various types are framed by paradigms and paradigms arise in part from actual
concrete practices embodied in exemplars and hence are not fully reducible to
rules or reasons, they argue that even in natural science, agreement could not be
gained purely by the producing of reasons. That is, Dreyfus and Rabinow
assume that Habermas's model for achieving a reasoned consensus is the now
generally abandoned one of Scientific Method which includes criteria of evaluation that are fully explicit, impersonal in application, and decisive in every case.
But there is no reason to predict ahead of time that, though lacking such a body
of principles, scientists could not come to a reasoned consensus on a particular
piece of work or theory. If they reach a consensus which follows from claims
and beliefs for which they produce acceptable warrants, then they have reached
an understanding in the matter (even if it turns out later they were wrong). As
Habermas repeatedly stresses, argument oriented toward reaching consensus
presupposes its own possibility, which is that the sense of best reasons will prove
sufficiently shared to produce agreement, and that the body of those participating in the argument should be indefinitely extendible (i.e., there should be no
reliance on beliefs or values known not to be general). The background (lifeworld) of shared beliefs and values required to achieve Verständigung need not
be complete, enumerable, or demonstrably universal.

Jonathan Culler concludes from the illocutionary/perlocutionary passage
that it denies the force of rhetoric, but he means "white rhetoric"—the "rhetoricity of language in general," "the uncanny, rhetorical, inhuman force"
("Communicative Competence," pp. 142–43)—the tendency of language to do
something other than it says, to be constantly subject to "perlocutionary"

cross- and countercurrents, however unintended. Culler finally concludes that Habermas's theory of communicative action is not a theory either of language or of communicative competence—which is exactly right: it is a theory of the formation of rationally grounded consensus. The point is worth repeating, for it also troubles Dreyfus and Rabinow: it is a theory of communicative rationality as argumentation.

Culler's criticisms are not entirely gratuitous, however, for Habermas must hold some theory of meaning and signification, and indeed others as well as Culler have accused him of foundationalism or an assumption of univocality in rational argumentation that cannot be had in human language. Michael Ryan, for example, elaborates arguments of Rainer Nagele to the effect that Habermas aims for the elimination of error, misunderstanding, and untruth in communication, but this could only be accomplished by "establishing absolute univocal meanings for words and by rigorously determining contexts so that a displacement of truthful meanings by a contextual shift would no longer be possible"—and this would be repressive, not emancipatory.[36] But again, this argument casts in absolute and semiotic terms what is, at least in *TCA*, principally an ethical agreement to coordinate actions through consensus arrived at in a certain way, and this process would not seem to require the elimination of error and misunderstanding in any sort of absolute or conclusive way. It is true, however, that Habermas does not probe very deeply into the corresponding ethical norm of sincerity and the problematic of intentions. When do we ever say exactly all and only what we mean with total sincerity? When can we be completely certain even of our own motives? If such is the requirement or presupposition of communicative rationality, actual instances of it must be vanishingly rare. Habermas's rather blunt and categorical statement that we know when we are speaking in good faith and when not (*TCA*, p. 286) seems to be his attempt to set limits to this corrosive subjective and intersubjective doubt.

There is more to Habermas's account of argumentation. The process of producing and scrutinizing warrants for one's statements, directions, evaluations, and expressions of feeling is crucial in maintaining communicative action. In UP he referred to this process or mode as *discourse*—surely an unfortunate term--and in *TCA* it is largely replaced by *argumentation* (though this term is somewhat broader in that it includes *critique*).

Certain general rules apply in argumentation: the exchange is to exclude all force except the force of the better argument, participants are to adopt a hypothetical attitude toward the problematic claim, each should have equal speaking rights. Habermas describes the slightly differing operations of argumentation according to the kind of talk that is being warranted: theoretical discourse for statements and programs of action (answers to "how do you know that?"; "what makes you think that will work?"), practical discourse for norms of action ("why should we hire more women?"; "why do you call what he did criminal negligence?"—Habermas includes legal discourse here); explicative discourse for clarifying or defending the comprehensibility of discourse ("why did you use that word?"). These three "discourses" have a special status for

Habermas in that the assent sought is on universal grounds—grounds, finally, that anybody would agree to, provided, he says, "the argumentation could be conducted openly enough and continued long enough" (p. 42). This is not the case for discourse-like arguments like esthetic criticism (which depend on values that may not be generally held) or therapeutic critique aimed at the patient's self-reflection. Such arguments he calls *critique*, noting that reaching understanding is possible if a special shared understanding is present. There is no reflective or argumentative mode for expressives, however, since one's truthfulness about one's feelings cannot be grounded in reasons—it can only be shown by one's actions. It would appear, then, that to the extent that lifeworlds or paradigms prove unmergeable or incommensurate, putative instances of discourse would reduce to critique. Although crucial as a guarantee that one is engaged in communicative action, argumentation is not communicative action per se, for it suspends the basic orientation toward harmonizing plans of action. For this reason, he classifies it as a type of conversation, defining *conversation* as communicative interaction when the weight is shifted away from purposive activity toward talk which makes communication possible and stabilizes it, or in general becomes an end in itself (p. 327).

Habermas is acutely aware that the modes of communicative interaction he has distinguished are ideal types, and toward the end of the "Intermediate Reflections" in *TCA* he lists some of the adjustments necessary to map the formal model onto actual stretches of talk and their surrounding personal and social interactions. Among the more articulated of these is the observation that a certain amount of strategic indirection and intimation ("perlocutions") may often appear when setting up what the parties intend to be a communicative action in order to establish a common interpretation of the situation, but as long as the overarching intent is not to manipulate the other, but rather to proceed on a reasoned and open basis, it remains communicative action.

Even with this proviso, a great deal of idealization remains in Habermas's model. The *telos* claim, as we have seen, is indeed a claim about the proper end of human speech, not its grounds—an end which is rarely fully or extensively realized. Indeed, it is a critical norm against which actual practices can be evaluated. It is true that Habermas follows Weber in viewing Western history as a process of rationalization, that is, of the extension of rationalized action to more and more domains previously governed by authority, tradition, ritual, or habit. But the casting off of these traditional modes of regulation also exposes these domains to new forms of manipulation and deceit; Habermas's view of communicative rationality differs from Weber's cognitive-instrumental model, functioning as a basis for critique of existing practices:

> Rationalization here means extirpating those relations of force that are inconspicuously set in the very structures of communication and that prevent conscious settlement of conflicts, and consensual regulation of conflicts by means of interpsychic as well as interpersonal communication. Rationalization means overcoming such systematically distorted communication in which the action-

supporting consensus concerning the reciprocally raised validity claims—especially consensus concerning the truthfulness of intentional expressions and the rightness of underlying norms—can be sustained in appearance only, that is, counterfactually.[37]

The distinctiveness and importance of Habermas's theory of rationality lies in its fusion of argumentation with ethical concerns for human freedom and emancipation. Communicative rationality is something we ought to endorse and engage in, if only because the alternative means of coordinating actions are so unacceptable. Rationality is a social bond because it depends on the acceptance by all parties of the obligations to speak warrantably (i.e., give accounts in terms of good reasons) and to assent to the force of best reasons.[38]

The criticism of Habermas's theory that most naggingly recurs is that it is too abstract, too general, and too idealized in the direction of discourses which rarely occur or are carried to conclusion. Critics have suggested, for example, that practical action (Aristotle's phronesis) is more the mode of everyday action, and it by its nature cannot be rendered with full explicitness and generality.[39] There may well be an absolutism implicit in the pursuit of best reasons; as soon as one adds "in the estimation of the other party," one seems to introduce the possibility of manipulation, fraud, fatigue, or folly, though in fact, given the non-demonstrativeness of most reasoning, actual arguments may come to a vanishing point of irresolvable indifference, the point at which the difference of lifeworlds becomes obscure. Rationality according to Habermas is on this point procedural or formal: it cannot prove that disputes are always resolvable according to some shared sense of best reasons, but only that argumentation in good faith presupposes it. But where wise and reasonable action depends on a sense of particular situations and precedents and is a fruit of individual, concrete experience, one cannot produce all one's reasons and warrants. At this point, Aristotle introduces a principle of authority: "Therefore we ought to attend to the undemonstrated sayings and opinions of experienced and older people or of people of practical wisdom not less than to demonstrations; for because experience has given them an eye they see aright" (*NE*, 1143b). Note that the authority here is not one of tradition but of experience. The point is amplified by Gadamer, who argues that there is such a thing as well-grounded authority which it is reasonable to accept. Reason is not always the antagonist of authority, Gadamer maintains, though Habermas's desire to recover the Enlightenment's strong sense of reason inclines him to that view.[40] Habermas would agree, I think, that believing or doing something because a wise person (a phronimos) said to may in certain circumstances be entirely reasonable. As David Ingram points out in discussing Gadamer's defense of authority, the kind of authority which for Habermas is inimical to communicative rationality is that arising from institutionally sanctioned privileges and norms that are binding only on one of the parties.[41] Further, speakers may legitimately acquire authority by virtue of their eloquence: "A natural kind of authority devolves to one who has a command of language and knows how to use it well. The privileged status of the rhetorician is not ipso facto nullified by the formal conditions of the ideal speech situation. . . . Hence, assuming that differences in educational background persist in the ideal communicative situation, one can expect that disparities in actual communicative power will result in an attendant stratification sanctioning the authority of some over others" (Ingram, p. 156). And yet further, Gadamer argues that actual argumentation articulates values and beliefs for hearers that they may not have known they hold. As Ingram phrases it, "reason-giving appeals intentionally or otherwise to the inchoate values, interests, and needs of the receiver while at the same time molding them. Far from being a dispassionate affair, the argumentative search for the truth invariably engages passions and prejudices at many different levels, and it is precisely the engagement of these prejudices that elicits recognition and agreement" (p. 156). What Gadamer and Ingram are talking about here is very close to what Chaim Perelman and Lucie Olbrechts-Tyteca call *presence*, the evoking of which they speak of as "magical" and as involving the imagination as much or more than the reason.[42] Obviously, an account of rationality that insisted on the impersonality of best reasons and Cartesian methodological doubt would cut rationality off from these traditional "proofs" based on the ethos and eloquence of actual discoursing subjects.

Habermas's great contribution to thinking about rationality is his shifting the discussion from questions of strategies for pursuit of ends and methodological canons for evaluating them to modes of argumentation in deliberating upon and justifying claims and actions. In so doing, however, he reinscribes the opposition of theoretical versus practical wisdom as an opposition between argument relying solely on logos and argument drawing more broadly on personal authority, implicit (and not completely formulizable) shared understandings, and expressive ability (eloquence)—what Gadamer and others would call rhetoric, here clearly cleansed of all negative connotations. One could suggest a compromise, with Habermas's rhetoric of pure logos being the rule in certain domains (such as philosophic and scientific theorizing), but with the more inclusive rhetoric being the normative standard for practical reasoning (the reasonable as opposed to the rational). There is, however, the suggestion in Garfinkel and more than a suggestion in Gadamer that the domain of the practical-reasonable embraces all social action, and scientific theorizing, being a kind of social action, also falls within this domain. This is not just or even primarily a matter of whether scientists and theorists in fact act like practical reasoners when they "do science" or theory, but whether there are a special set of norms that regulate their discourse. That is, it would not be sufficient just to reaffirm the impractical purposes of pure science in general; one should show that the specific argumentative practices are in some ways unlike those of ordinary practical reasoners. In the next chapter, we will examine several claims that just such norms exist, so that academic or scientific discourse can be said at least in part to institutionalize the principles and practices of communicative rationality. One of these writers, Robert Merton, refers to the set of norms as the "ethos of science," and the term is a reminder that the phrase "rhetoric of pure logos" is somewhat exaggerated. That is, one who discourses according to the ethos of science may be said to be instantiating it, and hence to derive the support of its very considerable power of appeal.

Although the four sections of this chapter spring from diverse perspectives on rationality, all of them seem to be haunted by the specter of what we have called strong rationality--the belief that best reasons in any given case can be determined by tracing them to abstract and general first principles and applied decisively without recourse to personal, subjective factors. And we have seen that the discussions all aim at limiting the domain over which this specter might rule and especially whether it might be confined to scientific theorizing (in the physical sciences), though we have seen that current philosophy of science rejects it as well, offering weaker versions of rationality which include the exercise of individual judgment. In the case of Habermas, this specter accounts for many of the misunderstandings that surround his work. As noted in the introduction, this specter is the antagonist of rhetoric, reducing it to some black version of subrational manipulation, obfuscation, or ornamentation, appeals to persons rather than to principles, and so on. With the withdrawal of its antagonist, rhetoric can no longer be kept outside of disciplinary discourse, and we are free to investigate the rhetoric of the disciplines without debunking, but we must find new grounds for distinguishing properly convincing arguments and appeals from limp, shoddy, devious ones. We may pass through a carnivalesque moment in which anything goes, but clearly not everything goes; if "best reasons" don't come pre-certified as such, how do scientists and scholars arrive at agreement about them in the discourse of their disciplines?

Even though we accept the view that, on the whole, individual acts of judgment are not compelled by the force of demonstrative arguments, they would seem to be guided by some faculty or faculties of mind that are developed through learning and experience. And one would expect to find everyday and scientific theorizing again differentiated according to the kind of judgment employed. The term *professional judgment* used earlier implies the institutionalization of certain discourses and inquiries, and recasts the question of contrasting rationalities as one of discursive guidance and regulation—in a word, as differences in *norms* governing types of discourse. The "attitudes" of scientific and practical theorizing, for example, presumably derive from the different purposes of the discourses, but they are clearly oughts for practitioners—one ought to scrutinize one's assumptions, check for consistency with other knowledge, and so on. And one can then think of professional training not merely as initiation into arcane mysteries and jargon, or apprenticeship in guild crafts and practices, but as the process of acquiring the norms of the culture and the tact, taste, and judgment to apply them. The various expert cultures do have specialized rationalities—specialized "logics" by which they make and support their claims—but they all have in common the potential for enacting communicative rationality. Or, indeed, of failing to do so.

Thus the discourse of the academic disciplines does not intrinsically incarnate communicative rationality. Argumentation and debate do not always appeal solely to the force of best reasons. The most one might claim for the discourse of the disciplines, especially of the "pure" non-applied type, is that they, like Habermas's *discourse*, are not constrained by practical purposes and applications and needs for feasible compromises. But we ought not to take that discursive freedom too lightly, or debunk it too readily as a concealed operation of power and branch of the ideological state apparatus; for many students, it provides a special opportunity to engage in argumentation when their efficiency, funding, reputations, jobs, and careers are not on the line, not to mention their loyalty and patriotism. It is, to be sure, only partial and subject to erosion, but as a human ideal, it is worthy of being practiced and pursued.

II

IMPERSONALITY AND ITS
DISCONTENTS

The cognitive-instrumental view of rationality treats it as an attribute of individual actors pursuing their particular purposes; alternatively, rationality may be attributed to various communicative exchanges or, we might say, to the discursive practices of communities. As such, it is related to the "attitudes" (kind of theorizing) and purposes of the community and to the collective commitment to conduct discourse in a certain way. One may think of it as embodied in the norms governing the discourse of the community, treating the discursive *community* as a "speech community" in the sense of William Labov: "The speech community is not defined by any marked agreement in the use of language elements, so much as by participation in a set of shared norms; these norms may be observed in overt types of evaluative behavior."[1] There is nothing concealed or unsuspected about such norms; they can be and sometimes are articulated—"one ought to keep one's promises," "acknowledge one's sources," and the like. There is only slight overlap between norms in this sense and what Foucault calls "discursive formation rules," i.e., well-formedness rules for statements that determine whether or not they make serious claims to truth within a certain discipline; rather, norms bind and guide individuals as they make and respond to arguments in the discipline.[2] We *can* follow Foucault in noting that norms have both a restrictive and a productive aspect: they set limits on a writer's palate of persuasive and stylistic techniques, but they open up possibilities for the individual and the community. By conforming to the norms, individuals can get perfect strangers to take their words seriously, even to cite them, and sometimes to assent. For the communities that employ them, these norms produce special, orderly exchanges pursuing a concern that welds together otherwise rather isolated individuals scattered geographically all over the world, that is universalistic in its appeal even as it is special and to various degrees impractical in its focus. They offer discursive possibilities which, if they did not exist, it would exceed the abilities of any individual to invent. Disciplinary discourse is literally utopian; it is the scholar's out-of-body experience. Thus knowledge-producing disciplines are disciplined both by their special aim and by the norms that guide their pursuit of that aim.

These initial reflections may make a prima facie case for the existence and importance of discursive norms in communities, but they provide little guidance in investigating them. Further, investigating them is rarely if ever a disinterested undertaking. Giving accounts of its norms is part of the self-reflection of academic communities, and the accounts are often part apology, part self-promotion, and maybe part ideological obfuscation. In this chapter, we will consider three such accounts, and traditions of account-giving, in the field broadly of academic, scholarly discourse and more narrowly in "science" (which we will allow to slide easily from *Wissenschaft* to laboratory to natural science)—namely, those of David Olson, Alvin Gouldner, and Robert Merton. These have been widely cited and applied, both as criteria for regulation and criticism within the disciplines and as guides for instruction insofar as it involves enculturation in them.

We will adopt the following queries as a checklist for interrogating these three discussions of norms for academic discourses:

(1) what is the relation of norms and practices? Can norms be read off from practices straightforwardly? Are the norms coherent, or do they conflict in some cases?

(2) what aspects of discourse do the norms govern? Do they hold in some contexts (e.g., formal, public forums) more than in others?

(3) what are the norms grounded on? Whence do they derive their normative force?

(4) what is the history of their formation? How uniform and widespread are they? What interests are served by them?

We will focus on a norm that under one name or another all three writers discuss, the norm, that is, that distinguishes contributions to public knowledge from that of private, personal expression and reflection, that separates the argument from its author and from its addressees, the norm of impersonality/autonomy/universalism. This is the troublesome norm that seems severely to restrict the rhetoric of academic discourse, and it is problematic in this chapter much as "methodology" was in the first.

Before taking up the three main accounts of norms for academic writing, however, we may rehearse the use of these four queries in regard to what might be called the minimalist account of the norms of written English, namely the rather old-fashioned and thoroughly discussed norm of Formal Written English (hereafter FWE), which for the purposes of this discussion should be understood in the "correct usage" sense—that prescriptive grammarian's heterogeneous bag of DON'Ts (. . . dangle prepositions or participles, split infinitives, use *which* as a restrictive relative pronoun [or with an entire clause as antecedent], confuse subjective and objective cases, use *whose* for inanimates, commit subject/verb agreement errors, use double negatives, use *like* as an adverb, say *anxious* when you mean *eager*, use *centers around*, etc.). In regard to the first question, these norms are said to have been extracted from the published writing of the best authors (from about the time of Dryden), though many critics have happily shown that not all the best authors always observed them, and they have of course been deliberately flouted on small or large scale.

There is thus a certain well-charted distance between norm and practice. These rules can be applied in a noncontradictory fashion: the main conflicts that arise are with further, stylistic norms of simplicity and naturalness.

The answer to the second question—the domain of application—is also fairly straightforward, since they are promulgated as rules for preparing written texts to circulate in formal contexts of exchange, though the attempt used to be made to extend them to classroom speaking.[3] These rules do indeed constitute a discursive norm regulating writers' practices over a wide variety of writing tasks; the community they define is the uninstitutionalized one of "those who care about language" or "the lettered." Their regulation of discourse, however, is essentially technical or editorial; even when observing the rules is made a matter of moral exhortation, their actual observation is a matter of the editor's pencil applied to an already-composed text, usually typed.

Answers to the third question—the grounds of the normative force—have been much more varied, ranging from a desire to arrest linguistic change and conserve the intelligibility of the great writers of the past to claims that the norms enhance the logic and clarity of expression. Occasionally it is even argued that observing them functions to indicate that one has been schooled, that is, initiated into the scribal culture. These different groundings are hardly consistent, and it may well be that the various prescribed practices of FWE do not all serve the same ends.

Finally, the history of their formation beginning in the eighteenth century is well known, as is their special development in American public education, the challenges to them mounted especially in the 1960s and early 1970s, and so on. Scholars also generally agree about the class interests promoting FWE, namely that concern with codifying and inculcating correctness was most widespread in the middle and lower middle classes as a means of displacing the norm of "well-bred" speech. That is, the prescriptive grammar movement promoted a classless norm which all could learn in school and hence provided a cure for linguistic insecurity for the socially aspiring and provincial. Thus, except for the question of grounding, we can be said to have a fairly thorough and adequate understanding of the norm of FWE.

One of the reasons that inculcating FWE almost defined the purpose of instruction in writing for many teachers was that it *is* technical; its rules are enumerable, finite, and mechanically applicable to a very wide variety of kinds of writing ranging from office memos to newspaper articles to essays and lab reports; they do not require reflection upon audiences and purposes, knowledge of special genres, conventions, modes of argument and kinds of proof, nor do they raise questions about the stance of the knowing subject or distinctions between legitimate and illegitimate appeals. They say nothing, that is, about the content of the writing or the conduct of the writer. As long as you don't dangle participles, commit errors of agreement, or strew commas where periods should go, you can do as you like.

Reflecting this technical orientation, the code of FWE does not directly address such norms as that of impersonality. To be sure, it does sometimes make superficial gestures in that direction (Don't use "I"), but such strictures seem arbitrary and unmotivated. The discussions of Olson, Gouldner, and Merton attempt a theoretical articulation and rationale for their norms. Olson's sketch of the the norms of Text (which govern "philosophic and scientific writing") is explicitly linked to the aims of education; Gouldner's sketch of the Culture of Critical Discourse describes many similar traits, but subjects the code to ideological scrutiny and critique; Merton's description of the ethos of science is a virtual apologia for science as a way of life. In the Mertonian tradition, the ethical and dramaturgical nature of discursive norms comes most to the fore.

1. "Text" as a Norm for Discourse

David Olson, Professor at the Ontario Institute for Studies in Education, is particularly concerned with the rationale for instruction in what he calls schooled writing which culminates in the prose expository essay. In his 1977 articles in the *Harvard Educational Review* and the *Journal of Communication* and in a series of subsequent pieces, he has characterized the set of conventions or code of the essay (or Text) as embodying the epitome of Western rationality: analytic thinking and the constructing of general, consistent models of the world (as in philosophy and science).[4] The value we place on observing and inculcating these conventions thus derives from the value we place on these activities as the evolved product of over two thousand years of Western cultural history.

Olson makes it very clear that these conventions go far beyond the "editing" conventions of FWE just alluded to and extend to the relations of readers and writers to texts. Indeed, they arise from three principles that differentiate the code of Text from other uses of language, especially those he groups under the term Utterance: the three principles have to do with meaning, truth, and function. With regard to meaning, Olson maintains that Text must be explicit about its assumptions and intentions so that it can contain and convey its meaning without any knowledge of the circumstances in which it was written. Text is said to be autonomous in minimizing its dependence on its context. The ideal Text would require no particular, personal knowledge of reader by writer or writer by reader in order to convey its meaning. In a sense, the writer and reader are anonymous—one of Olson's articles is entitled "Writing: The Divorce of the Author from the Text." In Derrida's terms, Text is emptied of presence. The writer should not use terms or refer to entities or events except those already known by her intended audience; otherwise, she is obliged to introduce and define them explicitly. She should not rely on the reader's inferences about her purposes or conclusions, but should state them fully. (That is, sentence meaning should fully realize utterer's meaning.) The ideal Text is a closed text which uniquely determines one reading of itself, a reading that exhausts it.

With regard to the second principle, that having to do with truth, Olson argues that Text is committed to a correspondence theory of truth, and truth in Text may run counter to intuition, commonsense, or authority. The writer cannot rely on personal appeals to the reader or his personal credibility and authority to make his point. As Hildyard and Olson put it, "the authority of rhetorical conditions are collapsed onto the truth conditions so that if a statement is true to the facts or to the text itself, that is sufficient condition for its being inter-personally appropriate. . . ."[5] Olson thus views the rhetoric of Text as one of pure logos. Clearly Text is a mode leaning heavily toward informative purposes, and it is a definition of expository writing that rather sharply distinguishes it from persuasion. In fact, he even refers to textbooks and primary school readers as the exemplars and typical examples of schooled language (written Text), noting also that their anonymity, combined with their use in institutions of instruction, gives them an aura of "objective" authority, enabling them to perform an archival and socially stabilizing function of presenting what "society takes to be the 'true' and 'valid' knowledge from which norms of thought and action may be derived" ("Divorce," p. 109).[6]

The third principle, that of function, emphasizes that Text is especially adapted to building abstract and coherent theories of reality, but not to all purposes:

> The development of this explicit, formal system accounts, I have argued, for the predominant features of Western culture and for our distinctive ways of using language and our distinctive modes of thought. Yet the general theories of science and philosophy that are tied to the formal uses of text provide a poor fit to daily, ordinary, practical, and personally significant experience. Oral language with its depth of resources and its multitude of paths to the same goal, while an instrument of limited power for exploring abstract ideas, is a universal means of sharing our understanding of concrete situations and practical actions. ("From Utterance to Text," p. 278)

Thus Olson does not claim the absolute superiority of Text over oral language (or Utterance), and the value he places on it is tied to the value we place on explicit statement and precise reasoning, which are essential for constructing abstract and coherent theories of the world. Clearly, Olson's opposition of Utterance and Text has close affinities to the Schütz-Garfinkel distinction of commonsense vs. scientific theorizing (here translated into norms for written discourse), and indeed Olson employs these terms in the *Journal of Communication* article ("Commonsense knowledge is related to theoretical knowledge in the same way that utterances are related to texts"—p. 15). And similarly, it has strong affinities to Basil Bernstein's distinction of restricted vs. elaborated code, as Olson mentions in this article, but differs from it in being grounded in "the structure of the media of communication," rather than in "underlying social structures in the family and the culture as a whole" (p. 15n1). The point at issue is that Bernstein argued that access to and use of elaborated code increased as one ascended the social class ladder, and correlated with "person-centered" family types (rather than position-centered).[7] That is, more generally, "Different speech forms or codes symbolize the form of the social relationship, regulate the nature of the speech encounters, and create for the speakers different orders of relevance and relation." Bernstein takes the essentially Marxian position that "the speech form is taken as a consequence of the form of the social relation or put more generally, is a quality of a social structure" (p. 161), though he immediately qualifies this by conceding that that speech form may in turn modify the social structure and may indeed free itself from its initial social moorings. Olson presents the code of Text as if it has freed itself of any social moorings.

Olson's account of Text norms has been found wanting on all four of our criteria. First of all, it has been noted that the relation of these norms to actual practices is anything but straightforward. The norm of explicitness, for one, is quite distant from practice and seems to be overstated: it cannot be fully and absolutely met, for observing it would swell any text to unmanageable dimensions. Olson freely concedes that the maxims of Text do not characterize all the uses of writing, and even that total explicitness may be an unattainable ideal, but he also argues that Text epitomizes the unique tendencies and potentialities inherent in writing. A course in Text is better for you than, say, one in political speech writing, for it better exercises your capacity for analytic thought and precise argument. Be that as it may, Martin Nystrand, Anne Doyle, and Margaret Himley have objected that Olson's account does not give the right sort of guidance to a writer, which is certainly not "approximate complete explicitness as an ideal within reason" but rather "be explicit about what needs to be said" given the intended audience and purpose of the particular text.[8]

Problems arise also with the second criterion having to do with the domain of activities governed by the norms. Clearly, not everything written is Text for Olson, but one might also note that some spoken monologues would seem to be governed by Text norms. This is a point commonly made—"speaking a written language"—and does not I think deeply unsettle the foundations of Olson's distinction. More unsettling is the range of terms he uses for examples of Text ("philosophic and scientific writing"): essayist prose, expository prose, textbooks, schooled language (this last is obviously tendentious, if the ultimate question is what language should be schooled). Getting Montaigne's *Essais* together with Locke's *Essay* as writing of the same type takes some doing; which scientists he has in mind are anyone's guess; and merging all of these with *"Discovering Our World"* textbook prose levels many important distinctions of author, audience, and purpose.

Unless we know what kinds of texts Olson has centrally in mind, it is hard to assess the grounding of the norms of Text, since Olson argues that these norms have arisen out of the practices of Western writers, especially since the development of printing. In fact, Olson relies heavily on the composite history of literacy, citing Goody and Watt, Havelock, Ong, and others.[9] Insofar as he defends Text as the means of doing philosophy and science, the grounding of the norms of Text becomes a part of the larger question of the grounding of those discourses, but this he is content to treat as self-evident.

With regard to the historical formation of Text, Olson does sketch some milestones in the internal history of the code, but he leaves the class and other social interests supporting and promoting Text entirely undiscussed.

The objections are not exhausted by these observations that Olson's sketch is overstated, vague, thinly grounded, and uncritical. More fundamentally, it can be argued that Olson's account is simply mistaken in its characterization of the inherent tendency of written, scientific/philosophic discourse to produce self-contained objects which can be scrutinized and evaluated in themselves, and hence that it seriously misdirects apprentice writers. Specifically, the code of autonomy of Text fosters a spurious belief in the possibility of attaining objectivity, turning the student's attention away from writing as a human action and transaction between human subjects and toward the construction of a perfect artifact that can't fail to win, or compel, assent. It obscures or denies the dialogic anticipation and answering back that Bakhtin emphasizes, and it ruthlessly intellectualizes the grounds on which belief and assent are actually granted. As a practical matter, Olson is right that student writing often tends to rely more on implicit knowledge, flexible word sense, and implicatures than academic writing expects. But the claim that implicit values and interests are irrelevant when writing and reading Text flies directly in the face of a leading tenet of "critical reading" (which also claims to represent the norms of academic, intellectual culture), namely, that readers should scrutinize Texts not just in terms of the quality of their evidence, precision, and explicitness of their reasoning, but also who is writing, in the service of what interests, and why now. And even if there were no "critical reading" movement, the claim would have trouble accounting for the practice of reviewers, who quite commonly evaluate scholarly works on the basis of their implicit political leanings, the author's previous works, incompletely articulated and unresolved conflicts, and the reviewer's own personal opinion of the matters discussed—*not*, that is, strictly on the grounds of explicit argument and evidence.

While Olson defends the code of Text as furthering a certain emancipatory ideal—its ability to resist received opinion and to innovate—his remarks on the quasi-objective authority of textbooks, which he seems to endorse, are distinctly chilling, since what textbooks contain is on his own account a kind of received opinion shored up with the anonymous institutional authority of the school. We may readily grant Gadamer's argument that all action, including intellectual inquiry, takes place against a background of shared understanding and does not profitably proceed by applying radical doubt to every term and concept in sight. Hence, we can see why Olson emphasizes the function of schooling to transmit tradition and prevailing consensus. But does not the tradition also include the techniques and habits of mind that we call critical?

Olson is not unaware of the one-sidedness of his discussion of textbook authority, for in a similar version of the article just discussed, he adds "an additional factor," namely that the right to criticism and dissent comes with membership in a peer group, so that academics treat the texts of their peers just as they would their face-to-face discourses: "And anything that could now be said directly to the author as an equal (perhaps even more) can also be said/ written against his text. That is, a peer group both invites the possibility of criticism and reunites the author with his writings."[10] Note that such dialogic arguing and answering back so characteristic of academic writing does not conform to Text! Qualification to act as a peer, Olson says, arises "at least in part from being a participant in that particular form of discourse, that is, through becoming a writer." Presumably, then, to urge *students* to engage in critical reading is to ask them to adopt an imaginary, counterfactual stance toward the text—to de-Textify it, and to imagine themselves as participants in a "conversation" with Plato and Luther, Locke and Kant, Marx, Freud, and Wittgenstein (or with other scholars currently arguing about them, if secondary sources are allowed). It appears that the student's transformation is now no longer one from a producer of Utterance to a producer of Texts, but from the respectful receiver of knowledge embodied in Text to a partner in academic dialectic. Here Olson teeters on the edge of contradiction, implying that academic discourse is actually quite Utterance-like and not the epitome of Text. We could avoid the contradiction by following the suggestion of a sequence: first the student leaves her original intellectual village of home, school, and peers and learns to produce textbook-like expository essays; then she acquires membership in a new intellectual village and can largely relax the constraints of Text.

It is far from certain that Olson would endorse this squaring of his accounts, and in one respect it is still inadequate, in that Text is not merely discarded in the final stage. Rather, it seems to function as a set of criteria not for constructing discourses but for evaluating and criticizing them. Thus one may say of a given text that it does not use terminology clearly and consistently, it makes unacknowledged special assumptions, fails to consider all the relevant facts, commits logical fallacies, merely reproduces accepted wisdom, and so on. And too it embodies a set of criteria which must not be invoked in academic debate having chiefly to do with the personal characteristics of the writer, unacknowledged implications, and unforeseen consequences of the argument. (This interpretation links up with work on the norms of scientific discourse that we will take up in the third section.) We might note, however, that "academic debate" is being used in a rather sanitized, normative way here: the polemical style of academic debate is not at all careful about sticking to what is actually said and leaving the author's mother out of it, as it were. But insofar as polemic is regarded as a deviation or violation of the scholarly code, it backhandedly upholds Olson's sketch, or parts of it.

Setting these subtleties and extrapolations aside for the moment, however, we can summarize the appeal of Olson's conception of "Text" as follows: it offers the individual writer a deal she can't or shouldn't refuse, at least if her aim is to make a serious contribution to science or philosophy. In return for bracketing out the particularities of her personal experience and point of view, she gets a potentially universal audience that will examine her argument on its own merits. Thus did Olson in the mid-1970s affirm the goal of writing instruction as the inculcation of Text as the culmination of the Western tradition.

2. The Culture of Critical Discourse

Alvin Gouldner's description of what he calls the Culture of Critical Discourse is in many respects complementary to Olson's view of Text and almost exactly contemporary with it. (*The Dialectic of Ideology and Technology* was published in 1976; *The Future of Intellectuals and the Rise of the New Class* in 1979.) The particular norms that make up that culture are very similar to Olson's, but Gouldner is principally interested in the historical and political implications of the Culture, precisely the dimension that is undeveloped by Olson. As a self-styled Neo-Hegelian sociologist, he unfolds his analysis as a discovery of limitations and contradictions, so that a more complex attitude toward this culture and its norms emerges.

The Culture of Critical Discourse and its norms are a relatively recent historical formation, Gouldner says. It embodies the basic commitment to rationality shared by intellectuals and the intelligentsia, technocrats, and bureaucrats in the modern state. The technological innovation of printing contributed to its formation (here he is in perfect agreement with Olson), but equally important was the emergence of the modern, and especially of scientism and positivism, in opposition to traditional authority and institutions. "This is a culture of discourse that rests on the sociological premise that the coercive power and the public credit of societal authorities has been undermined, restricted, or declared irrelevant, and that the use of manipulative rhetoric is limited either by institutional and moral restraints or by the prevailing technology of mass communication" (p. 39). Its essence is compounded of two main impulses—toward self-groundedness and toward self-reflexiveness—and Gouldner presses these to the point of dialectical contradiction. The impulse to self-groundedness leads to the formation of Text very much as Olson describes it: discourse is to be addressed to a public of unknown others, is to spell out all its premises, bracket out the personal interests and biases of the writer, pursue knowledge for its own sake, employ words with fixed, lexical senses, make a serious, carefully considered argument, and submit it to the scrutiny of the relevant public, with its acceptance to depend solely on the force of its reasons. Following this impulse leads to "defocalization of the persons to whom the text is addressed and of the speaker making the address."[11] It thus aspires to the self-groundedness of a mathematical demonstration.

The culture, however, is also animated by the impulse toward self-awareness and self-criticism: "This prizes the speaker's capacity to speak the assumptions of his perspective, to know the rules to which he submits. Rationality is here construed as the capacity to make problematic what had hitherto been treated as given; to bring into reflection what before had only been used; to transform resource into topic; to examine critically the life we lead" (p. 49). This capacity may be developed in individuals to various degrees, but it is also collectively enacted in dialogue, in which others scrutinize and challenge the assumptions of the speaker.

> The grounding of such a rationality can therefore be secured only in the right of the listener to question and critique the speaker's assumptions. Such rationality, then, depends not only on the speaker but, no less, on the listener and on their *inter*relationship. Rational discourse entails a kind of *rotating* division of labor, the speaker of the moment having a vested interest in *his* assumptions, while the listener challenges, and, indeed, has a vested interest in his capacity to challenge, the assumptions made, and so on. Such rationality, then, is in the *dialogue* and in rules that permit assumptions to be examined regressively. But one should note that under these rules the particular set of assumptions at any given moment—the cultural *status quo*—is always subject to challenge. Inherent in this structure of rationality, then, is potential revolution in permanence, the "permanent revolution." It is the drive toward unending perfection, that unceasing restlessness and lawlessness, that was first called *anomos* and later *anomie*. (p. 49)

And thus the fact that speakers have interests and assumptions—that no discourse is self-grounded—cannot finally be repressed: "Objectivism is that pathology of cognition that entails silence about the speaker, about his interests and his desires, and how these are socially situated and structurally maintained" (p. 50). Hence the much vaunted capacity of Text to resist the taken-for-granted and challenge its groundedness applies finally to itself. By making self-awareness itself persuasive, Gouldner turns the tables on any instance of Text, canceling its status as permanent, monologic artifact by highlighting its status as one moment in a potentially endless dialectic.

If the Culture of Critical Discourse sets a high value on questioning assumptions and received wisdom, it is not epitomized in the problem solving activity of Kuhnian normal science; Gouldner even cites Kuhn to the effect that "it is precisely the abandonment of critical discourse that marks the transition to a science. Once a field has made that transition, critical discourse recurs only at moments of crisis."[12] One of the crucial properties of paradigms, of course, is that they allow disputes to be settled and consensus formed (provisionally, to be sure) by securing certain assumptions of the status quo from challenge. Hence, for many technical endeavors, Gouldner suggests, CCD is there only as a "latent but mobilizable" resource.[13] This conception sounds much like Habermas's view of *diskurs* as a mode for resolving difficulties in normal endeavor, though one can see that, given Gouldner's peek into the *abyme* of reflexive scrutiny, the resolution would not have the appearance of conclusiveness that paradigms provide. Paradigms function as what Latour and Woolgar call black boxes—whole complexes of concepts and reasons that were at one time argued and may be so again, but for the nonce can be taken for granted to get on with business. Thus the tenet of universal questioning, which Gouldner as much as Schütz and

Garfinkel take as central to the attitude of scientific theorizing, is variably applied, it would seem, even within science. The workaday research report is neither very "scientifically theorized" nor very self-critical.

Gouldner pursues the two-sidedness of CCD on both the psychological and the social levels. In relation to personal psychology, CCD is a "classical" discipline of restraint or "self-editing" which buys "commendable circumspection, carefulness, self-discipline and 'seriousness' " at the cost of a disposition "toward stilted convoluted speech, an inhibition of play, imagination and passion, and continual pressure for expressive discipline" (*Intellectuals*, p. 84; see also *Ideology*, p. 60). The result can be ·a certain inflexibility in the face of changing situations and an insensitivity to persons in favor of tasks. On the social level, CCD is the core consciousness of the New Class which is emerging all over the world; on the one hand, it is *the* progressive and emancipatory force in modern life, but on the other, it is elitist with its own hegemonic designs: "Even as it subverts old inequities, the New Class silently inaugurates a new hierarchy of the knowing, the knowledgeable, the reflexive and insightful. Those who talk well, it is held, excel those who talk poorly or not at all. It is now no longer enough simply to be good. Now one has to explain it. The New Class is the universal class in embryo, but badly flawed" (*Intellectuals*, p. 85). The CCD is particularly prone to lapse into being the ideology of technocrats when it forgets its commitment to self-awareness, as it tends to do in the public school system, where it serves the school's need for an impartial mode of public discourse that rises above the particular interests of the students and forces in society. Nonetheless, one might elaborate Gouldner's point by suggesting that the critical impulse in CCD is a kind of surplus; it was originally directed on the social world as it found it, namely as a product of traditional and authoritarian views, but now it is directed on the new social order that supplanted the old, and the new order is much of its own making, including the new body of received opinion.[14] It thus inevitably becomes more reflexive, since its targets for critique are the results of its own work.

There is little doubt how Gouldner would view Olson's Text, namely, as one moment in the dialectic of CCD. Olson's account of Text is thus a clear illustration of the impulse to self-groundedness. The principle of critique had to be brought in from outside, as it were, since Text presents only an edited silence about its writer and reader, declaring them irrelevant for the proper making and reception of Text. And, for certain purposes— say of working science—they may be relatively so. That is a question we will refer to the next section on the norms of scientific discourse. But insofar as it is so, the writing moves away from the center of CCD by limiting the horizon to which universal questioning applies. The special interest of Gouldner's dialectical account is that the critical principle for him is not outside the historical formation of CCD but a part of it, not that which poses the limits to the culture of Text but rather that which brings them into consciousness; further, the critical principle does not in itself provide a superior alternative to Text. Rather, it, together with Text, poses a problem, well nigh a dilemma, for the modern consciousness to overcome.

Unfortunately, Gouldner's suggestions about the direction of resolution (of *Aufhebung*) are incompletely worked out. We will see some other struggles with this conflict and attempts at resolution in the next chapter.

The complexity of Gouldner's conception of CCD can be highlighted by comparing it to a recent discussion of disciplinary discourse by Robert Hariman.[15] Hariman focuses on disciplinary discourse in relation to professionalism and expertise as sources of anti-traditional power. Hariman's professional experts have much in common with Gouldner's New Class, except that Hariman's account is less philosophical, more social: the place of positivism is taken by professionalism—the code whereby the middle class displaced aristocrats and attained administrative power for themselves. That is, knowledge for its own sake is not the real goal of the contemporary academy, which really has no place in its structures for serious self-scrutiny and reflection. Hence there is no effective principle of critique built into the contemporary academy or ethos of the professions, and it must come from the outside, via "rhetoric," where rhetoric is conceived not as an academic discipline but as deliberately unprofessional, marginal, and insurrectionary—an intellectual populism or gadfly. Clearly Hariman's view feeds the "monolithic" conception of disciplinary discourse as producing a culture of complacent experts and bureaucrats. Such a view makes the inculcation of disciplinary discourse an unappealing (because unworthy) goal of instruction.

There is one reason, I think, to prefer Gouldner's more complex view of CCD: Hariman's view has no place in it for serious disciplinary self-critique, but, as the following chapters will show, there is plenty of that, and anxiety and sense of crisis, within the disciplines. This does not mean that everything entitled "Rhetoric of . . ." is a critique of disciplinary practices and purposes, but much is, and deserves the "rhetorician's" attentive study and support. As Gouldner suggests, academic discourse is a lot more open, self-conscious, and self-critical on the inside than Hariman thinks.

3. The Norms of Scientific Discourse

Gouldner's account of CCD makes it a unique, emergent formation of a New Class and a new elite. When scientists come to reflect on their own code, however, they have traditionally described the organized pursuit of knowledge as epitomizing long-standing humanist values. Here, for example, is Jacob Bronowski, writing some thirty years ago in his immensely popular *Science and Human Values*:

> By the worldly standards of public life, all scholars in their work are of course oddly virtuous. They do not make wild claims, they do not cheat, they do not try to persuade at any cost, they appeal neither to prejudice nor to authority, they are often frank about their ignorance, their disputes are fairly decorous, they do not

confuse what is being argued with race, politics, sex or age, they listen patiently
to the young and to the old who both know everything. These are the general
virtues of scholarship, and they are peculiarly the virtues of science.[16]

This is an assorted mix of virtues—most apply to discursive behavior, the two
exceptions being not cheating and patient listening. Quite a number of sketches
have been given of the *ethos* of science, which ties very directly in to the ethos of
the scientist: the ethos of science comprises the values that the particular
scientists should uphold or appear to uphold in their papers, articles, books,
and lectures as they enact their membership in their professional community.
Quite possibly, they should also uphold them in their conversations with
colleagues in their laboratories and offices and in the corridors. As a
spokesman for scientists, Bronowski sounds quite complacent and self-satisfied,
partly, I think, because his list is made up almost entirely of negatives—practices
commonly enough engaged in which scientists eschew. We shall quickly see,
however, that some scientists and sociologists of science have been much more
probing and critical. Very broadly, the public image of science suffered a severe
blow to its innocence with the publication of James Watson's *The Double
Helix: A Personal Account of the Discovery of the Structure of DNA* in 1968
from which it may never recover.

Bronowski's remarks share with Olson's and Gouldner's accounts the property of being extremely general: none of them are intended as an initial sketch
for investigation and refinement—as an empirical theory, in the very broad
sense, of how norms govern the way scholars and scientists behave. There is
such a theory, however, and tradition of application, challenge, refinement, and
extension stemming from the work of Robert Merton. This work is a valuable
resource for carrying our discussion beyond the provocative obiter dicta of
Olson and Gouldner.

In the early 1940s, Robert Merton wrote essays on what he called the
normative structure of science; these have proved extremely seminal in the
sociology of science and are still being discussed.[17] Merton sketched four
norms of pure, academic science—cultural values and mores which he believed
governed the activities termed scientific. He held these norms to be binding "not
only because they are procedurally efficient, but because they are believed right
and good" (p. 270). These were Universalism, "Communism," Disinterestedness, and Organized Skepticism. Very briefly,

Universalism insists that scientific findings and theories be evaluated without
regard to personal facts or attributes of their proponents; this norm is more
conveniently called "impersonality" and is very similar to Olson's norm of
autonomy of Texts.

"Communism" refers to the paradox that a scientist can only "own" a theory
by disseminating it publicly; hence arises the obligation to publish one's
findings and an antagonism to secrecy.

Disinterestedness does not refer to personal motives of scientists, but to the submission of findings and theories to professional judgments of merit ("rigorous policing"), which should be rendered without regard for whatever coterie, social, or ideological interests might seem to be involved. In the tradition of commentary on this norm, it is frequently taken to bar scientists from pursuing their work for personal gain or fame.

Organized Skepticism is chiefly skepticism applied to sacred cows—that is, any natural phenomenon can be subjected to scientific scrutiny and theorizing. This is a limited form of methodological doubt.

In constructing this list, Merton drew upon a tradition of apologies for science, as Thomas Gieryn notes, as well as on Talcott Parsons's writings.[18] The list itself is something of an apology, and builds a case for science as democratic, progressive, and emancipatory. Elsewhere, Merton wrote a full-length study of the emergence of the scientific ethos in the seventeenth century under the crucial influence of Protestantism.[19] Hence Merton does not ground the norms in any sort of logical or conceptual analysis of communication or social bonds, but rather regards them as a particular, fragile, and contingent social formation. Scholars, among them Marlon Blissett, have noted that norms also support the autonomy of science from the social and political forces and processes of particular societies. Scientists not only *can* conduct and regulate their activities themselves, but *must* be allowed to do so.[20]

Merton's essays and the immense body of commentary and criticism they elicited provide fairly full answers to the questions posed by our four criteria. Much of this commentary and application has focused on the relation of the norms to practices, on conflicts between the norms (and possible counter-norms), and on the precise aspects of discourse they govern (and hence on how they are manifested). Sociologists and ethnographers have observed instances when the personality and reliability of particular scientists were invoked in evaluation, when hoarding results seems common, when scientists struggle to advance their own theories and those which they think will support them, and when scientists act like commonsense reasoners relying on a large number of implicit, uncriticized assumptions. We will trace the general lines of this elaboration and critique by following the discussion of the first norm, that of Universalism, since it ties in most directly to the question of subjectivity in discourse and is central to the norms as they govern discourse.

Merton explains the norm of Universalism as: "truth claims, whatever their source, are to be subjected to *preestablished impersonal criteria:* consonant with observation and with previously confirmed knowledge. The acceptance or rejection of claims entering the lists of science is not to depend on the personal or social attributes of the protagonist; his race, nationality, religion, class, and personal qualities are as such irrelevant" (p. 270). (Note that this norm would help account for Foucault's claim that the author[s]' names do little to establish value in modern science).[21] Merton applies this norm by showing how it rejects nationalistic, especially Nazi (and later Soviet) attempts to discard some science as non-Aryan or otherwise "bad." And from it he also derives a mandate for equal opportunity for careers in science regardless of caste. Far from being unique to science, he argues that universalism is a dominant guiding principle of democracy as such. From his examples, it is clear that this norm is a rule about what criteria may not be applied when evaluating, especially rejecting or delegitimating, a piece of science. Lest one suppose that the passing of Hitler and Stalin has rendered the issue thoroughly passé, note should be taken that it was recently raised by the neuropsychologist John C. Marshall in his review of Peter Gay's new book on Freud (*Freud, Atheism, and the Making of Psycho-analysis*): Freud's personal life and attitude toward his heritage are of little importance to psychoanalysis, *precisely insofar as it is a science*—a position Freud always upheld when speaking as an apologist, but which conflicts with a number of his other remarks and with Gay's account of "the making of psychoanalysis."[22]

Subsequent commentators have noted that this norm, and the others, are often violated in some of the off-the-record behavior of scientists, particularly with regard to assessment on personal grounds. As Barry Barnes and R.G.A. Dolby note, scientists flip through journals reading only the "big-name" articles and avoiding the work of people they consider unreliable;[23] personal estimates of the credibility of particular scientists are a common rule of thumb (so also Rom Harré[24]). For neither Barnes and Dolby nor Harré is this a serious violation of the norm, however. Barnes and Dolby distinguish between *criteria* (Merton's word) and *indicators* of reliability, the latter being these and other rules of thumb that scientists employ as liberally as the rest of us, at times perhaps erroneously. In fact, they regard Merton's 'non-Aryan' example as a foolish rule of thumb applied by a mistaken Nazi. Harré sees personal assessments of credibility as a reasonable induction over previous encounters with the scientist's work. He draws a distinction similar to Barnes and Dolby's, this time between the "strict system of assessment" and the actual one, noting that the strict system is best understood as a moral injunction. Both of these distinctions seem somewhat fragile, especially insofar as they do not spell out the relation of the two systems in practice or address the possibility of blurring. These distinctions are similar to the frequently drawn one of context of discovery vs. context of validation usually attributed to Hans Reichenbach (with the Mertonian canons applying only in the latter context), but Karin Knorr-Cetina and also Derek Phillips have assailed it as untenable in practice: considerations of the origin or discovery of findings are constantly raised by scientists evaluating each other's work (or proposed work, in the case of refereeing grant applications).[25] Indeed, Marlon Blissett, reporting on a survey of 789 academic scientists and mathematicians regarding the perceived behavior of other scientists, says that 65 percent of the scientists *disagreed with* the statement that "acceptance or nonacceptance of scientific evidence does not in any way depend on the social position of the one who submits it (that is, his institutional affiliation), his degree of recognition, those under whom he has studied or worked" (*Politics in Science*, p. 72).

Ethnographers who have interviewed scientists concerning their work and that of controversial colleagues have turned up many accusations of bias, prejudice, ineptitude, and other selfish and self-aggrandizing motives (see Mitroff, Gilbert and Mulkay, Latour and Woolgar, Collins[26]). In one study of the gravity wave controversy, Harry Collins compiled a list of eleven "nonscientific" sources of attitudes toward the controversial scientists which includes such things as "Faith in experimental capabilities and honesty, based on a previous working partnership," "Personality and intelligence of experimenters," "Inside information," "Size and prestige of university of origin" and "Nationality"(!) "Replication," p. 105). However, Collins is careful to note that scientists also criticize themselves and each other for not doing science proper at such junctures ("Replication," p. 106; "Son," pp. 46–47).

Collins and Trevor Pinch analyzed mainstream scientific response to research on paranormal phenomena in terms of two forums, the constituent and the contingent.[27] The constituent forum is the formal, public one of presentation and criticism in professional journals and (perhaps) formal conferences. The contingent forum is made up of "the contents of popular and semipopular journals, discussion and gossip, fund raising and publicity seeking." Their use of this term seems similar to Gilbert and Mulkay's "contingent repertoire" (which contrasts with the "empiricist repertoire"), where we find frequent references to personal factors influencing the doing of science that are edited out of the official story. If they are not edited out, David Travis notes, they may give rise to damaging suspicions that the scientist is unserious or even contemptuous of the discourse he is participating in.[28] Cross-classifying this distinction is another between implicit and explicit opposition. Implicit opposition, they note, is common in the constituent forum (theories are just ignored and allowed to die), and explicit opposition is generally couched in terms of method and theory, rather than the personalities or motives of the scientist. J. M. Ziman[29] describes the rule of muted opposition ("It is thought to be unkind and professionally unprofitable to point out another man's error in public; better simply to hint that his claims are not quite substantiated and then to give one's own more positive and correct version," p. 115) and uses it to argue for referees applying tough standards "without deference to the identity of the author or his corporate backing" (p. 117). That is, it is just because errors are not vigorously denounced once an article appears that submissions must be rigorously screened by referees.

In regard to paranormal phenomena, however, Collins and Pinch note that personal considerations are raised in the constituent forum, suggesting that the normal courtesy accorded to colleagues in print is not extended to those with notably deviant beliefs. So for example Thomas Szasz writes in *Psychiatric Quarterly* that the identification of ESP with the occult "is responsible for the obscurantism which pervades this area of inquiry and which makes its companionship unwarranted in the larger field of scientific disciplines" (Collins and Pinch, p. 246) Similarly, J. Hanlon writes in the semipopular *The New Scientist* concerning parapsychological researchers at Stanford, "Targ has worked in the parapsychology area on and off for fifteen years. Puthoff has gone through encounter groups and other West Coast fads, and is now a scientologist (as is Inigo Swann [one of the psychics used in the experiments])" (Collins and Pinch, p. 255). In more recent work, Collins and Pinch detail further extraordinary accusations leveled at the paranormal researchers—surreptitious alteration of equipment, recruitment of non-expert allies (professional magicians), publicity seeking in popular journals, unscientific motives, and insincerity.[30] But again, Collins and Pinch regard these efforts as atypical of normal science, reflecting an extremely vigorous form of border patrol seeking to protect science from contamination from an alternative world view or paradigm.

We might conclude that Merton's universalistic norm operates as a rule of scholarly decorum governing public presentations and published assessments and critiques. This conclusion would sort well with Merton's subsequent description of the extremely unruffled facade that modern science maintains (pp. 336–38). Warren O. Hagstrom develops this point, noting that professional journals generally proscribe "polemics" and "speculation," though these are more likely to be entertained in review articles, popular and semipopular writings, and symposia.[31] Ziman notes, however, that even in review articles "courtesies forbid that errors should be bluntly confounded" (p. 122), and he gives a short guide to the circumlocutions which in the vernacular mean " 'Damn fool!', 'Idiot!', 'Nincompoop!' " Concerning this public decorum, Ziman concludes: "Yet the norms of ordinary Science strongly discountenance the *argumentum ad hominem*, the vitriolic personal attack, the public mudslinging that is quite commonly observed amongst historians, philosophers, theologians and other quite respectable scholars" (p. 135). This good behavior, he argues, derives from the scientists' overriding desire to maintain a free consensus.

If indeed the canon of universalism (impersonality) applies only in the most formal and public of settings, and governs assessment only or principally in the act of refereeing, then one might suppose that scientists would experience considerable conflict when the techniques of the contingent forum are employed on a colleague in print or at formal meetings. Indeed, Pinch has examples of such discomfort at techniques used by one scientist (called Quest) to discredit a proponent of gravity waves (Weber). Participants at a crucial conference made many comments critical of Quest for vindictiveness, obnoxiousness, and dogmatism. One explained the code a little more: " . . . I felt that was a very inflammatory issue. It was clearly a case where Weber had tripped himself up because of his data analysis and I felt that it spoke for itself, and that those few people who knew about it were enough. But Quest did not feel that way and he went after Weber . . . and I just stood on the sidelines covering my eyes because I'm not really interested in that kind of thing, because that's not science" ("Son," p. 46). (Quest himself acknowledged that his campaign to kill the high-flux gravity wave research went far beyond "science.")

All of the analyses so far formulate the issues in terms of a basic opposition of the *ought* and the *is*, as if scientists all accept the norm of universalism, at least as it "governs" their public, official roles, and struggle to keep it from being mere window dressing. The question is rendered more complex, however, by a current of thought which raises questions about the *ought*. To trace this, we need to return to the ideological appeal of universalism.

Apologists for science repeatedly celebrate its anti-authoritarian, anti-traditionalist impetus. As Bertrand Russell said with characteristic bluntness, "The triumphs of science are due to the substitution of observation and inference for authority. Every attempt to revive authority in intellectual matters is a retrograde step."[32] Galileo is the great culture hero. Assessing a piece of science impersonally and on its merits as science blocks the importation of personal factors, as we have seen, and also such extrinsic criteria as compatibility with current ideology or religious dogma. Hence the great demons are the Spanish Inquisition, creationists, Nazi science, and Lysenko. But, as M. D. King[33] points out, a view that denies any personal or social grounding to scientific ideas also denies them any personal or social consequences:

> The scientist can entertain ideas without putting himself personally or socially at risk. Scientific ideas can be discredited without threat to the authority of science or scientists. This is one aspect of the notion of scientific objectivity: scientific ideas are treated as morally and socially neutral things, as objects or commodities rather than as states or attitudes of mind. They pass from mind to mind as economic goods pass from hand to hand. Their value is judged against impersonal standards of scientific merit, rather than in terms of their human or social significance. (pp. 9–10)

King is characterizing the positivist view of science, which, she notes, employs a Manichaean polarity of rational science and irrational tradition. It depends crucially on the scientific criteria being clear and decisive in particular instances. If they were, scientific articles might well claim the status of apodictic demonstration.[34]

But apparently they are not, if we accept Polanyi's account of the role of professional judgment in scientific assessment. If assessment makes use of reputation, "credibility," judgment, and authority, the canon of impersonality would seem at most an injunction to resist personal and ideological prejudice in assessment and to struggle to be fair by applying the same standards to the work of the unknown and the known.[35] As Cournand and Zuckerman rather blandly conclude (and in a footnote!), "It should be evident that the principles of authority and of universalism are not wholly consistent with one another."[36] If the "ought" of universalism/impersonality is at least qualified by another, contradictory "ought," scientific discourse is not its special and peculiar home, as some of the apologists claim. It would seem, then, that interpreting impersonality as a norm binding referees and other readers to blind, anonymous reading is somewhat naive.

Alternatively, impersonality may be viewed in a rhetoricizing way as the decorum of scientific (or scholarly) discourse in its formal, official setting. It distinguishes the allowable from the disreputable things you can write and say in public, forcing at times wonderful circumlocutions, impersonal obliqueness, and other highly coded expressions of "Idiot!" or "Nincompoop!" While the complexity of the issue is great, and one might imagine a sharp split between norms and practices, public and private, or some such dichotomy, it is not clear that locating it between a china shop etiquette and raging bulls snorting ego and contempt is the right place. That would suggest a cynicism which is on the whole not characteristic of scientists. Impersonality may be a set of gestures, but they do not appear to be entirely empty ones, or ones radically at variance with the true state of affairs. Michael Mulkay observes that the norms are invoked by scientists when criticizing the behavior (not just the writing) of other scientists and defending their own. He suggests viewing the norms "not as defining clear social obligations to which scientists generally conform, but as flexible vocabularies employed by participants in their attempts to negotiate suitable meanings for their own and others' acts in various social contexts" (*Science and the Sociology of Knowledge*, p. 72). On this interpretation, the community would be those who employ these norms in their accounts and evaluations of their own and others' work (though, for Mulkay, observance or nonobservance of the norms would not be the basis of the actual evaluation made). This returns us to Labov's definition of a speech community: the scientific discourse community is not necessarily those who observe the norms in their own writing, but who employ them in judging and reacting to the writing of others.

Finally, some of the normative force of impersonality would seem to arise from its association with impartiality, rather than with objectivity as such: impersonality enjoins readers to be fair and unprejudiced in applying their standards of assessment and writers to try to get everything that is relevant down on the page, so that the readers will have sufficient information to make a fair and unbiased assessment. Clearly such an interpretation does not impute objectivity in an absolute sense on the part of reader, writer, or Text.

It is interesting that the distinction drawn repeatedly by the ethnographers between a contingent repertoire (laboratory talk, practical daily life theorizing) and an empiricist repertoire (official, public science) would seem to align closely with Olson's contrast of Utterance with Text, the first a mode of talk, the second a mode of writing. This tour through the study of scientists' work thus helps to unfold and specify what is meant by the rather general term "doing science." It does reduce the claims one might make for Text, as for example that its mastery helps the student writer to think more deeply or clearly—to construct coherent, general models of the world. It makes us think of Text more as a social code and institution—at once rhetorical and ethical—than as a machine for thinking.

As noted above, many of the same probings of norm and practice have been applied to the other Mertonian norms with a similar pattern of results. The theme of rigorous refereeing and scrutiny, for example, ties in to the fourth Mertonian canon—Organized Skepticism. For Merton, this canon is also a pillar of the anti-traditional edifice of science: since it essentially urges (when doing science) "suspend judgment and scrutinize beliefs in terms of empirical and logical criteria" (1973, p. 277), the scientist is no supporter of received wisdom or dogma.[37] In the Mertonian tradition, this canon is often taken as a charge to challenge and scrutinize the assumptions, evidence, and inferences of one's own work and those of other scientists—a sort of standing call for warrants and good data in scientific argument. Ethnographers report somewhat divergent observations in their studies of laboratory life. Michael Lynch finds such scrutiny notably absent in his experience of scientific shop talk, where an apparent "preference for agreement" and for "getting the work done" overrides "any possible usability of extended 'questioning' or 'dispute' as a *general* organizing feature of the work."[38] On the other hand, Karin Knorr-Cetina found exactly such a fierce challenge and scrutiny being applied to successive drafts of a research paper within her research institute, as documented by marginal queries and objections and responses (*Manufacture*, ch. 4). It would appear that Organized Skepticism is preeminently a feature of the preparation of formal scientific Texts, rather than daily laboratory life, though the latter would surely be guided by an awareness of the scrutiny that will be applied when it's time to write it up. It is clear that scientists have acute senses of what is challengeable in their work, and devote much energy to countering possible challenges and objections with both procedural and rhetorical devices. Bruno Latour and Françoise Bastide also emphasize this anticipation of objection as a cardinal feature of scientific composition.[39]

Taking the domain governed by the Mertonian norms as principally the public one receives some support from the debate concerning norms and counternorms. Pondering the major discrepancies between the high Mertonian norms and the ways scientists talk about their own work and that of their peers, Mitroff, following certain suggestions in Merton's later writings, proposed that the norms were in fact paired with counternorms, which, though inversions of their matching norm, were nonetheless norms insofar as scientists endorsed and applied them in evaluating each other's work (albeit in interviews, not review articles). So Universalism is countered with Particularism, "Communism" with Solitariness (or Miserliness), Disinterestedness with Interestedness, and Organized Skepticism with Organized Dogmatism. This suggestion has not been well received, partly out of a concern with rendering the norms vacuously or irrefutably applicable. Both Roger Krohn and Harriet Zuckerman[40] have argued that Mitroff's evidence for the counternorms is drawn almost entirely from private contexts and from questionnaires about the behavior of other researchers prior to the public presentation of their findings, and hence that the different stages of "doing science" may be governed by different norms.[41]

In a recent article entitled "The Rhetorical Construction of Scientific Ethos," Lawrence Prelli reports on a case study of the rhetoric of legitimation/delegitimation in the area of primate language studies, where certain voices speaking for orthodox science (Thomas Sebeok) oppose the purported discoveries and achievements of certain innovative researchers (Francine Patterson and Eugene Linden).[42] Prelli argues that Sebeok faults Patterson for not projecting a credible scientific ethos as sketched by Merton, and that Patterson responds by affirming the counter-norm values listed by Mitroff. Prelli suggests that the Mertonian norms and other standard assumptions and procedures favor orthodox, mainstream science, and that those who wish to present significantly unorthodox claims and employ novel techniques of observation might almost be forced to challenge the prevailing ethos of science. Unfortunately, Prelli's case is blurred by the fact that Sebeok's attack on Patterson, which was cast as a book review, massively violates the norm of impersonality, attacking Patterson in terms of her lack of institutional credentials, bias, fuzzy thinking, and ignorance. Prelli's wading through this controversy does remind us that Labov's phrase "evaluative behavior" can refer to some pretty rough stuff.

One factor that complicates the personal/impersonal dichotomy is that scientists become public figures and acquire reputations. Supplementing the major Mertonian norms, Harriet Zuckerman ("Deviant Behavior") has suggested, are certain rules of etiquette which also govern the scientist's discourse as a public figure. As a tentative first sketch, she lists four DON'Ts: eponymize yourself (a sign of recognition by the community not to be claimed by the individual himself), underacknowledge a collaborator's contributions to joint research, attack ad hominem in scientific discourse, and seek publicity. She shows that these norms are violated, and their violation reprehended, and indeed she touches on a tender point for Mertonians: if the reliability, qualifications, and theoretical orientation of the researcher are relevant to the best assessment of the work, is it not the obligation of the assessor to bring these matters up (at the cost of infringing on "universalism")—not, that is, as a convenient rule of thumb, but as a criterion? It is still presumably out of bounds to cast aspersions on the personal character of the researcher, or the chastity of his mother, but there will evidently be a hazy area where character as person merges into character as scientist rather than a categorical proscription against taking the identity of the researcher into account.

In one sense, the sketches of discursive norms discussed in these sections are complementary. Olson enumerates the qualities and norms of academic ("wissenschaftlich") writing in terms of its artifacts or products, while the Mertonian tradition discusses norms for the producing and reception of texts by human agents. One can object to Olson's sketch that it is arhetorical, but that dimension is clearly central to the Mertonians, and one can see how "autonomy" might arise as a property of texts as well as the ways in which it needs to be qualified: it is not so much that the text breaks free of its writer, reader, and practical context of application, as that the writer (and reader) are engaged as public, "professional" figures restricted in the kinds of appeals and responses they can make. The ethos of science thus becomes a quintessentially rhetorical concept, the counterpart for the modern, scientific forum, of the "reasonable man" sketched by Aristotle as the most persuasive figure to cut in the Greek forums of public deliberation.

The Mertonian norms for the professional evaluation and public discussion of scientific claims do require that these claims be treated as self-grounded, in Gouldner's terms. They place little value on the scientists' awareness of the complexities of their stances as knowing subjects—the sorts of considerations that might have influenced their choice of topics, for example, or the social significance and ramifications of their claims, or the feelings their project aroused. The Mertonian picture of discourse in the natural sciences is compatible with Gouldner's suggestion that normal science does not develop the full potential of critical self-awareness. CCD seems more pervasive in the less "normalized," more preparadigmatic academic disciplines. In the human sciences, for example, many disciplines have seen the emergence of proposals for new rhetorics to replace the rhetoric of impersonality—rhetorics that would more directly reflect the actions and passions of human subjects as they set out to investigate the world. Instead of accepting (conspiring in?) the rhetoric of impersonality, they attempt a different rhetoric for the human sciences, a rhetoric of self-awareness, and it is to that development that we now turn.

II
Applications

III

IRONY AND REFLEXIVITY
RHETORIC AND SOCIAL CONSTRUCTION

> For the textualists, the literary artist's
> awareness that he is making rather than
> finding, and more specifically the ironic
> modernist's awareness that he is responding to
> texts rather than to things, puts him one up
> on the scientist. Both movements treat the
> scientist as naive in thinking that he is doing
> something *more* than putting together ideas,
> or constructing new texts.
>
> —Richard Rorty[1]

> When socially minded observers of scientific
> activity come to think about the role of
> language, our current concepts of language
> offer no strong clues about how language
> talks about anything other than itself.
>
> —Charles Bazerman[2]

To recapitulate the view of academic discourse built up in the first section of this book, it may be said to present two aspects—a technical one and a critical one. The technical one stresses knowledge making as incrementation of a body of public, authorized statements. In order to pursue this incrementation, scientists and scholars tacitly agree to operating with black boxes—sets of assumptions and procedures not currently open to systematic doubt. In addition, foundational, epistemological, social, ethical, and political reflection is suspended; the status of the knowing and discoursing subject is not in question. As a result, rhetorical innovativeness is rather narrowly channeled. Somewhat paradoxically, certain of the traits of "scientific theorizing" are not much in evidence, especially organized skepticism applied to itself, and discourse is limited to sufficiency for the practical purposes at hand. Thus, under its technical aspect, disciplinary discourse has certain traits of commonsense understanding—commonsense, we might say, applied to uncommon questions.

Academic discourse, however, has a second aspect, a critical and dialectical one which sets out to scrutinize basic assumptions—to open the black boxes periodically. Each discipline has its "theory," and in addition in recent years there has been a vigorous efflorescence of inter-, cross-, meta-, and pan-disciplinary discussion under such rubrics as "Theory" in the post-structuralist, "textualist" sense of the first epigraph, "social studies of science," and "rhetoric of" particular disciplines. In these discussions, the role of the knowing subject—the analyst—in relation to the world of practice she investigates is very much in question. The discoursing subject is, most broadly, an outsider who struggles with a sense of marginality or arrogant intrusiveness. Even within disciplines, theory is often regarded with suspicion and hostility, and the analyst must contend with an extremely deep-seated sense that to study someone or some group is to try to be one-up on them, again in the spirit of the first epigraph: unreflecting practice is naive. The analyst may begin by waving the Socratean motto about the unexamined life but had better be mindful of the community's ultimate response. And, beyond melodrama, ordinary disciplinary practice may find the outsider's position not a resource but a serious limitation, insofar as the outsider lacks the practitioner's acquired judgment and tact that cannot be grasped by analytic techniques.

Critical reflection has a problem not only with justifying its practice but with grounding its findings, which, when offered as some kind of public knowledge, are themselves subject to the same reflective scrutiny. Thus critical reflection, which in this chapter will be represented by "social studies of science," has to scramble inventively to justify its own epistemic privilege as it examines the grounds for the privilege claimed by scientists. Since social studies of science are a branch of social science, they make scientific claims about how scientists make scientific claims, and whatever they say about scientists making claims applies mutatis mutandis to their own claims.

Such is the nature of this reflective skid that it makes everyone self-conscious about their stances and claims. As we observe and attempt to assess writers observing and assessing the discourse of scientists, are we not in the dubious position of outsiders ourselves, lacking the implicit knowledge of practitioners and not sharing the disciplinary purpose? How can we understand the rhetoric of a particular piece of writing without being in some sense members of the community, which is to say members of the relevant audience? One can of course project oneself imaginatively into that audience, and this is not hard to do when the discourse is interdisciplinary, pre-paradigmatic, and relatively nontechnical (as is the case with social studies of science), but a reality check is still useful: our confidence in our imaginative projection is enhanced if we find practitioners in the discipline seeing what we see and responding as we do. This principle is well recognized in literary criticism under the rubric of "reception aesthetics," where aesthetic interpretation and response are in question, and it can be extended to questions of scholarly persuasiveness as well. This chapter will examine three books in the fairly closely knit field of social studies of science—Joseph Gusfield's *The Culture of Public Problems*, Bruno Latour and Steve Woolgar's *Laboratory Life*, and Nigel Gilbert and Michael Mulkay's

Opening Pandora's Box—and it will make use of the scholarly reviews and responses to these books, to use the more informed responses of colleagues to scrutinize their arguments and assess the impact they have had in their particular communities of expertise—their own persuasiveness, as it were. "Social studies of science" is hardly an example of normal science conducted within a stable paradigm, or even of an emerging discipline; it receives contributions from those who characterize themselves as historians, philosophers, sociologists, and rhetoricians of science. It does not have a lot of technical black boxes lying about. Further, it is an area of inquiry that has proved increasingly inclined to treat its own methodology and claims to knowledge as principal objects of study, with approaches ranging from quite traditional correspondence models of "getting it right" to innovative social construction theories that link up with strong textualist positions that it's all rhetoric. Thus there is a decent hope for us, as outsiders, to enter the discourse without stumbling over our ignorance and naivete at every turn.

These three books are major events in the emergence of the social constructionist approach, which can be said to take its impetus from the decision to study science not in order to understand how it successfully models the world but in order to understand how scientific discourse works and whether its claims of cognitive privilege are warranted. If they are warranted, for the social constructionist, it is not because they are demonstrated objectively: Peter McHugh's declaration in his "On the Failure of Positivism" has been widely cited as expressing the main thesis of the movement:

> We must accept that there are no adequate grounds for establishing criteria of truth except the grounds that are employed to grant or concede it—truth is conceivable only as a socially organized upshot of contingent courses of linguistic, conceptual, and social behavior. The truth of a statement is not independent of the conditions of its utterance, and so to study truth is to study the ways truth can be methodically conferred. It is an ascription. . . . Actually, this principle applies to any phenomenon of social order.[3]

Social constructionist analyses concentrate on three major themes: those of sociological irony, the stance of the knowing subject, and the rhetoric of reflexivity. Sociological irony results when the sociologist determines that a particular formulation of the facts could have been otherwise and offers another account of the matter. That is, one shows that the prevailing account is underdetermined by the facts, so one then may question how it comes about that it and not another is accepted as the right one. The alternative account causes the prevailing one to lose its self-evidentness and is said to ironize it, often to debunk it if it has lofty aspirations to represent the clear truth of the matter. Controversies and disagreements are preferred sites for investigation because they are in a sense self-ironizing. For example, the pesticides Aldrin and Dieldrin have been banned as carcinogenic in the USA but not in the UK. But where there is no alternative account, the analyst invents one. The answer to how the prevailing account has come to enjoy its success is usually given in terms either of its rhetoric—the ways its proponents have made it appealing and plausible—or in terms of social and political factors operating within a discipline or on the discipline from larger forces in society. This second line is the one preferred by Gillespie, Eva, and Johnston in the case of Aldrin/Dieldrin,[4] but the books we will examine prefer the first line of explanation rather than the second and hence might be said to be central works in the rhetoric of science. To examine how they set up and conduct their arguments is to study the rhetoric of "science as rhetoric." It is a kind of metarhetoric. Put another way, the procedure of ironizing has much in common with Marxian critique of ideology, but these writers pull up short of specifying what class, corporate, or material interests are served by the prevailing account, beyond observing that the accounts are comfortable to the prevailing ideology (support the myth of public order, for Gusfield) and legitimate the claims of their holders for power, prestige, and material support.

So the analysts set up or discover a discourse that ironizes a prevailing one. How can they get us to take their account seriously enough to entertain it? How can they see what so many others have missed, including expert practitioners in the discipline? They may attempt to capitalize on their outsider status: if they were insiders to the scientific discourse (that is, fully ratified practitioners) they might be incapable of exercising critical distance sufficient to give an explicit, unbiased account of their own practices. Therefore the analyst trying to discover how scientific discourse really works might begin in a conventional, outsider stance of scientific observer; he or she might do surveys of working scientists or case studies or field work or citation counts, studies large scale or close in, but sooner or later the sociologist will have to give some answer to the insider's query: how can you, an outsider to our community, claim greater insight into our tacit knowledge and grounds of assent than we have? In short, what privileges the stance of the analyst? What is the status of his account? The philosophical dialectic of stance has been incisively summarized by Habermas; our concern is with the ways the issue is raised and handled by writers who are not principally philosophers but practicing analysts of scientific discourse.[5]

If the answer is, "he is a social scientist," then his own account can be taken as part of the object of study and hence can be subjected to the same critique—that it too is socially constructed, underdetermined by the data, and so on. Social constructionists could of course exempt their own activity from critique by fiat, but they have preferred to grasp the nettle firmly, maintaining that the axiom of the social construction of all knowledge includes their own discourse and is exemplified by it. Their superiority lies in acknowledging it reflexively, hoping in so doing to demonstrate at least the honesty and consistency of their position. They thus cultivate a rhetoric of reflexivity in various ways, though they stop short of debunking their own debunking, while at the same time claiming to do science, to offer all the knowledge about scientific discourse that there is to have. They are not cynics nor are they indulging in the spirit of carnival and frivolous play—they are scientists struggling to do justice to their claim that scientific discourse is rhetorical to the core.

Though all of these books thus share the same program of criticizing and reducing the special discursive power of scientific discourse, they differ in the domains examined and the aspect of scientific discourse addressed. Gusfield tackles the discourse of social problems, specifically that of drinking-driving, where the pursuit of purely scientific understanding is complicated by its bearing on the formulation of public policy. Latour and Woolgar look for the special quality of scientific discourse in the circulation of talk and texts in the laboratory setting ("science in the making"). Gilbert and Mulkay concentrate rather on accounts both in writing and in interviews given by scientists participating in a major controversial area in biochemistry. None of them claim the status of an insider (though Gusfield is one, to a considerable degree) and hence do not claim to be able to evaluate the knowledge claims being made, though, as we shall see, they all present arguments that no definitive account of the way things are is possible anyway. This chapter will not attempt to resolve this epistemological conundrum; rather, it will examine the ways these books posit and resolve the struggle between the unreflecting discourse of practical science and the denaturalizing sophistication of rhetorical consciousness in the domain of science.

1. The Rhetoric of Public Problems: Joseph Gusfield

The Culture of Public Problems: Drinking-Driving and the Symbolic Order (University of Chicago Press, 1981) is the second of Joseph Gusfield's major books, the first (*Symbolic Crusade: Status Politics and the American Temperance Movement*, University of Illinois Press, 1963) was well received and has been acclaimed as "among a handful of works that transformed the sociological study of deviance in the 1960s."[6] Parts of *Culture* appeared earlier as articles in journals, notably "The Literary Rhetoric of Science: Comedy and Pathos in Drinking-Driver Research" which was published in the *American Sociological Review* in 1976, was greeted with a "critical celebration" by Michael Overington, and subsequently several times cited as a pioneering effort in the rhetoric of science.[7] Judging by the reviews, *Culture* is a complex object wielding authority and expertise both in the practical, problem-oriented domain of accident prevention and as an illustration of the sociological theory known as symbolic interaction or social construction (or definition), which studies problems not as objectively existing phenomena requiring solutions but as they are identified, symbolized, and as it were created (constructed) in discourse. The book's basic picture of the emergence of drinking-driving as a social problem and its critique of the prevailing account has been taken as authoritative in articles appearing in such journals as *Deviant Behavior, Accident Analysis and Prevention, Social Problems, Journal of Criminal Law,* and *The Sociological Quarterly*.[8] The authors of these articles appear either not to be interested in the book's sociological theory, or to accept it without reservations. On the other hand, certain writers have been very concerned with the book's theory and its rhetoric as examples of the tensions and perplexities which they see as inherent in social construction theories. A social scientist who exposes the "literary rhetoric" of another social scientist exposes his own writing to the same critique, and Gusfield deliberately invites such scrutiny, calling attention to strains and problems in his own stance as knowing subject. These analyses of theory and rhetoric, by Steve Woolgar and Dorothy Pawluch and by William Tam, are the ones of greatest interest to us.

Woolgar and Pawluch touch on Gusfield's book only insofar as it illustrates the problematic move they call ontological gerrymandering which they see as endemic in works taking the social constructionist position.[9] In what might be described as a classical confrontation of the attitudes of scientific and everyday theorizing, the social constructionist attempts to demonstrate that certain key concepts in the everyday or commonsense characterization of a phenomenon are not natural or given or just plain there but are the result of acts of naming and symbolizing and selection and, as Gusfield puts it, could be otherwise. In regard to drinking-driving, for example, Gusfield argues that various components in the definition of the problem clustering around identifying the irresponsible killer drunk as the cause of highway fatalities are not necessitated by the facts: the involvement of alcohol in highway fatalities and the responsibility for it could be conceptualized otherwise, as involving for example the location and operation of bars and the roles of liquor companies and the state. But, Woolgar and Pawluch note, a thorough adherence to the principles of social construction requires one to acknowledge that there are no facts in this simple, atheoretical sense, since any account of the facts is also an account, a construction involving acts of naming, symbolizing and selection. "Ontological gerrymandering" is their term for the argumentative move whereby some statements are granted the status of unconstructed facts even though, according to theory, there cannot be any such. So, they observe for Gusfield (at least in the earlier article in 1975), "the actual number of deaths per year from automobile crashes assumes the role of a given" (p. 217). (By the bye, Gusfield by 1981 is quite aware of some of the social construction involved in such statistics—pp. 68–69.)

Woolgar and Pawluch examine one social constructionist study of child abuse in detail and cite a number of others of various degrees of sophistication, showing various stylistic/rhetorical devices that have the effect of reintroducing the theoretically abjured plain facts and things in themselves. A few of these bear mention: one is the use of inverted commas/quotation marks ("objective," as in "the same 'objective' condition may be defined as a problem in one time period, not in another"—Gusfield, p. 8; "discovery"—"The 'Discovery' of Child Abuse"). These marks work in the usual way of allowing the writer to evoke a common manner of speaking while withholding her endorsement of it, suggesting there is something wrong with it.[10] So for example, one might write of the "discovery" of child abuse, implying that it was not properly a discovery for one or more reasons (it was constructed, not discovered; we knew about it all along; or there is no such thing). Similarly, Gusfield makes the gerrymandering move with "objective" while showing he is aware that he has no privileged access to the facts. In scholarly writing, which frequently involves summary, citation, and restatement of someone else's claims, and where frequently the rightness of the term is one of the points in dispute, quotation marks tend to proliferate, especially if the scholar wants to position himself outside the fray. When Lawrence Hazelrigg wrote a commentary on Woolgar and Pawluch's article (Is There a Choice between "Constructivism" and "Objectivism"?), he placed both theoretical terms in quotes, adding a footnote of explanation:

> Placing "constructionism" (and "objectivism") in quotation marks is meant to forestall any taken-for-granted or matter-of-fact reading of what counts as "constructionism" (or "objectivism"). It is a way of cautioning "Let's not prejudge the question of its meaning in its full logical extension." But repeated use of quotation marks for such purpose becomes tiresome—all the more so in recognition that the use can purchase no guarantee—so I shall mostly refrain.[11]

Indeed, and Woolgar and Pawluch show that the marks often get shed in the course of the arguments, "objective" becoming objective, and so on. Another technique is closely related, namely, the use of certain ambivalent words like *putative* and *imputation* (the meanings of which are close to the inverted commas). They also note subtle discriminations made between things which are said to be interpreted, conceptualized, or claimed and those which are acknowledged, recognized, or exposed (e.g., gynecologists were said to have "discovered" [with inverted commas] and then claimed that menopause was a "deficiency disease," but feminists are now exposing the sexism in women's health care.) Finally, one might in their spirit note that the word *myth* is supposed to have a special, non-negative connotation in social construction theories, but in phrases like "The Myth of the Killer-drunk" or "the legal myth of social order" the word easily recovers the connotations it is not supposed to have. One critic does read it this way ("To speak of 'the *myth* of the "killer-drunk" ' suggests that there is something *false* about that picture"); officially we can say the critic is obtuse, but does the word not perhaps have that effect unacknowledged by us from time to time?[12] Gusfield plays a pretty close and consistent game of social construction, but he does drop his hedges when contrasting "Reality" as he as a scientist knows it with the facts, certainties, and clear-cut categories public deliberation requires: "Reality is too ambiguous, uncertain, and inconsistent to correspond to categories which render it unambiguous, certain, and consistent" (p. 69—et passim). It is the intellectual's credo, certainly a highly constructed piece of work! And, just as Woolgar and Pawluch predict, by page 80 he can say, without commas, "The world of objective reality is, like much of natural behavior, confused, ambiguous, and unobtainable. . . ." In fairness to Gusfield, and to all others who may have committed ontological gerrymandering, I should add that total adherence to the principle that all accounts are only accounts, even the one one favors, is an austere and difficult undertaking, especially when one is required to give equal treatment to evident stupidity and pernicious folly.[13]

Applications

Woolgar and Pawluch thus show how constructionist writers manage to achieve some of the rhetorical appeal of objectivism— the claim to a privileged access to the facts and an unconstructed account of them—even while disavowing it. Equally tricky is the rhetoric of reflexivity. From the social constructionist point of view, its own accounts are as little founded and as much constructed as those it analyzes and calls naive. The accounts it analyzes are naive because they do not realize their nature as a construction. Accordingly, the social constructionist reminds us from time to time of his greater sophistication—he indicates his awareness in gestures such as the following from Gusfield's analysis of the rhetoric of a paper by Julian Waller published in 1967 in *The Journal of the American Medical Association*.[14] Noting that exemplifying a whole body of writing from one example is an instance of the "literary device" of synecdoche, Gusfield says the paper was chosen

> for two conscious reasons: (1) it has been influential, frequently cited by other research persons and in government documents as a base for advocating particular policies and (2) it represents a number of studies and papers which, in recent years, have operated as persuasive elements in a transformation of strategy toward the control of auto accidents associated with alcohol use. This too is fictional since each study and each interpretation has its uniqueness. (p. 86; cited in Tam, p. 186)

In effect, "my fiction is superior to yours, for it knows itself to be one, and scrupulously refuses to pull the wool over the reader's eyes." Such reminders are a paradoxical self-authenticating device familiar in fiction from Fielding and Sterne down to John Fowles and even Margaret Drabble. They are authenticating in at least two ways: first, they capitalize on a general positive value we assign to consciousness, and second, they are dues paid to the theoretical limitation which can then be forgotten, as if one pinches oneself and then sinks back into dreaming: one is momentarily de-illusioned, but not disillusioned. The imagery is Nietzsche's and the theme a favorite one of deconstruction, and indeed, the writer of Woolgar and Pawluch's case study, Stephen Pfohl, replied to them in a piece entitled "Toward a Sociological Deconstruction of Social Problems," by citing Gayatri Spivak's introduction to *Of Grammatology* concerning the "provisional forgetfulness" of the deconstructive critic who, all protestations to the contrary, "necessarily assumes that she at least, and for the time being, means what she says."[15]

Woolgar and Pawluch make it clear that they are not scolding various writers for slipping up or back into old modes of thinking, for they maintain that social construction theories must achieve some sort of privileged access to the facts to show the versions are only versions. Their only objection is that social constructionists must acknowledge that their own explanations are also social and no more "logically necessary" than the accounts they have exposed. Thus they should not be surprised when Hazelrigg notes that their own article exemplifies this unwarranted appeal to the simple facts: they surveyed numerous articles of a social constructionist stripe and found these recourses to a reality-behind-or-beneath-all-symbolizing in them all—but the articles surveyed were of course not simply given, or found, but selected, named, etc. Hazelrigg agrees that it is hard to avoid lapses into objectivism, but adds the observation that such lapses are the source of the social scientist's rhetorical power: "The priestly voice of expertise vitally depends upon the esotericism of object's own standpoint" (p. 511).

But Gusfield does not want to claim a technician's authority; he sees his role more as "an artistic developer of an ironic sense of alternatives" (p. 195). Calling Gusfield a symbolic interactionist (and the book was awarded the Charles Horton Cooley Award for 1983 by the Society of the Study of Symbolic Interaction), William Tam likens him to Erving Goffman and both of them to Kenneth Burke.[16] Tam points out that the kind of knowledge which Gusfield offers is the awareness of possibilities, alternative ways of seeing—not, to be sure, a definitive or authoritative knowledge, but, as Richard Rorty might say, an edifying one. Gusfield characterizes his own work and sociology in general as ironizing: it sets out to deprive the given and the assumed of its self-evidentness, and this loss almost always threatens the legitimacy of the given—it is no longer taken for granted. Sociology takes the position of an outsider or "stranger," and its analysis almost always debunks, even when it disavows any such intention. But the case is more complicated for Gusfield, for he takes on not just received opinion, but the social-problems discourse of drinking-driving manifested variously and epitomized in the article by Waller. How can Gusfield establish himself as the outsider to the community to which he belongs, in part by virtue of appearing and speaking as "a presumed 'alcohol studies expert' " (p. 7—his inverted commas), seeking and receiving grants, reporting results, and so on? This is one point where Burke becomes valuable to him technically—the pentad provides a neutral, commonsense analytic scheme—but also I think temperamentally and strategically, encouraging a dramatization of writing and stylistic preferences for irony, paradox, oxymoron ("There has been some transition from stigma to insurance"—p. 118), analogy (scholarly article as three-act play), metaphor ("We live in a forest of symbols on the edge of a jungle of fact"—p. 51), anecdotes, anthypophora (the posing and answering of questions), and in general a foregrounded authorial subjectivity. There is something subversive about taking your case to the educated layperson directly, laying aside the mantle and the decorum of expertise.

Not everyone has been delighted with the result: one British reviewer remarks with that special archness American works attract, "If alcohol loosens inhibitions, so too, it seems, does alcohol research."[17] This is mere stuffiness, but the reviewer also touches on an uneasiness that Gusfield himself discusses and is manifested in other reviews. If the experience the book gives us is the delight and refreshment of what used to be called free thinking, in which the world-shaping and world-disclosing powers of language are very much in the fore, is not this autonomy bought at the price of engagement and responsibility? Are we not invited to ignore, for one thing, the struggle for power of various interests in the formation of social problems discourse? Gusfield did analyze the discourse of the Temperance Movement in terms of class interests struggling to maintain cultural hegemony, and MADD has more than a passing resemblance to the Bluestockings. (He does acknowledge, however, that MADD's successes have changed the picture he sketched in 1981.) The point is that we do not learn from Gusfield's book, or the responses to it, what material and historical forces have constrained the formation and selection of the "facts" that have become commonsense. Gusfield did promise another book addressing this aspect of the problem, but it has not yet come forth.

The deepest uneasiness, about which Gusfield is overtly defensive, is that the disengaged, outsider perspective of the "Olympian ironist" (his term for his stance) is irresponsible in having nothing better to offer (as opposed to the "utopian ironist," who does). Tam suggests that this concern arises because the discourse is one of public problems: "When the subject of study bears on the construction of moral orders and the arbitrary ways these moral orders may be put together, audiences implicitly demand that the writer make social policy recommendations" (p. 178). And Gusfield resists that, at least in this book, as if the analyst's disengagement is crucial to his appeal—he really does have no preconceived opinion, no hidden agenda, no designs upon us, no ax to grind. It is the ethos of the scientist, and Gusfield invokes it eloquently, along with impartiality and open-mindedness, in order to contrast it with the atmosphere of debate over drinking-driving issues in which the audience is hostile, narrow-minded, and unimpressed by the nuances and qualifications of scientific method (p. 80). The imagery is of a prizefight. And too, the ironist who takes a relativist/constructivist position cannot easily make moral or policy recommendations without having the grounds of *his* position subjected to scrutiny. The position is more problematic when it is a matter of saying what is better and what should be done. This is a recurrent theme in responses to Foucault's genealogical writings,[18] and it is a complexity the Olympian ironist avoids. When it is a matter of laws and lives, the stakes are different and in some ways higher, and one can easily understand the note of distress in Barry Schwartz's question at the end of his extremely favorable review of the book: will we always have to choose between social science after the model of Waller ("a ritual instrument of cultural affirmation") and social science as Olympian irony?[19]

2. The Rhetoric of Laboratory Studies: Latour and Woolgar

Originally published by Sage Publications in 1979, Bruno Latour and Steve Woolgar's *Laboratory Life: The Social Construction of Scientific Facts* presents us with a particularly rich network of textuality, for it has been widely cited and responded to; in addition, it has been reissued by Princeton University Press with a Postscript in which the authors respond to their critics, giving us another turn in the scholarly dialogue. The form of the book is somewhat strange, a product in part, the authors reflect in the Postscript, of its being a collaborative effort between a French philosopher and an English sociologist of science (and based on field work done by Latour in the laboratory of his fellow Burgundian, Roger Guillemin, at the Salk Institute in San Diego).

Laboratory Life opens with a fable of strangeness in which a semi-fictional "observer" finds himself in the position of an anthropologist arriving to study a strange tribe and trying to make sense of the laboratory activities he observes which seem to him chaotic and disorderly in the extreme. Perhaps because he is fortified with Bachelard, Bourdieu, Derrida, Foucault, Lyotard, and Serres, the observer quickly comes to see the laboratory as a complex machine for processing and generating texts, the objects dealt with as statements (not hormones or rats' brains), and the basic dynamic of doing science as the moving of statements up and down a five point scale of "factuality" ranging from wild speculation (level 1) through unattributed textbook fact (level 4) to tacit knowledge (level 5). He also sees the facts arise out of material practices and negotiations among researchers as to how good or how reliable they are for the purposes at hand. His own fable of textual dynamics is thus an ordering that makes sense to him of what seemed at first a chaotic swirl of activity, and he sees his work of order-making as parallel to what the scientists do to nature.

Obviously, such a crossing of cultures is rife with possibilities for debunking, and many stereotypes and models of science are undermined by what the observer observes: science as following an orderly line of march regulated by method, the exemption of the technical from social influence or explanation, the Mertonian norms, especially of universalism and disinterest, and even the distinction of scientific vs. commonsense theorizing. Opposition to this last distinction is a particularly sustained theme in the book: initially they doubt scientists are more rational than outsiders; they find the Schütz-Garfinkel distinction tendentious, and eventually suggest that "the mysterious thought process employed by scientists in their setting is not strikingly different from those techniques employed to muddle through in daily life encounters" (1986 ed., p. 166).[20] If scientists are commonsense reasoners, then they argue to persuade particular audiences, rely on common topics such as personal credibility (ethos), manipulate their data and sources to make their reasons look good, and in short put their pants on, like the rest of us, one leg at a time. So, paradoxically, what started out as an endeavor to "make strange" the unreflected-upon assumptions and practices of scientists which are concealed by scientists' own accounts and reports for outsiders, turns out to reduce the strange otherness—the "exoticism" (p. 29)—of science to zero.

As is the case with many of the books we are studying, reviews in journals of broad or peripheral audiences have been more welcoming and less critical than those in the specialty, namely sociology of science (Princeton University Press puts "Science/Sociology" as an identifier on the jacket). Often it is grouped together with other social studies of science, especially of the social constructionist kind, and welcomed precisely for its debunking of exaggerated images of Science. So the *Journal of Marketing* runs an article "Is Science Marketing?" and *Studies in Higher Education* offers "The Intimidating Bastion of Scientific Knowledge: A Way to Breach the Ramparts."[21] The more substantial criticisms from within the specialty, however, examine some of the assumptions and theoretical underpinnings of Latour and Woolgar's argument and question whether the reduction of scientific or laboratory discourse to commonsense reasoning follows from the data they cite and interpret. These criticisms are in the best tradition of academic debate, for they help to clarify theoretical terms that may be used in too "commonsense" a manner. In particular, they amount to the claim that Latour and Woolgar have not adequately grasped what might be said to be crucial and special to scientific discourse; hence their examples purporting to show no difference misfire, miss the target, or even boomerang.

The sharpest criticism—that their examples boomerang and inadvertently illustrate qualities special to scientific discourse after all—has been made by Nicholas Tilley in a review article to which Latour and Woolgar respond.[22] Basically, Tilley argues that the conversations reported in *Laboratory Life* do exhibit the application of self-criticism and radical doubt, the refusal to take anything for granted or on authority, that is one of the cardinal tenets of scientific theorizing. They are skeptical of the findings reported by other investigators they consider unreliable, but they test them anyway. Tilley sketches a six point "non-positivist, non-mechanical, neo-Popperian account" characterizing "big science" and then argues that *Laboratory Life* confirms that each point applies in the laboratory work they investigate, if the passages of conversation are interpreted somewhat differently. Latour and Woolgar concede in their reply that they lack the "resources" to force their interpretation over Tilley's. Tilley's "kidnapping" of their data to support an interpretation diametrically opposed to the one intended stands as an uneliminated possibility. This exceptionally mild and candid reply is consistent with their social-constructionist position: the facts, of course, do not speak for themselves; many interpretations are possible that cannot be ruled out on the basis of logic or evidence.

The matter of critical stance is also central to Michael Lynch's discussion of social scientists' approaches to working science ("Technical Work and Critical Inquiry: Investigations in a Scientific Laboratory").[23] In general, Lynch notes, when a social scientist studies laboratory work, he brings with him his own attitude of scientific theorizing (or critical inquiry) which enables him to make explicit at least some of the tacit, taken-for-granted knowledge and assumptions that are embedded in the unreflecting practical work of the laboratory. Crucially, he is and must remain an outsider, or "stranger," to use Alfred Schütz's term and discussion.[24] As Schütz points out, the stranger cannot merge his commonsense understanding with that of the target culture—that is the very root of his experience of strangeness. Instead, he is forced to fall back on his capacity for scientific theorizing, for systematic and fully conscious analysis of what is implicit and taken-for-granted in the target culture. A test of his having cracked the code of implicit knowledge in a particular area of the culture is his ability to function, albeit with deliberate consciousness, in it. As long as he remains a stranger (and Latour and Woolgar insist their observer not "go native"), he will be able to see things members of the culture do not, but he will never see things as a member of the culture or be able to operate as a native in the culture. His understanding of the culture will always be of a scientifically theorized kind, as he cannot experience how it works from within. Since his account of what he observes is always a translation into his model of society, it always involves a displacement or parody of the original—if not with debunking effect, at least with critical effect which reinscribes his strangeness. (A similar point has been raised by Renato Rosaldo, who notes that natives who are sufficiently bicultural as to understand the anthropologist's scientific account of their culture often find it obtuse or ludicrous.[25]) "Critical inquiry" is exactly what commonsense understanding lacks; it is the contribution of scientific theorizing.

Now Latour and Woolgar fail to detect signs of critical inquiry in scientists' conversations; from this it follows that in the laboratory they must be employing commonsense theorizing and it is very like "our own"—scientists are content, that is, not to probe matters further than necessary for the practical purposes at hand, to take various operations and procedures for granted, forgetting that each had been and still could be subject to challenges. That is, they treat various tests and procedures as "black boxes," assuming that they do what they are said to do and do it reliably (though they are able to assess different procedures in terms of their strength as evidence when arguing). Hence the reduction: scientists are commonsense reasoners (and rhetoricians) just like us (when we're not doing science). But what if there were a culture that did embody critical inquiry in its commonsense practices, but so deeply and implicitly that an observer would never find it as long as he remained an observer? This, Lynch suggests, is exactly the case with scientists, and he attempts to show that it is so with some conversational data from his own observations in a neuroscience laboratory. To be sure, Lynch's approach has its own theoretical problems (some of which are noted in Latour and Woolgar's Postscript); in addition, Lynch has severe difficulties finding a language to convey the workings of technical practice and, as he later notes, his own efforts to convert them into a text introduce artifacts.[26] But what his argument suggests is that when Latour and Woolgar label their observer a "fiction," they mean something more than just "this ain't quite the way it happened." They mean that the postulate of otherness, along with the experience of strangeness, is ultimately abandoned. The culture is not a different culture; the observer was deluded, sent to study a group that were just a minor variant of the folks back home. Any ethnographer who produced that result would be strongly urged to seek another profession!

The "stranger" device has been objected to also by Paul Tibbetts and Patricia Johnson on somewhat similar grounds for attempting to bracket the implicit knowledge in the context of the scientists' discourse, but not that of the sociologists' own endeavor.[27] Such a move, they argue, cannot but fail to capture the practical reasoning of scientists (because it is context dependent); they advocate instead aiming for a Gadamerian merging of horizons between the sociologist and the scientist through dialogue. Woolgar replies that *dis-*

course in *Laboratory Life* should be understood in the French, especially the Foucaultian sense, as including practical, material practice. Well and good, but their own displays of laboratory discourse give greatest visibility to statements and conversational exchanges.[28]

The observer is, then, a didactic or argumentative ruse: with the maximum expectation of finding difference, he finds almost none. QED. Lynch, by contrast, takes the two cultures analogy seriously, noting that the social practices in his neurobiological laboratory were oriented toward disclosing neurobiological phenomena, and "To abstract the 'social sciences' of scientific work from their technical context on the basis of common language resources or the application of schemata of general analytic theorizing and literary exegesis, immediately omits questions on how the technical work of the laboratory exists in a discovering relation to its phenomena. In the absence of an orientation to such questions, the work of science becomes defined in terms of institutional networks, or refined applications of commonsense or natural language theorizing, and becomes indistinguishable from what sociologists already know by virtue of being sociologists" (*Art and Artifact*, p. 277). That is to say, an account of doing science such as Latour and Woolgar's observer's, which describes the movements of statements and the generation of texts, could as well describe an endeavor that is not natural science, or only a pseudo-science. He concludes, "As a research *policy*, therefore, it is worthwhile to presume a difference between the particular natural science investigated and the social science resources of the investigator if such a presumption motivates an ongoing inquiry into the practices studied, instead of a facile reduction of those practices to a ready-to-hand social science schema" (p. 279).

Another consequence of the ruse may be to give what Richard Whitley finds to be an excessive image of disorder, contingency, and veering about from project to project.[29] In part, he suggests, this impression may simply be an artifact of the micro-level of analysis—the focus, that is, on the individual actions and remarks of scientists and technicians. Laboratory life, so considered, is not necessarily the quintessence of science as a social activity—which, of course, Latour and Woolgar are willing to concede. Their claim is only that if you are looking for a special rationality in science, you will not find it in the lab. Further, Whitley notes, the order that Latour and Woolgar make of the disorderly lab is cast in terms of a social model that is something less than forced upon them by the data. Laboratory life seems a competitive, Hobbesian hustle of each against all for the payoff which is "credit." I'm not sure I agree with Whitley that they are "unwilling to follow the consequences of their rhetoric," however, for they too acknowledge that they can only try to make their fiction plausible, to make it seem to be the "real story about what is going on." The rhetoric of debunking, to be sure, invites the interpretation of replacing error with truth, but Latour and Woolgar know that they can only claim to offer another story; in that, they are—they claim—doing the same thing that the scientists do ("building up an account, . . . staging concepts, invoking sources, linking to arguments in the field of sociology, and footnoting . . . to decrease sources of disorder and to make some statements more likely than others, thereby creating a pocket of order"—pp. 257–58). The scientists' stories about the structure of peptides are more credible only because they have a laboratory—image of vastly greater resources and investment in their endeavor. Their textual power is immensely greater because they can marshal reports and results of the endeavor of hundreds of researchers, employ instruments and techniques that have taken years to develop and have been subjected to thorough scrutiny. Lacking such resources and investments, *any* argument in the sociology of science will be less creditable than one of the lab's research reports—there just aren't enough weighty arguments and robust findings around to force preference of one story about science over another. Hence, Latour and Woolgar say in the Postscript, they described their work in manuscript as "ultimately unconvincing," but the original publishers made them strike the phrase, "because, they said, they were not in the habit of publishing anything that 'proclaimed its own worthlessness' " (p. 284). Again they strike a note of uncommon modesty—though less modesty about knowledge claims and more modesty about the interpretations of their examples might be more convincing.

In addition to the Postscript, and partly as a sketch for it, Steve Woolgar wrote an article defending their "reflexive" approach to the sociology of science and discussing reasons why *Laboratory Life* had been mainly read as an "instrumental" account of what laboratory science is really like. The intended reflexiveness, he explains, examines science work for its illumination of "practical reasoning in general."[30] The misreading of the work as an objective account can be attributed to preconceptions that that is what it should be (what sociology of science is), to its report-like format, and to a working assumption that in practice sociology of science can be "doggedly non-reflexive" while acknowledging that its approach can of course later be applied to itself.[31] Perhaps one might add on the one hand that explicit reminders that the account is a fiction can be taken as mere conscientious dues-paying to trendy theories (one reviewer calls them "at times obtrusive"[32]) and on the other that readers as well as serious publishers do not know how to weigh arguments that claim they are beset by fallibility—a problem that Woolgar says "is insoluble and unavoidable, and that even efforts to examine *how* it is avoided are doomed in that they entail an attempt to avoid it!" He calls for the exploration of "forms of literary expression whereby the monster can be simultaneously kept at bay and allowed a position at the heart of our enterprise" (p. 489). Thus Woolgar in a later article ("Alleged Distinction") lists *Laboratory Life* among studies that invite misreading because of its report-like format, and especially misreading by Anglo-Saxons, who do not understand the French sense of *discourse* and *representation* which pervades their work. (Anglo-Saxons assume a distinction between discourse and praxis, and apprehend "textual representation as representation *of something*," p. 314.) Subsequently, other writers in the field, notably Michael Mulkay, have experimented with other forms, such as dramatic dialogue, "which can do justice to the creative, interdependent and self-referential character of participants' and analysts' discourse about social action in science, yet which is not itself undermined by its acceptance of reflexivity."[33] In some of the most recent work, these writers are referring to scientific accounts, including their own, as "stories." But of course it is fashionable to refer even to philosophical theories in this manner, and once again one suspects the issue has been deferred: there are some stories that aren't worth the time of day, some that are suggestive, even plausible, some that are important, and some so serious and urgent that it is worth going to the wall to defend them.

In any case, one might say the jury is still out on the rhetoric of reflexivity. Certain critics such as Harry Collins argue that a reflexive acknowledgment of the fallibility of one's own account is neither necessary when doing sociology of science nor sufficient to exempt one's work from criticism.[34] Others have reaffirmed the stubborn and it may be Anglo-Saxon expectations of readers, as for example Ellsworth Fuhrman and Kay Oehler: "The presence of reflexivity in the text is often viewed as a kind of narcissism. Reflexive presence can be, and sometimes is, the basis of dismissal of a text. It is not surprising that so few published texts discuss the nature of their own construction."[35] Martin Hollis goes even farther, arguing that reflexivity compounds the problem rather than saving the argument.[36] Perhaps the fullest account of reflexivity as a problem to be "managed" in ethnographic writing is Graham Wilson's, though Wilson provides no simple formula or resolution.[37]

If, as Woolgar and Pawluch argue, many social-constructionist analyses appeal by allowing some contact with "the way it really is" to leak through their official commitments, how does Latour and Woolgar's own attempt to contain the monster fare? The complex web of commentary and clarification suggests that it is an unstable product, owing a good bit to pan-textualist theories current in the late 1970s and making demands of its readers that many were unable to meet. Perhaps the sociology of science is too close to its object not to develop an abiding case of physics-envy, an aspiration to make knowledge claims, stories with no monsters. On the other hand, it is interesting to observe the difficulties that dissenters such as Lynch experience and the caution they exercise in arguing that scientific discourse has some special property that arises from its orientation toward making nature yield up her secrets. Lynch explains at some length why he cannot simply say what it is, and in the course of doing so evokes nature in an especially modern way: "The struggle with the re-calcitrant phenomenon, a struggle which validates the experience of [it] as 'independent,' emerges as the insufficiency of the author's resources adequately to 'contain' or apprehend the phenomenon. Simultaneously, the phenomenon is available as an obscured presence, a baffling presence, or a series of failures, corrections, and refutations of the author's mode of addressing [it]" (p. 280—brackets in text).

Reflexivity, with its capacity for reversal and re-framing, is a dialectician's dream, a topic on which no one can have the last word. It has become the topic of books and collections of articles; in one such recent collection, *Knowledge and Reflexivity*, Latour backs away from some of the more extreme claims and assumptions we have observed—what he calls "meta-reflexivity"—especially the view that readers are naive believers in unproblematic reference who need to be reminded of the textuality of text: "Readers seem to be much more devious, much harder to take in, much cleverer at deconstruction, much faster in fiction-making than is assumed by those writers who, with some arrogance, believe that others believe. Here, too, 'we need to play down the exoticism of the other.' Scientific texts prepare themselves against a much more likely outcome: that of *not* being believed by their readers, or worse, that of not *interesting* anyone."[38] Latour recommends replacing methodological warnings with "style," especially the style of the English and French eighteenth-century philosophers and natural scientists, rather than that of nineteenth- and twentieth-century German or French writers (p. 170). Where will the next turn take us?

3. The Rhetoric of Scientific Accounts: Gilbert and Mulkay

The discussion surrounding Nigel Gilbert and Michael Mulkay's *Opening Pandora's Box: A Sociological Analysis of Scientists' Discourse* is in most respects continuous with that of *Laboratory Life*. *Pandora's Box* is also a contribution to the sociology of science; pieces of it were published as articles and discussed in *Social Studies of Science* before it appeared; it is often co-cited with *Laboratory Life* for its commitment to social constructionism; and it too is involved in the reflexivity discussion. It differs from *Laboratory Life*, however, in being a study not of scientists' talk when they are doing science in the laboratory ("science in the making") but of their talk when they are discussing their own work and that of others—in other words, their reflective account-giving. It is based on interviews with most of the principals involved in a particular controversy in biochemistry (oxidative phosphorylation). In the interviews, the scientists give their own accounts of the controversy, their role in it and that of others. Gilbert and Mulkay use this material not, as they say, as a resource (instrumentally) to construct their own account of "what really happened," but as itself the object of study. What principles can be discerned in the ways scientists construct accounts of science? Their first finding is that these accounts are extremely variable and flexible according to the situation; their second is that there are two modes or repertoires for account giving—the empiricist and the contingent—which assume contradictory things about the doing of science, one minimizing the acts and decisions of individual scientists and the role of accident and circumstance (the empiricist repertoire, or official face of science) and one that maximizes these factors (the contingent repertoire). Thus accounts in the contingent repertoire debunk the official stories of the empiricist mode, but, since it is the scientists themselves that provide both accounts, the writers' own stance does not come into question. As Woolgar notes, reflexivity is not a crucial issue for them, and they do not call attention to their own interpretive activity or the reliability of their account.[39] At the beginning of the book they announce their desire to function as pure passive conduits of scientists' discourse:

Applications

> Most sociological analyses are dominated by the authorial voice of the so-
> ciologist. Participants are allowed to speak through the author's text only when
> they appear to endorse his story. Most sociological research reports are, in this
> sense, univocal. We believe that this form of presentation grossly misrepresents
> the participants' discourse. This is not only because different actors often tell
> radically different stories; but also because each actor has many different voices.
> In this book, we will begin to lift the lid of Pandora's Box in order to give some of
> these voices the opportunity of being heard. (p. 2)

Gilbert and Mulkay's account of their own procedures is very much in what they
call the "empiricist" repertoire, which represents or symbolizes the object
world as acting on its own: "The guiding principle of this repertoire appears to
be that speakers depict their actions and beliefs as a neutral medium through
which empirical phenomena make themselves evident" (p. 56); and somewhat
earlier: "A style is adopted in formal research papers which tends to make the
author's personal involvement less visible; and the existence of opposing scientific perspectives tends to be ignored or depicted in a way which emphasizes
their inadequacy, when measured against the 'purely factual' character of the
author's results" (p. 47). A little reflexive consciousness does seem in order here:
Gilbert and Mulkay appear to be enjoying the discursive power of the empiricist
mode even as they declare it to be a rigorous editing out and denial of the
author's personal involvement! No wonder that critics have taken it upon
themselves to remind Gilbert and Mulkay that *Pandora's Box* depends on
much interpretive activity and is in fact offered as a "best account" of their
findings concerning account-giving by scientists! Note too that Gilbert and
Mulkay are not about to scale down their authorial privilege to the extent of
turning their transcripts over to readers for them to interpret and make sense of
as we can. They will let the scientists speak, but not let readers interpret.

This is not a frivolous suggestion, Harry Collins argues, for the interpretation
of the passages is not self-evident; lifted out of context in the book and given to
others for interpretation, the passages received some readings like those given
them by Gilbert and Mulkay, and other, rather different ones as well.[40] It is
important to raise this question, Collins argues, for the readings given to the
scientists' elicited accounts of the controversy are very natural and straightforward seeming. That is, we don't sense any interpretive effort, nor is very much
required of us, so that the scientists seem to be making their meanings and
speaking for themselves. This effect depends crucially, Collins argues, on the
fact that Gilbert and Mulkay are not talking about science "but only about such
things as how scientists apportion blame, account for their own successes, cite
philosophers, make jokes and so forth," and thus "their work requires a
minimum of esoteric abilities to produce *an* interpretation. The preferred
interpretation will therefore seem immediately reasonable," and hence, "A
reader . . . will then feel immediately at home with the material, and feel that
there is little more that needs to be known about science per se in order to have
a grasp on the whole situation under discussion" (p. 103). Collins is arguing not
that Gilbert and Mulkay's work is defective or unreliable, but that it is reliable

for reasons they do not acknowledge—namely, that they have a privileged position in writing their account arising from their extensive field work with the scientists (including gathering the scientists' comments on their analyses) and at least a grasp of the general outlines of oxidative phosphorylation. In short (and Collins does *not* say this), they make the reader seem smarter than she is, by minimizing the work of selecting and interpreting that they have done. By way of contrast, Latour and Woolgar, because they call attention to their own activity, leave the reader uncertain how smart she is, or the "observer" is; Lynch, finally, succeeds in affirming the profound ignorance of all "readers" who lack technical skills.

Despite this pose of merely recording the voices that arise, Gilbert and Mulkay do not smuggle in "the true account of what really happened." Rather, they advance two methodological claims that place any such "true account" in question. First, they maintain that *neither* empiricist nor contingent accounts, or any other, is to be taken a priori as truer or closer to the facts: "The informal talk whereby actions and beliefs are constituted at the laboratory bench is not regarded as having primacy over any subsequent reinterpretations around a coffee table, at a conference, in a research paper or in an interview" (p. 14). Second, the degree of variability in accounts is so great "that no degree of craftsman's expertise can enable the sociologist to sort out the interpretive dross within participants' discourse from what is sociologically valuable" (p. 10), hence "For traditional sociological analysis of social action, then, participants' interpretive variability causes fundamental, and perhaps insoluble, difficulties" (p. 13). Variability thus performs for them the role of the stranger, severing the discursive practices of account-giving from any referential connection to the facts of the matter and foregrounding them as the object of study.

This position has been felt to be a rather severe methodological stricture, ruling out the use of scientists', or anybody's, accounts as a resource for describing what really happened, as for example is done in the history of science as well as traditional sociology, and strongly suggesting that any such account could not be "definitive" (a word they repeat), but only, of course, one more account. Steven Shapin objects that these tenets do constitute a "restrictive program" which radically narrows the historian's goals and procedures.[41] Speaking for historians, Shapin says, "We do not label our accounts as imaginative fictions because we hope they are not. Our goal is indeed telling it *wie es eigentlich gewesen*. If this is what Gilbert and Mulkay mean by seeking to offer 'definitive accounts,' we should be proud to plead guilty" (p. 127). Shapin also notes a softer line which he calls the "inclusive" program, which takes attention to the principles of account-giving as "a necessary prelude to the satisfactory resolution of traditional questions" (*Pandora's Box*, p. 15). This second line is the one Jonathan Potter chooses to emphasize in his defense of Gilbert and Mulkay. It is, as he says, "hardly an earth-shattering claim."[42] But, as Shapin notes, that scientists' accounts are only accounts is pretty well understood by historians already: "E. H. Carr has surely supplanted Leopold von Ranke in historians' favor" (p. 127). Gilbert and Mulkay sound quite skeptical that anyone could reasonably extract a coherent and well-supported account of what really went on from the materials they gathered, but they back away from claiming to have shown the impossibility of doing so.

Gilbert and Mulkay have been called skeptical and relativist, and the restrictive interpretation of the program certainly is that, but it should be noted that scientists' accounts are not held to be totally inadequate; in fact, the scientists' modes of accounting constitute "a range of flexible techniques which enable them to make sense of whatever is going on in a way that is adequate for most practical purposes" (p. 13). That is to say, these techniques are those of practical reasoning—contextually defined arguments aimed at settling immediate problems. It is only when one pushes them toward consistency, coherence, and comprehensiveness that their variability emerges as a problem: "this kind of everyday reasoning is not sufficiently grounded in data to be satisfactory for analytic purposes" (p. 13). (Note the strikingly empiricist language here.) When it comes to accounts of what is going on in their work, Gilbert and Mulkay seem to be saying, scientists are not scientific theorizers, and, so would seem to be the implication, if they're not, what makes us outsiders think we can make theory out of their practical accounting?

The term *variability* thus seems to be functioning as a code word for *inconsistency*, since only the latter would be an embarrassment for scientific theorizing. That is, as Woolgar points out, variability in itself is no great theoretical problem: it just shows the accounts in different repertoires are adjusted to the situation in which they are given (formal publication, say, vs. answers to questions from Gilbert and/or Mulkay). To be problematic, the accounts have to be of the same reality and they have to be inconsistent/incompatible. But allegations of inconsistency are notoriously hard to make good. First, how do you know when you've detected one? Fuhrman and Oehler suggest that some readers/interpreters may discern inconsistencies that others will not.[43] Second, how do you nail someone for it? Inconsistency is indeed a grievous fault in scientific theorizing, and accusations of it are resisted with great ingenuity and vigor. Well, that's what logic is for, one might say, but in the case at hand, the alleged inconsistencies are between scientifically theorized accounts (the empiricist repertoire) and commonsense accounts, or between commonsense accounts, where the principles of consistency might be expected to work differently. The commonsense equivalent of inconsistency is "speaking out of both sides of the mouth," which may be regarded as anything from a character flaw to a necessary accommodation to a complex situation, but is not the knock-out rule in commonsense reasoning that inconsistency is in scientific theorizing. However, the scientists bail them out of some of these difficulties, since the transcripts indicate that when they are generalizing about the progress of science, they do try to give consistent accounts, hedging, drawing distinctions, modalizing and adjusting emphasis to avoid the appearance of a flat out contradiction. That is, the scientists themselves are following the canons of consistency and compatibility with other knowledge that governs scientific theorizing. But they also seem to regard themselves as the best judges of that.

Woolgar reports, "My own attempt to confront a leading scientist with 'discrepancies' in his account of the discovery of pulsars was met with the comment that any scientist worth his salt could *see* that *in fact* the accounts were quite consistent. Clearly, ideas of 'discrepancy' and 'consistency' are no less amenable to treatment as social constructs than the accounts themselves"[44]—and, one might add, less ready to hand for the analyst to invoke.

Gilbert and Mulkay do maintain that the two repertoires yield inconsistent or potentially inconsistent accounts of how science progresses. Their discussion of scientific humor as a means of reconciling these two incompatible views in a sense provides evidence for the felt sense of conflict among scientists. Even more, they describe what they call the "truth will out device" (TWOD), which enables scientists in their interviews to continue to uphold their (empiricist) view that theories ultimately succeed by garnering the preponderance of the evidence in the face of their own (contingent) accounts of bias, maneuvering, naivete, error, and sheer cussedness on the part of individual researchers. The passage of time is the heart to this device ("in the long run the weight of the facts becomes decisive"), but more than this Gilbert and Mulkay do not tell us, leaving the impression that the TWOD is some sort of invisible hand in which scientists believe as an article of faith. The use of the term *potential* with inconsistency is a wonderful move that finesses the problems raised in the previous paragraph. There seems little doubt, however, that Gilbert and Mulkay think there are inconsistencies abounding, given the radically opposing assumptions of the two repertoires; the inconsistencies are potential, it seems, as long as the scientist herself keeps trying to wriggle out of them; a real inconsistency would occur when the scientist just throws up her hands and acknowledges it.

Thus Gilbert and Mulkay pull up just short of saying that accounts from the two repertoires are inherently and pervasively inconsistent and mutually undermining (or debunking), but the book invites the reader to make just those conclusions. Further, since debunking is generally asymmetrical, with the more prestigious language or account being undermined by the lesser or repressed, the less prestigious account comes to seem more adequate or true to the real facts of the matter. One can see the empiricist repertoire as blatant ideology, blinders that are carefully put back in place (with TWODs) as soon as they start to slip and with scientists sustaining a terrible burden of *ketmen*[45] which only humor can occasionally relieve. The book carefully avoids saying that. But the contingent accounts are the news of the book, and the acts of eliciting and displaying them seems very like the scientists' paradigmatic act of uncovering/discovering the non-evident truth.

Let us now draw together these three books in a general review and assessment of the social constructionist program. A social constructionist study begins by denaturalizing the so-called natural attitude of mundane reasoners that there exists an objective world, that is, a world of objects and relations that exists independent of observation and interpretation and that is not greatly altered by endeavors to study it. The natural attitude flourishes in relation to nature and the natural sciences, where the objects of study are not obviously produced by hermeneutic, interpretive work. The attitude can be taken in the social world, though there, as we can see from Gusfield's anatomy of drinking-driving, it is much easier to shake or displace. Gusfield can readily produce the history of the emerging definition of the problem and cite controversies disputing the interpretation of key studies (such as the notorious Scandinavian studies) and statistics. Gusfield does not have to make vigorous gestures severing his study from those in the drinking-driving discourse—it could, after all, lead to an improved conceptualization of the problem, which is probably why he has been supported in his research and invited to speak at conferences. Social problems discourse is less oriented toward experimental confirmation and disconfirmation than natural science and more oriented toward effective intervention. He strikes the pose of Olympian ironist without a great deal of fuss over the epistemological grounding of such a position (Olympus itself, one supposes, or the academic ivory tower); the fuss and worries are rather directed to the moral responsibility of furthering the end of effective intervention. Gusfield's Olympian disdain for the "utopians" makes him an outsider, not his demonstration that "the problem" could have been conceptualized otherwise and that the way it *is* conceptualized fits very comfortably into the way people want to see themselves and their world. In the studies of natural science, however, the attack on the natural attitude takes a more radical and vigorous form. The analysts are not concerned with the adequacy of scientific discourse as a model of nature; indeed, they acknowledge they are incapable of evaluating that. Rather, they are concerned with the ideology of the natural attitude, as it were—with theories about how scientific discourse works which scientists as well as laymen and some philosophers hold: that it is guided by a special set of theorizing attitudes (critical questioning and scrutiny of all assumptions, rigorous pursuit of internal consistency and compatibility with the rest of scientific knowledge, and so on) governed by norms of universalism, disinterestedness, a readiness to change one's mind in the face of evidence, and the like. If this theory were an accurate model of how scientific discourse worked, then acceptance or rejection of claims would be on a far different footing than in other kinds of discourse: personal factors and appeals, presentation and timing and the cunning to make one's case appear stronger and the opponent's weaker, would have very little impact. Scientists would persuade by the purest of rhetorics, the rhetoric of best reasons where assent is given to theories supported by the preponderance of the evidence which no one can gloss or deny.

It is indeed a powerful rhetoric (as well as a lofty one), but it is one social constructionists cannot wield themselves without giving the game away. They refuse to pattern their studies after that of the scientists, as though they were trying to build accurate and progressively more definitive models of scientific discourse. They ironize their own stances, discovering even as they do so that readers still take them as offering reports about what doing science is really like, or, more critically, as availing themselves of the empiricist repertoire and natural attitude even as they try to diminish its force. They do succeed in casting doubts on the loftiness and impartiality of scientists and the systematic or-derliness of laboratory life and scholarly debate, but ironically their success may arise from the device of the candid observer: "I went there without preconcep-tions and studied and listened and this is what I heard." Reflexive rhetoric is a very fallible weapon to employ against the big bear of Scientific Inquiry: it may simply not fire at all, and when it does, it may hit the foot. As Graham Wilson recapitulates: "It bears reiterating that the reader consults an ethnographic text for news of the world conveyed to him by an accredited reporter. If he suspects that news brought to him is conveyed, not by a qualified professional social scientist, but by a layman, then he will not warrant it as anthropology; he will deem it unsifted raw material of undetermined validity and significance. So an ethnography in which the writer continually confronts and displays his essen-tial reflexivity, thus prompting the reader to question his authority, is a contra-diction in terms. This is the vexation of an ethnography which takes reflexivity seriously" (p. 37).

In his discussion of the insider/outsider problematic mentioned above, Habermas argues that to get beyond the dialectic of rhetoric and counter-rhetoric, insider and outsider, the analyst needs to share the orientation toward knowledge or policy of the community he is studying (to take it seriously, that is, according to its own definition of its seriousness) and then to construct an account of how one could get from those aims to his own, not by contrasting them, but by figuring how one set could grow into the other given the appropri-ate historical development or learning process. This suggests that social con-structionists who refuse to acknowledge the scientist's aim to understand the world, or who relate it to their own aim only by bracketing it, will remain locked in irresolvable conflict with the object they hope to understand. They will be left wondering by what devices the scientists' truth will out.

IV

ARGUMENTS AND APPEALS
RHETORICS OF THE SOCIAL SCIENCES

The books to be examined in this chapter share with those of the last the goal of highlighting the rhetoricity of disciplinary discourses and thereby of reducing the distance between them and less specialized discourse. All of them with varying degrees of polemical zeal oppose scientism, positivism, and objectivism in their disciplines (economics, sociology, and anthropology). These studies are somewhat more conventional than those discussed in the previous chapter in that they do not attempt to probe "science in the making" and are content to analyze examples of science already made in the form of published articles and books. They are content to focus, that is, on the constituent forum, treating it as the site of argument, and to articulate their views of the writtenness or rhetoric of the discipline by analyzing published works. They do case studies to show that common rhetorical appeals and tactics underlie the success of these published works even when official pronouncements say otherwise. At the same time, however, their books urge a refocusing of the purposes of the disciplines to bring these official pronouncements into closer relation to actual practices. Why, that is, promote a rigorous-objective-science account of your discipline when that isn't really the way it works?

In the course of describing how it *does* work, they touch on how the special purposes of the discipline differentiates its discourse from other specialized ones (ranging from literature and literary criticism to natural science) and also from commonsense, practical discourse. They do not follow the social constructionist procedure of ironizing and denaturalizing the dominant "scientific" account, which as we have seen tends to minimize the difference between the disciplinary discourse and that of commonsense. Rather, they foreground the "writtenness" (or rhetoricity) of the writing by drawing on the categories and insights of rhetoric—traditional and New—combining them with some traditional stylistic analysis and some use of textualist and philosophical arguments. The resulting rhetorics of the disciplines diverge considerably, and it is not always easy to distinguish the differences reflecting actual differences in the disciplines from those the writers happen to fasten on. These analysts do not take the role of stranger with respect to the disciplines they study; they write as "insiders," some more distinguished and authoritative than others, but they nonetheless appeal to a broader audience, virtually the "candid reader" of general academic discourse. (Pieces of Donald McCloskey's and Clifford Geertz's arguments appeared in *Daedalus* and *The American Scholar* respectively.) In part, such an appeal necessarily is made when the purposes and means of a discipline are in question: even if the only readers were in fact the members of the particular profession, they must be addressed as general members of the concerned educated public so that they will be able to set aside their habits and preferences as working practitioners. As Perelman and Olbrechts-Tyteca would put it, the writers may be particular persons addressing particular others, but they address them as members of the universal audience, though one might add as especially literate and intellectual members of that audience.

Not the least of the differences in the "rhetorics of" that emerge are the definitions of rhetoric and persuasion themselves. Donald McCloskey, as befits an economist (and econometrician), relies heavily on the metaphor of the marketplace of ideas to characterize the constitutive forum of economics. This represents the contentiousness of academic debate as competition for value, and gives him very concrete and public measure of the success or persuasiveness of an argument—citation counts—though, as we shall soon see, this criterion is not without its problems. Ricca Edmondson and Clifford Geertz, as befits interpretivists, employ a much "softer" definition of success, namely, being taken seriously as offering understanding. Edmondson even declares that her focus is on "suasion" rather than persuasion, but we shall see that this maneuver has its own costs, which not all members of the disciplines appear to be willing to pay.

1. The Rhetoric of Economics: Donald McCloskey

Like Social Problems, Economics is strongly oriented toward application and intervention in practical affairs. In universities, it has been observed, it is generally the largest and best funded department in the social sciences, and usually the best housed, but, unlike most academic disciplines, the successful economist may have a career that would take her out of academe and onto the Council of Economic Advisors; a Nobel Prize is awarded in it annually. Its object of study seems the realest of the real world with a givenness approaching or equaling that of the natural world. That is, the social construction of many social problems (e.g., child abuse, chemical dependency) is easy enough to point to and is sometimes a source of humor, but it would be much harder to denaturalize inflation or competition or taxes. Also, as there are no atheists in foxholes, with medicine as with economics, we may grumble and snipe and flirt with heretical ideas, but if there might be trouble with the body, we run to the doctor. Economics is both influential and prestigious (as academic disciplines go) and its principal capital assets are its claims to knowledge. It is not known for its spirit of play; it is the dismal science.

Like Joseph Gusfield, Donald McCloskey was securely established as professor and grant recipient by the time he published *The Rhetoric of Economics* and, like Gusfield, he had published a sketch of the argument in an earlier article and had received a largely favorable response—one reviewer said that it "caused the biggest methodological fluttering among economists since Friedman"[1] (the reference is to Milton Friedman's "The Methodology of Positive Economics"—1953). The book has been widely reviewed and cited, though with differing levels of precision and care. It has its highly polemical stretches, which may have induced some readers to see in the book a rather simple-minded opposition of Methodology and Rhetoric, with Methodology being bad and Rhetoric good. Such a simple opposition quickly generates dilemmas: how can one criticize as bad or inferior works or styles of writing that have been accepted (have proven "persuasive"), or for that matter account for good work that was neglected? If it's all rhetoric, why won't McCloskey tell us how to distinguish good rhetoric from bad, or true rhetoric from false?[2]

These Methodology bad/rhetoric good readings, which one might simply dismiss as sloppy work, may reflect unfamiliarity with current textual theory or a tendency to charge at some of the many red flags McCloskey has scattered about. A great deal of the book had appeared as articles by the time it was published, and McCloskey is not terribly explicit about the structure of his argument, which is considerably more sophisticated than the "polemical" reading discerns. The book investigates the rhetoric of economics in two rather different senses: in regard to discourse justifying its knowledge claims (to outsiders, essentially) and in regard to the success or failure of various pieces of work (in house, as it were). McCloskey maintains that the self-justifying discourse (Methodology with a big em) still leans heavily on what he calls modernism—positivist notions of objectivity, prediction, falsification, and quantification that have been largely shed in the other sciences and should be abandoned forthwith as deleterious to Economics—a suit of armor for the developing science that has now become a straitjacket as it has been outgrown. (The metaphor is a little blurry, but let it pass.) McCloskey's eagerness to jettison modernism alarms one professor, who notes that it may be intellectually passé, but it still pays the bills:

> If it were the case that abandoning modernism in favour of rhetoric had no implications for economic doctrine, why have not the high priests already given up their incense and incantations to become common rhetors; perfectly anticipated modernist methodology should allow no advantage over the stable values of rhetorical discourse. Abandoning the concept of an ever forward march of scientific advance toward "Truth" in economics will at the very least have costs for those who profess to know it, costs that are likely to outweigh the benefits of more civilised methods of argument.[3]

Professor Kregel does not spell out what those costs might be, but we can guess. Perhaps he could not reasonably be expected to spell them out in an academic journal.

Even though he wants to shed Methodology, McCloskey does not thereby adopt an "anything goes," let-the-market-decide anarchism. There are two other types of discursive regulation that he wants to keep intact—top level Sprachethik à la Habermas and methodology with a small em, the latter being the mostly "homegrown" rules of good procedure about the use of statistics and the like—the special topoi of economics. And in fact one of his most cited chapters—"The Rhetoric of Significance Tests"—is not entirely about rhetoric, but is an example of a methodological argument. This point has been made by Michael McPherson, who notes that McCloskey is assuming a reasoned stand-point from which he can criticize the treatment of items from a time series (e.g. annual incomes since the late 1940s) as if they were a sample from a universe (of possible incomes). That is to say, McCloskey is assessing the persuasiveness of statistical significance tests and ruling some of them out as unpersuasive on methodological grounds. One may try to catch him in a contradiction here, but he can escape since he takes a basically Polanyian and Habermasian position that qualified people in the field can settle these matters by argument and debate (of which this section is one round) without being able to state what makes sense or is reasonable ahead of time for all cases: "We believe and act on what persuades us—not what persuades a majority of a badly chosen jury, but what persuades well-educated participants in the conversations of our civiliza-tion and of our field *and justly influential people in our field*."[4] The Polanyian touch appears in the italicized words which concluded this quotation in the 1983 article form. They were vigorously criticized by Caldwell and Coats in their "Comment" as "uncharacteristically conservative" and seriously question begging. (Who are the justly influential? What distinguishes them from the unjustly influential? What if they hold diverse views?) Rather than tackle that issue, McCloskey apparently drew in his horns and deleted the offending phrase from the book.

The argument of *The Rhetoric of Economics* is not only that Economists should shed the straitjacket of Methodology, however; it also executes several case studies of particular books and articles to show that the way they are written accounts for their persuasiveness/success or failure within the discipline itself. If the demonstration were convincing, it would be a major breakthrough and shot in the arm for writing teachers, who still harbor nagging doubts about writing badly enough to please. But on this point, alas, a number of reviewers remain unconvinced that how a piece is written has very much to do with how it is evaluated as economics. Part of the difficulty seems to be the polemical style of the book which does not conduce to clear drawing of distinctions. In particular, *rhetoric, style,* and *well/badly written* tend to overlap in ways that muddle the line of argument. The chapter on a noted article by John Muth illustrates some of these difficulties.

In 1961, John Muth published in *Econometrica* an article, "Rational Expec-tations and the Theory of Price Movements" (29: 315–35) which was relatively neglected for a decade, but then became heavily cited, partly through its use by the economists Robert Lucas and Thomas Sargent. So it is a case of early neglect and later recognition of the kind that interests historians of science, suggesting some shift in the overall prevailing winds (not to say paradigms). McCloskey does not take this avenue of explanation, however; for him, both its early neglect and its later success were the result of the way the paper was written. "The paper took a long time to be recognized as important because it was badly written" (p. 88), by which he means "badly organized, with ill-motivated digressions and leaps from large claims to lame examples. Little distinction was made between minor points of form and major revisions of economic thinking. Though no reader of *Econometrica* would have stumbled over the inelegant mathematics involved, he probably did wonder what exactly it was supposed to prove." McCloskey then performs the old "translation" trick of citing Muth's text in one column and a plain-English-concrete-subjects-and-active-verbs version of it in the other—though he quickly points out that this version would have failed as a scholarly paper. He then proceeds: "The question is how Muth's argument achieves credence. Now of course it did not achieve credence easily, because it was obscurely written. Its obscurity, however, became a rhetorical advantage once it had been made the holy writ of a faith. It is composed in a foreign language, but the language is a sacred one, like Old Church Slavonic. Its style is the key to its rhetorical appeal, because it is the style of scientism" (p. 96)—namely, avoiding "I," using the passive voice, hedging claims decorously, using jargon and mathematics, and bowing to empiricist idols. These features hardly distinguish Muth's article from hundreds of others that did not achieve the status of holy writ, and one is left wondering whether McCloskey has shown that the writing has much to do with the case. Especially so for he provides other information that offers a more plausible explanation for neglect-and-recognition of Muth's article, namely that it questioned a major assumption prevalent at the time it appeared and drew heavily on unofficial arguments (based on analogy, aesthetic criteria, and the like) that positivists did not find convincing but that he does. It might be a story of radical contents cloaking themselves in conventional form in order to obtain any sort of hearing at all. There are in fact a number of other accounts one might construct of the Muth story (Arjo Klamer, for example, describes what Lucas and others added to Muth's article when extending it to macroeconomics, thereby catapulting it to prominence[5]). Why should we believe McCloskey's account of the writing as both reducing and then enhancing the impact of the article? And, for that matter, why shouldn't we assume that other economists now find Muth's article persuasive and important for roughly the same reason McCloskey does and not because they are rhetorical "dopes" genuflecting before its now canonized scientistic prose? The scholarly conversation calls for warrants here and the casting of doubt on alternative explanations, not bald assertion. Note that McCloskey avoids the practice (common in technical discourse) of repeating a term, and thus creates a dubious string of equivalents: be recognized, gain credence, become important/influential, attain status of holy writ.

In his eagerness to illustrate the use of rhetorical figures in his own writing, McCloskey does not single out the ones that are called fallacies, as for example in this paragraph early in the chapter which is both a petitio principii and a rather silly argumentum per contrariam: "The paper took a long time to be recognized as important because it was badly written. The case illustrates by an argument from contraries the importance of successful writing in successful science. Galileo was a master of Italian prose; Poincaré, Einstein, and Keynes influenced science and society as much with their pens as with their mathematics" (p. 88). The term *success* is a little blurry here and in many other places in the book. This is unfortunate, for it is crucial to identifying the effect of rhetoric. One would suppose that in disciplinary discourse, success might begin with favorable mention and review and ripen into "accepted as true" or as "fact" (as Latour and Woolgar would have it) as registered by inclusion in textbooks in the field. McCloskey, however, seems to accept the citation-counting definition of success/impact ("spawning a large literature"—p. 117, and see the citation tables for the Muth and Solow articles, pp. 83, 87). Nonetheless, in his case study of Robert Fogel's *Railroads and American Economic Growth*, he states that Fogel's piece did not succeed, except among young scholars ready to commit themselves to a novel faith (p. 124), and aroused annoyance and fear in older scholars. McCloskey apparently knows a lot more about success than citation counts alone would tell him. Though McCloskey never discusses citation counts as an index of success or importance or impact, there is a considerable methodological literature which emphasizes the crudity of unanalyzed numbers, at least in the history of science.[6] But this instance may just reflect McCloskey's basic contention that statistics don't usually ground arguments in economics; they just illustrate them.

The Fogel case study does use one of the devices of the rhetorical critic who is trying to zero in on the effects of the rhetoric, namely comparison with a roughly parallel case where different rhetoric occurs with different effect. But McCloskey does not face, or even address, the crucial problem for rhetorical analysis, namely that of abstraction of principles from complex concrete cases; that problem was at least addressed in Economics by Milton Friedman in the famous methodological essay mentioned earlier:

> A hypothesis is important if it "explains" much by little, that is, if it abstracts the common and crucial elements from the mass of complex and detailed circumstances surrounding the phenomena to be explained and permits valid predictions on the basis of them alone. To be important, therefore, a hypothesis must be descriptively false in its assumptions; it takes account of, and accounts for, none of the many other attendant circumstances, since its very success shows them to be irrelevant for the phenomena to be explained.[7]

Since McCloskey rejects "valid prediction" as a measure of success for a hypothesis in Economics (and presumably in *The Rhetoric of Economics* as well), his abstraction of the causes of an article's success is strictly after the fact, and the basic structure of his argument is that of assertion plus illustrations of the hypothesis. And that form of argument is not persuasive when alternative accounts of particular cases spring to mind and are not dismissed. When he suggests that his own style is similar to Fogel's, it is not perhaps quite the puzzle one reviewer finds it to be: McCloskey may be making do with the same argumentative aggressiveness and "charisma" that he discerns in Fogel. I am spelling all this out, for, like some of the reviewers, I am not convinced by McCloskey's case studies that writing accounts for success or failure in Economics, and I am disappointed, because I would like to be able to cite a sound argument that it does and will not be satisfied with assertions supported mainly by an authoritative, well-read, fair-minded ethos.

Underlying McCloskey's assumption that he can isolate writing (rhetoric, style) as the cause of success is the image of the disciplinary forum of economics as already fairly closely approximating the ideal of the free marketplace of ideas. Thus Methodology for him is a kind of arbitrary constraint on what may be offered for sale and purchase—an annoying restraint that distorts the market. This market is free in several senses: first, it is not significantly historical— that is, a good argument should sell anytime it is offered, even if it questions or flies in the face of received wisdom, prevailing tendencies, assumptions, vested interests, or paradigms. (Hence he thinks he need only scold the "typical economist" for a penchant for dogmatic adherence to his church—religion for McCloskey being the image of irrational adherence, shades of Tom Paine!) Similarly, writing well is a matter of following the precepts given in the purist handbooks—these are good for all times and occasions. Second, it is free of political or ideological commitments and constraints—it is academic. This view wholly brackets its role as the handmaiden of business and government. McCloskey's own ethos is that of the consummate academician (and Renaissance man, as Klamer notes[8])—the book begins with a witty Latin dedication "Ad universitatem Iowae, montuosam, humanam, urbanam, quamvis in fustibus positam" (*fustibus* literally translates idiomatic American English "sticks"), which is followed by a preface about his move from the University of Chicago and its intellectual community to Iowa. Third, the marketplace image only scratches the surface of the notion of knowledge as socially constructed; for McCloskey, the social character of knowledge is reflected in the fact that it is certified by communities and not everyone in the community is necessarily persuaded (as they should be if economic arguments had demonstrative force) (p. 100). Of the notion that the basic metaphors prevailing in a discipline might promote blindness as well as insight and serve the interests of certain parties he says nothing. These points have been raised by Adrian Winnett, suggesting that McCloskey might take his post-modernist stance further in the critical direction sketched by Foucault, noting both how the discourse of economics defines what is "out there" and how it positions the economist as knowing subject. Similarly Arjo Klamer notes that the basic metaphors or analogies of Economics—such as the marketplace and rational man—have their own ideological appeals and systematically exclude other, conflicting metaphors (e.g., economy as workplace, not marketplace). That is, McCloskey does well to call attention to the role of analogy and metaphor in Economic argument, but stops short of discussing how they are selected and why they work (or don't work).

The reviewers, properly, do not proceed to sketch the missing account, but McCloskey's discussion and Klamer's response to it suggest the following possibility. The basic "metaphors" of neoclassic model building in economics, those of Rational Man and the Law of Demand, for example, have their roots in ordinary commonsense understanding and are believable partly for that reason. But as they are developed in the expert discourse of microeconomics, they take on aspects that make them less recognizable and self-evident to the layman, man of business, or even to the student of economics, so that the model becomes less "intuitively" believable or relevant as an extension of common-sense reasoning. Klamer, for example, describes an economist talking about preference functions, constraints, and game strategies when a pizza is to be divided and says he always finds it interesting to observe who cannot laugh at the joke. Those that do not laugh either fail to perceive an incongruity or to judge it to be witty. For those who do not perceive (all economists, presumably), the microeconomic elaboration of the basic story has become a second com-monsense and the pizza a handy occasion for applying them. For others who are not amused, the remoteness of the language from the common practical concern may cause bewilderment or uncomfortable strain—incongruity fades into irrelevance. Economists, one might say, are commonsense reasoners who are content to have certain of their notions elaborated and specialized for the purpose of doing economics, but if the expert discourse goes too far from its roots, or if commonsense should happen to change (as it notoriously does), everybody might *not* believe the Law of Demand or conclusions drawn from it, particularly if it runs into competition from another economic school, which may to be sure be nothing other than another elaborated variant of common-sense understanding. But McCloskey does not align himself with the "what's wrong with economics" approach to disciplinary account-taking (which is rather highly developed), and the thought that its dependence on appeals to untheorized commonsense might expose economics to ideological uses never crosses his mind. It is not enough, we will see Ricca Edmondson arguing in the next section, to acknowledge that the appeal of your argument draws strength from its metaphors; you have to take responsibility for them.

2. Rhetoric in Sociology: Ricca Edmondson

One might illustrate the complexity of McCloskey's assumptions about rhet-oric and "success" by comparing the reception of his own book to that accorded a similar argument in sociology by Ricca Edmondson. Like McCloskey, Ed-mondson's book opposes impersonal, positivist methodology and offers instead rhetorical sophistication, arguing that methodology distorts and conceals how good sociology actually works. Like McCloskey, she develops her sketch of how good sociology does work by rhetorical analyses of selected well-received books. There are, however, many differences: *Rhetoric in Sociology* is her first book (and is a revision of her Oxford dissertation); its argument was not announced in an earlier article; she is not an established authority or insider in the field (though the book bears an endorsing preface by Anthony Heath, who is); the book is predominantly nonpolemical and only lightly debunking; the book was published by British Macmillan in 1984 (and printed in Hong Kong); it was not promoted by placing it in an intensively advertised new series by an American university press; it is about Sociology, where less perhaps is at stake in the way of power and prestige arising from knowledge claims; the author is professionally young, British-educated, and a woman. She cites Schütz but not Garfinkel, Richard Rorty, or Foucault, and she keeps her distance from the consensualist view of truth, which she associates with Kuhn, Polanyi, and Toulmin. Which of these factors might account for the relatively modest and slow impact of her book? The reviews in the professional journals (*American Journal of Sociology, Contemporary Sociology, Quarterly Journal of Speech*) were uniformly welcoming and approving. I turned up one citation, in the Fuhrman and Oehler article on reflexive rhetoric. Though modest and careful, the book deserves attention, both for its particular conclusions, and as a model of what a nonpolemical disciplinary rhetoric might look like. To some degree, I will be supplementing the rather stinting published analysis and commentary with more of my own.

Edmondson opens her book with clear initial formulations of the kind of knowledge sociology offers and what she means by rhetoric. The purpose of sociological writing is to enhance the reader's understanding of the individuals or group studied, and the sort of understanding she has in mind involves a sympathetic appreciation of the reasonableness of other people's attitudes and actions. This is not always explicitly or fully acknowledged by particular sociologists, but it is the underlying purpose that makes sense of their tactics and choices in their books. The arguments of sociology, then, are oriented toward evoking understanding in the reader, but understanding is deliberately not Habermas's *Verständigung*: "I do not claim that arguing necessarily aims at agreement or community of purpose, but I do take arguers standardly to want the import of what they say to impinge on others, to be taken seriously by them" (p. 5). This goal she calls "suasion," citing Gadamer's view "that rhetoric presents considerations which are *einleuchtend*: plausible in such a way as to illuminate the question for the hearer" (p. 6). One might say that this understanding is not fully propositionalized—it is in the nature of a "grasp" of the people and situation, a sense that one knows one's way about in the situation and could function practically in it, although sociological understanding is not really oriented toward preparing them to do so. This position is only sketched at first, but the rest of the book develops it in detail.

Edmondson then proceeds to give a clear account of the analytic tools she takes from the rhetorical tradition, especially as it is developed in Perelman and Olbrechts-Tyteca's *New Rhetoric* with its encyclopedic listing of general purpose lines of argument (technically, these are topics which function as warrants for claims). Broadly, these include an attention to ethos ("self-presentation," she prefers) and pathos ("sensitization"). She further extracts from *The New Rhetoric* eleven figures of arguing that are especially salient in her corpus of texts: order (e.g., making the object attractive before discussing more troubling aspects), presence (e.g., making aspects of the object vivid as through description or dialogue), emphasis, repetition, amplification, hypotyposis (vivid description), metaphor, example, humor, argument from authority, and reticence (allowing the reader to draw the implications, carrying the reasoning, she frequently says, "off the page"). Several of these figures imply a view of the text that contradicts the norm described by Olson (Text), especially metaphor, arguments from authority, and reticence. She points out that these figures allow authors to convey evaluations in ways that their methodological statements might rule out: that is, they provide a way around the stance of neutrality—which, one might note, is attractive not only because of the restrictions of methodology but because it enhances the credibility of the author as impartial, fair-minded observer. Such passages come about as close to debunking or suggesting duplicity as Edmondson ever goes, and even then she stresses that authors couldn't fulfill the requirement of strict objectivity even if they wanted to: "A sociological text with no communicative attitudes would be one with no attitudes toward people. This would be very odd indeed and much more harmful than what is actually the case" (pp. 143–44).

The sociologist thus is socially and politically engaged, though not primarily oriented toward intervention or policy change; the sociologist's text is not Text, since it taps into all kinds of implicit assumptions as it leads the reader to "off the page" inferences and evaluations. If it were candid, therefore, it would renounce the admittedly powerful rhetoric of impartial objectivity (the rhetoric of "anti-rhetoric" in the sense of McGee and Lyne), hold authors responsible for their personal communicative attitudes, and acknowledge that it is perfectly legitimate to criticize a work of sociology on personal and political grounds. Thus she would criticize some of the arguments found in McCloskey not because they were based on metaphors, but because they made questionable assumptions and led to some objectionable implications. We are here at a level beyond McCloskey's arguments that economists use metaphors and rely on them, just like everyone else; assuming that, the question is that of discriminating good metaphors from bad ones. She cites a passage from Blau and Duncan's *The American Occupational Structure* (1967) which I repeat here because its content is a prime example of the kind of buoyant bourgeois liberalism cum cognitive-instrumental rationality that supports the inculcation of Text:

> Objective criteria of evaluation that are universally accepted increasingly pervade all spheres of life and displace particularistic standards of diverse ingroups, intuitive judgements, and humanistic values not susceptible to empirical verification. . . . The attenuation of particularistic ties of ingroup solidarity, in turn, frees men to apply universalistic considerations of efficiency and achievement to ever-widening areas of their lives.

Applications

> Heightened universalism has profound implications for the stratification sys-
> tem. The achieved status of a man, what he has accomplished in terms of some
> objective criteria, becomes more important than his ascribed status, who he is in
> the sense of what family he comes from. (Cited from Edmondson, pp. 69–70)

Of this she says "It would not be an objection against this passage to point out
that it functions rhetorically. It would be an objection to assert that it is not
true, or that the social and political judgements it embodies are—for social and
political reasons—incorrect" (p. 70). She does not spell out the objection
further, or even outrightly *object* it herself, presumably because she does not
want her own political views to get in the way of seeing the example as a
specimen. Though Edmondson emphasizes the active reader, she usually assumes he is very cooperative, dutifully making the off-the-page inferences set up
for him (as for example here, that, being free to apply universalistic criteria,
men do apply them, and not just substitute, say, the ethos of their corporation
for the ethos of their family and village). But a reasonably strong-minded and
alert reader, like Edmondson, would not only not be seduced by the rhetoric of
this passage; she might even be put off by it. Edmondson is saying, don't object
because it is rhetoric or metaphor. This discussion does suggest that metaphor
has dubious standing in the code of Text because it does implicate values and
assumptions that are not explicitly stated—not because it is useless ornament,
or even because it is unruly.

In her practical analyses, she makes most use of order, presence, example,
and reticence, and in so doing, she becomes engaged in distinguishing sociological discourse from that of natural science, on the one hand, and literature
on the other, and, less successfully, in relation to commonsense practical
understanding. Her discussion of how examples work in her texts (as "actual
types" and "epitomes" and in rhetorical induction) is particularly thoughtful
and worthy of the praise the reviewers do give. Her writers are fond of extended
description and citation of particularly articulate subjects, even though they are
sometimes explicitly described as atypical. Of this last practice, she says "By the
standards of the natural sciences, it is as if someone claimed to have made a
discovery about the amount of interferon needed to cure cancer in his or her
patients, but exhibited in support of this claim a patient who had reacted
differently from all the others" (p. 50). Even when they are not atypical, they are
selected without much regard for criteria more important in the natural sciences, such as sampling to guarantee representativeness of a population, quantification, precision, and well-defined variables, and trade heavily on their
concreteness and vividness so that we can sense them as we do others in our
daily life. This is the general shape of what she calls rhetorical induction, which
is a generalization not to all cases, but to all reasonably similar ones, and
depends ultimately on the credibility of the writer. "Trust me," the argument
says, "the actual case is typical and this incident epitomizes the phenomena in
question." True, the writers do attempt to provide statistics and "hard facts" to
back the claim up, or test its consequences, but it is the judgment of the writer

upon which we finally depend, hence the crucial importance of our assessment of his practical wisdom, his social competence and judgment. As she says parenthetically toward the end, rhetorical induction is the basis of the force of her own book, which is intended not merely as a set of rhetorical analyses, but as the laying out of how it works in this neck of the textual woods. Rhetorical induction from the actual-typical case is of course the way Gusfield's "fiction" of representativeness works in his analysis of Waller's article.

Actually, she may be making her case harder than she needs to on this point by ignoring her own emphasis on the active reader. It may be that we depend on the judgment of the writer, but we will assess her claims according to our reading of the evidence presented and in relation to what we believe or have read about what is described. That's why we like to have substantial descriptions and quotations and indications of how they were elicited. It is interesting that Jonathan Potter, defending Gilbert and Mulkay against the charge that they foreclosed the reader's interpretive activity by giving just one definitive interpretation of their citations (their own), says, "Readings are made, but the reader is not asked to take them on trust. Instead, large chunks of extract are presented. Inevitably these will be to some extent selective; yet selections will attempt to cover the diversity of textual materials examined."[9] The first sentence points to the reader's engagement, though the second returns to the "trust me" mode. In general, the less knowledgeable we are, the more dependent on the writer's judgment and competence, at least until we become more knowledgeable. But we can also rely on the presumably more informed judgments of the editor and referee(s) as well as the author's awareness that there are *some* other expert readers who might take him to task if he seems willfully selective, ignores what has been said on the subject heretofore, and so on. Here Edmondson seems to slight the public nature of publication.

So important are these portraits of people and sketches of landscapes in the rhetoric of sociology that she goes so far as to say, "Just as it is hardly feasible to write intelligibly about social situations without using actual types, it seems implausible that an author could show what a group of people is like without exhibiting anything they say—that is, without using quotations that function in an actual-typical manner" (p. 98). These works use novelistic description to set the feel of a world, "actual type" presentations of real people including quotation of their very own words. If sociologists draw upon the ability to make their objects lifelike and their situations vivid, how does sociology differ from a novel? Here Edmondson does not invoke fiction/fact directly: "sociologists show what people are 'like' in relation to predicaments which are not chosen only according to the author's personal inclinations, but whose interest derives from their location at the intersection of identifiable social forces. Sociological epitomes examine people's behaviour in a fashion which gives priority to their responses to these specifically social predicaments" (p. 99). One might scruple at "author's personal inclinations" as missing the point of aesthetic design, but Edmondson seems mainly concerned to contrast the artist's imaginative freedom with the sociologist's constraint which is imposed by real ("identifiable") social forces and circumstances. What she says here could be taken as a formula for a particularly ghastly form of social realism, which I'm sure she does not intend, and so we are left a little uncertain as to why *Middlemarch* is not a classic work of sociology despite its subtitle ("A Study of Provincial Life") but *Middletown* is.

Rhetoric in Sociology argues that sociological writing engages its readers as commonsense reasoners (or "understanders"); within our framework, the question thus arises of sociology as scientific theorizing—what is the status of the understanding it produces, what is its potential for critique? Although rhetorical inductions depend on the reader's commonsense wisdom—his phronesis—they are not oriented toward practical action: "Sociological rhetorical inductions deal more pointedly with the interpretation of situations than everyday ones need do, and they connect these situations more selectively with phenomena of social, political, and economic interest" (p. 159)—again the word *interest*. The passage does suggest some abstract theorizing going on, though it doesn't say much about its status. With regard to the second question, Edmondson very carefully shows that sociological writing does not merely make the strange and deviant familiar and reasonable, making everyone into ordinary persons as the reader comes to the text thinking of them. Sociology does make that move, which she calls the "ordinary person" enthymeme, but it also aims at displacing stereotypes and prejudices against others by calling certain of them into question, removing them or at least reevaluating them in the reader's assumptions of what constitutes reasonable behavior given other assumptions. Thus she cites one study of Japanese industry which argues, against British "commonsense," that it is reasonable of Japanese engineers not to seek professional certification, given their assumption that their place and status is in the company which will employ them all life long, not in a profession. (She shows, in fact, that the argument can be read in two subtly different ways, depending on whether the reader is ready to agree ahead of time that Japanese engineers are likely to be reasonable men—their not seeking certification is either an illustration of their already assumed reasonableness or a proof of it, if not assumed.) And she concludes her study with a brief analysis of Erving Goffman's systematic thrusts at the reader's commonsense assumptions, his repeated efforts to defamiliarize and redraw the reader's initial maps. Also, the sociologist's perspective enables him to understand the reasonableness of actions and attitudes better than the participants themselves do; he is not limited to their own horizons of commonsense understanding, since his task is not that of making explicit their implicit social competence, but of making sense of their actions and attitudes in terms the reader will accept, even if his participants would not. How, one might ask, does sociological writing get such power? Not by its scientific methods, Edmondson argues, but by the usual form of arguing the "reasonable man" enthymeme: the oddities of asylum behavior, Goffman argues, become quite understandable once one grasps the way the asylum undercuts both its own seriousness and that of the real world. Thus sociological writing can work to challenge and change the reader rather than merely to confirm all of his initial assumptions, but not by force of its statistics and large scale studies, or its superior scientific theorizing.[10] And the understanding produced by this process is nothing less than the real thing:

> In showing that given actions, views and feelings *are* reasonable, reasonable person enthymemes show in what light we should see them; the proper sort of response to make to them; and how they fit in with daily assumptions and standards which reader and subject share (or can be brought to share). It seems to me that if one knows as much as this about someone's conduct, and if one has undergone sensitising processes dismantling barriers against comprehension of this conduct, it would be absurd to claim that one did not understand it. (p. 139)

How could one argue with that?

Perhaps the reader has already begun to imagine how an instrumentalist or realist might challenge this view of sociology. One could imagine that it would always be possible to show that actions, views, and feelings (which are hardly "given" but already produced by the writer) are reasonable and therefore understandable (with all the tolerance that implies), and perhaps possible to give several different accounts that would make it reasonable. Which then to choose? And why defer to the reader's possibly ethnocentric or class-bound views of what's reasonable? Sure, we can understand them, but do we understand them correctly? Just because we couldn't understand them before and now we do? Edmondson does point out that different reasonableness accounts will be persuasive to different readers: "there are different ways of perceiving what is true and different ways of truth-telling" (p. 165). Nonetheless, she argues, we can still reject some accounts as false; it is not clear, however, that she has made a distinction between false and merely implausible—a badly executed demonstration of reasonableness. There is no denying that Edmondson's conception of reasonableness is culture bound, and indeed, in one sense culture defining, and so her scheme would seem to lie open to the sort of problem illustrated by Perelman:

> The Supreme Court of Belgium in a judgment of 11 November 1889 justified the inadmissibility of women to the bar in spite of the absence of any law to this effect, affirming that "if the legislature had not excluded women from the bar by a formal disposition it was because it was too self-evident an axiom to state, that the service of justice was reserved to men." This affirmation which seemed self-evident, thus certainly reasonable, a century ago, would be inadmissible, even ridiculous today. The reasonable of one age is not the reasonable of another, it can vary like common sense.[11]

For this reason, Perelman argues for a dialectic between the rational, with its potential for critique and innovation, and the reasonable. Put another way, the reasonable seems tied to what Gadamer calls prejudice, and his attempts to rehabilitate prejudice have not been wholly successful.

But one might be demanding too much here. Edmondson's most ambitious claim is to characterize sociological writing as such. To do that, she gathered a group of representative books that had been cited in answers to a questionnaire sent to randomly selected members of the British Sociological Association (in 1973 and again in 1980) asking them for the titles of "at least three sociological works containing explanations which [they] regard[ed] highly" (p. 167). From these titles, she selected her list according to considerations she describes. There are plenty of opportunities for skew in this process, and one suspects that, as one reviewer suggests, they are weighted toward a particular style of sociology, one which is rather highly qualitative and interpretive and liberal in its assumptions and politics. Edmondson tries to guard against this interpretation by including two studies which are notably scientific/positivist in their language and claims, but, she argues, are "replete with features which disappoint expectations that they might form neutral, unrhetorical and unpersuasive examples of scientific impersonality" (p. 62). One does sense something of a polemical straw man in these "expectations" and the chapter, which concentrates on showing that the books have particular argumentative contexts, strong points to emphasize and weak ones to mitigate, and lead the reader through experiences of theory-building and testing, makes what seem fairly obvious points. Because the works do not fit so neatly into the model of sociological/personal understanding, the exposé of their working on the reader is not as enlightening as her other discussions of more sympathetic works. As the reviewer Joachim Matthes says, "Might it not be useful, in looking at rhetorical analysis, again from a *sociological* perspective, to differentiate social "systems" or "games" of rhetoric instead of letting rhetorical analysis be guided by one concept of rhetoric?"— or, one might rather say, one concept of understanding, and, hence, of sociology.[12] The chapter in question comes off as something of a tu quoque move by an interpretivist against the "scientist/positivists" (who in addition exhibit a hamfisted and tactless use of metaphor). But if we accept the limitation of the scope of the study to interpretive sociology, and further accept interpretive sociology as a going concern rather than try to ground its claims to science, then *Rhetoric in Sociology* stands as a model of a serious and thoughtful discussion of how language is used to effect understanding and "suade" readers. One supposes the anti-positivist noises had to be made—how else to get people to take the book seriously?

The partiality of Edmondson's account can be seen in a slightly different way by noting the rather different discussion of one of her cases, Paul Willis's *Learning to Labour*, by George Marcus.[13] Willis is one of Edmondson's first examples of an interpretative, qualitative sociologist. There is, she notes, a vein of neo-Marxist theorizing in the book, but she treats that as a purely contingent matter. Marcus, however, takes the work as an exemplary experiment in trying to fuse ethnographic, interpretive "micro" analysis with a much wider, "macro" concern with social forces and social action, going so far as to say, or to say that "we might say," that "the representation of working class experience is not at all Willis's primary goal" (p. 184)— and he too uses Willis as a "case" for studying textual strategies! The different treatments do not witness against the interpretivist program, but they are a reminder that interpretation is going on even when cases are selected and analyzed, and that interpretations tend to be plural.

In one sense, Edmondson's argument supports Habermas's emphasis on the purposes of the expert discourses: the rhetoric of sociology works to further the end of sociology, which is understanding as she describes it. Since it does not work by constructing and testing abstract models, it has no need of the procedural and methodological canons that would be appropriate in a discipline that does so proceed. On the other hand, by running up the magnification on the particular discipline of sociology, her argument shows a level of conflict and dissensus about its purpose within the discipline itself. There can really be a rhetoric of sociology only to the extent that the schools and branches of the discipline agree about the purpose of the discipline and the kind of knowledge it produces. There have been attempts such as Richard Harvey Brown's *A Poetic for Sociology* to give a unified and comprehensive grounding for sociological discourse on a "cognitive aesthetic" "symbolic constructionist" epistemology, but this attempt on the whole was not too well received. There are doubtless numerous traits and commitments that bind sociologists together, but an articulated purpose may not be one of them. One wonders how much dissensus of this kind underlies McCloskey's scolding about sects in Economics.[14]

3. Ethnography as Art: Clifford Geertz

Works and Lives: The Anthropologist as Author, the most recent of Clifford Geertz's works, appeared while I was planning this study and is animated by many of the same questions and concerns, including an inclination to resist the self-conscious suspending of truth claims for ethnographic writing. Writing ethnography, Geertz feels, has become very hard to do in recent years as a result of anxious, reflexive scrutiny of the stance of the writer, the act of writing, and the status of the resulting account. Here, for example, is his assessment of the windowpane problematic discussed in the previous chapter:

> The pretense of looking at the world directly, as though through a one-way screen, seeing others as they really are when only God is looking, is indeed quite widespread. But that is itself a rhetorical strategy, a mode of persuasion; one it may well be difficult wholly to abandon and still be read, or wholly to maintain and still be believed.[15]

This nervousness about its own textuality and knowledge claims is especially troubling to enthnography because it is already scrambling to reposition itself after the collapse of colonialism, which after all provided the undergirding for the positions of observer, observed, and audience in classical works. The only possibility of cure, he feels, will emerge from a direct confrontation of the literariness of ethnographic writing; *Works and Lives* advances this program

by examining the style and textual strategies employed by four master ethnographers in less self-conscious times.

Geertz has long been one of the principal voices advocating and articulating
"interpretive anthropology," which in the course of his career has successfully
challenged the traditional "positivist" and objectivist approach and is now
thoroughly established, at least within the (major) branch of anthropology
called ethnography.[16] As much as eight years ago, he was carrying his message
to the wider audience of *The American Scholar* with "Blurred Genres: The
Refiguration of Social Thought."[17] Accordingly, he sketches his general view of
anthropology, which has much in common with Edmondson's program for
interpretive sociology, with a few quick strokes of the brush. He dispatches the
scientistic myths about how ethnographic studies manage to be taken seriously
and to persuade in less than two pages—clearly it is *not* the sheer weight of facts
on the one hand or the conceptual elegance of its general theories on the other.
Rather, the source of their persuasive power is their ability to convey that they
have "been there," having had "close-in contact with far out lives" (p. 6). He is
also supported by a rather vigorous body of self-analysis within anthropology.
There is no more mileage to be had beating Positivism or Scientism; the view
that ethnography is written by human subjects out of the experiences of human
subjects and intended for the complex uses of other subjects is not hot news, at
least not in anthropology in the mid-1980s.

The relevance of Geertz's book for our study seems manifest. *The New York
Times Book Review* identified Geertz when the book came out as a professor of
rhetoric at Princeton's Institute for Advanced Study.[18] Nonetheless, *Works and
Lives* is finally most relevant for what it does not do. What it *does* is to offer
close analyses of the textual strategies and literary qualities of four of the great
writers, each in their way authors or founders of the discursivity known as
ethnography (Claude Lévi-Strauss, Bronislaw Malinowski, Edward Evan Evans-
Pritchard, and Ruth Benedict) with a view toward discerning the sources of
their power, a power which is so drastically diminished in recent ethnographic
writing. Wielding this power is the proper goal of ethnography; it is the power
of enlarging "the sense of how life can go" (p. 139) through a "rendering of the
actual, a vitality phrased" (p. 143); by means of this power, it can "enlarge the
possibility of intelligible discourse between people quite different from one
another . . ." (p. 147). Good ethnography is a work of the imagination, "the
imaginative construction of a common ground between the Written At and the
Written About" which is "the *fons et origo* of whatever power anthropology has
to convince anyone of anything—not theory, not method, not even the aura of
the professorial chair, consequential as these last may be" (p. 144). It is the
Defense of Ethnography as Poesy.

But, and there is a but, what it does *not* do is to develop ethnography as a site
of argument, specifically argument about the accuracy or fidelity of the master's
accounts to the purported objects of their studies. Interesting to see how Ruth
Benedict's portrait of the Japanese is fashioned as a critique of American
commonsense, yes, but is she right about the Japanese? What do other scholars

say? How do they argue with her? Geertz finesses this one in a complicated parenthesis, but what is missing is enormous, once noticed. Geertz does discuss responses to the writings of his masters, the strengths and limitations of their textual strategies, and he does also expose the weaknesses of the recent genera- tion, but it is always in terms of the strategies and implied personal qualities of the writers—the adequacy of the texts in resolving the tensions that underlie them—never in terms of the accuracy or insightfulness of their particular observations and especially never in relation to other observations. Geertz simply does not concern himself with claims that ethnography adds to public knowledge even as accurate description, not to mention explanation. He is not, as Paul Shankman points out, concerned with offering criteria of assessment so that we could choose on principled grounds between competing accounts; this becomes a serious matter when there are competing accounts, as there are of the Balinese culture Geertz has described.[19]

Geertz's equating "taking seriously" with "being persuaded" in *Works and Lives* thus skips a step: we can certainly take something seriously and argue against it; in fact, we don't bother to argue against things we don't take seriously. Being taken seriously in Foucault's sense ("well-formed" in a knowl- edge seeking discourse) is only the first step; being taken as true, or the best available account, requires something more. Thus one might take the impres- sion of having "been there" as the criterion for taking an ethnographic work seriously enough to bother to subject it to serious critique; it is what determines the acceptance or rejection of manuscripts, perhaps. But Geertz seems to imply it is the *only* criterion that matters all the way to incorporation in textbooks and absorption into the tacit knowledge of the profession. And, consistent with this downplaying of even small em methodology, he treats Benedict's employment during World War II in the Foreign Morale Analysis Division of the Office of War Information, which was trying to understand the enemy's alien mentality, as reflecting the touchingly well-intentioned naivete of the times. He certainly would not want ethnography to produce knowledge useful to advancing Amer- ican cultural (or political) imperialism.

That said, it can also be acknowledged that *Works and Lives* is not only a restatement of Geertz's program as an apology for ethnography; it is also an argument against the nervous, reflexive, self-ironizing modern fashion of writ- ing ethnographical accounts that arises from the current "epistemological hypochondria." It proceeds by examining the stances and devices of the four masters as they appear first in minor or peripheral, especially personal, writings and then in their major writings, employing a strong and traditional con- ception of the author as one whose unique traits are manifest in all his or her writings—private journals as well as public tomes, ephemera and unpublished "remains" as well as signed monuments. He even develops a term for these traits—the " 'being there' signature." These unique formulae, or stances, how- ever, are not necessarily coherent and harmonious solutions to the problematic textuality of ethnography; in fact, Geertz treats them as ways of negotiating between conflicting commitments which often involve veering from one emphasis to the other or even of equivocating, as, for example, he shows Malinowski doing between Absolute Cosmopolite and Complete Investigator. And he frankly acknowledges the limitations that arise from the special purposes the masters form for themselves—that Evans-Pritchard, for example, was out "to demonstrate that nothing, no matter how singular, resists reasoned description" (p. 61), where reasoned description is that of the "of course" of the Oxbridgian Senior Commons Room. Yes, they were culture-bound and limited by temperament and sensibility, he seems to say, and we can clearly see that, but they were not disabled by their limitations or transported to grand, "pumped up and febrile" theorizing about textuality and representation.

Geertz's position is thus solidly Tory, combining reverence for the Ancients with contempt for the Moderns, and when he writes of the appeals of the Oxbridgian "of course," there is a note of nostalgia, even yearning for the old code of simple subject-verb-object sentences, the purity of the English idiom, and the refusal to flaunt one's "culture" or knowledge of other tongues—the sort of solidity of Sir Arthur Quiller-Couch, Henry Fowler, and William Strunk all rolled into one. And he finds similar virtues in the American Benedict who developed "a powerful expository style at once spare, assured, lapidary, and above all resolute: definite views, definitely expressed" (p. 108). But the times are much altered, and Geertz's own style is not so simply centered. *Works and Lives* provides many examples of the tendency toward the "late Gothic" involution and virtuosity that Shankman sees emerging more and more strongly in Geertz's writing. He does often achieve the lapidary effect, as well as turning out many of his superb antitheses and scattering with profusion *bon mots* and allusions of dazzling diversity, but many of the sentences have trouble cutting through the thicket of qualifications that parenthetically interrupt them. Consider these two sentences, that follow a two-page anthology of Japanese/American contrasts from Benedict's *The Chrysanthemum and the Rose*:

> The empirical validity of these various assertions, taken from ten pages, not unrepresentative, in the middle of the book, aside (and some of them do sound more like reports from a society supposed than from one surveyed), the unrelenting piling up of them, the one hardly dispatched before the next appears, is what gives Benedict's argument its extraordinary energy. She persuades, to the degree she does persuade—significantly so, in fact, even among the Japanese, who seem to find themselves as puzzling as does everyone else—by the sheer force of iteration. (p. 120)

(This passage, to be sure, is not from the first four chapters, which were orally delivered as the Harry Camp Memorial Lectures at Stanford in 1983, but examples could be cited from them as well.) One would not want to take the parentheses out *tout court* (as Geertz might say), for there is a whole second, and third, discourse at work in them. Recall the *fons et origo* citation above, with its contrasting "not theory, not method, not even the aura of the professorial chair, consequential as these last may be." What are "these last" and how consequential are they? But the desire to reflect on what is said from several angles, some of them critical, to fend off the anticipated objections before they are made (fig.: procatalepsis), and the somewhat anxious alertness it induces in the reader, all of these are the unmistakable signature of Geertz's unacknowledged master, the Old Pretender and mandarin's mandarin, Henry James. And, if the style achieves a rich, deliberative reflectiveness, it also exasperates at times with its swirl of conditionals, qualifications, and interruptions. *Are* Benedict's assertions about the Japanese empirically valid? *Do* the Japanese accept her account of them? And, for that matter (don't look back!) what exactly is Geertz's position on the windowpane problem? If Geertz persuades, what does he persuade us *of*?

In citing James as the unacknowledged master, I do not mean to suggest direct influence or imitation, nor even that Geertz reinvented the style in response to the same discursive needs. Rather the opposite, in fact, for Geertz is taking an extremely public, highly institutionalized role as critic of current ethnographic writing and is trying to fashion a persuasive ethos. One may speculate, as many have, about the psychological pressures and conflicts that may have motivated James's late style, but the forces Geertz is contending with are more apparent. Geertz is speaking from a position of privilege, but it is, on his own account, fraught with jeopardy. To be distinguished, out of sympathy with the trends, and bent on reading the rising generation a lecture on how to do ethnography would be enough to arouse some guardedness. In addition, the audience and larger scene are populated with eccentric French theorists given to hyperbole in one quarter; disillusioned "I-Witnessers" pondering their estrangement, hypocrisy, helplessness, and domination in another; in yet another, metaethnographers noting that "[What] has become irreducibly curious is no longer the other, but cultural description itself";[20] and from all quarters withal the objection "that concentrating our gaze on the ways in which knowledge claims are advanced undermines our capacity to take any of those claims seriously. Somehow, attention to such matters as imagery, metaphor, phraseology, or voice is supposed to lead to a corrosive relativism in which everything is but a more or less clever expression of opinion. Ethnography becomes, it is said, a mere game of words, as poems and novels are supposed to be" (p. 2). Smarty-pants debunkers everywhere ready to catch the earnest, reflective ethnographer and pin ears and a tail on her! Nonetheless, the hero accepts the task and ventures forth with zeal. Never mind if the picture is somewhat overdrawn, the monsters are partly imagined, and some pitfalls have been paved over—the sense of the thing is right.

Though light-hearted, the previous sentences do suggest how Geertz sets up what is at stake for his argument, what is serious and important in what he has to say, even if it is not knowledge. But in a sense it is—exactly the kind of knowledge ethnography affords. *Works and Lives* can be seen as an ethnography of ethnographers: a going There to the worlds of Malinowski and Evans-Pritchard, Benedict and Lévi-Strauss, an imagining of a common ground bridging them to the Here and a recovery, through his writing, of their possibilities of writing ethnography for the edification of the Now. And the strains borne by his style are symptoms of the heavier burden of authorship, his writing a model for the recovery of authorial nerve.

Shankman concludes his response to the responses evoked by his article by commenting on Geertz's own textual, or argumentative, strategies in his writings since 1963, suggesting that they were designed to avoid controversy, but now that the interpretive program is on the table, controversy is unavoidable and would be salutary. In this circumstance, Geertz's strategies begin to seem evasive, even to him: "Argument grows oblique, and language with it, because the more orderly and straightforward a particular course looks, the more it seems ill-advised."[21] Shankman urges him to join the debate by refuting the criticisms raised in his article and in the responses: "If the claims he makes for the interpretive program are to be persuasive, interpretive and conventional social science approaches should be compared using the same case material. An open exchange of ideas and evidence of this kind would be neither evasive nor unreasonable" (p. 278). Granted that making a great to-do over criteria of assessment before the fact smacks of Methodology, and that communities can arrive at particular assessments on a case-by-case basis by arguing in part for the criteria to be applied, and granted too that controversies often deadlock, leaving participants with a diminished sense of the rationality and good will of their adversaries and a desire to do something else altogether, nonetheless, answering one's critics is certainly one of the moves involved in academic persuasion; otherwise "Being there" begins to sound like mystification and conjuring. Such a position, Shankman seems to be saying, works well to counter a positivism that represses it; as a way of doing business and settling disputes in the discipline, it leaves something to be desired.

What is at issue here extends well beyond Geertz's general obligation as a scholar to keep up his end of the dialectic. Insofar as the entire interpretivist program for anthropology and other of the human sciences is in question, the debate is one that leads directly to the most fundamental levels of reflection—what Habermas calls the meta-theoretical, meta-value level and the level of self-reflection.[22] If we view disciplines as defined by the purposes, or "basic tasks," or "fundamental goals" shared by practitioners (as Habermas as well as Stephen Toulmin have it[23]), then the argument between the interpretivists and the empiricists brings this shared sense into question, and, on Habermas's view, should trigger discourse at higher levels: the question "which approach best advances the purposes of anthropology" requires discourse on "what should the purposes of anthropology be?" and perhaps even discourse on the highest level: "what kind of knowledge of culture is possible/desirable?" As Brant R. Burleson observes, at this level, questions of theory and value merge. Again, it may seem excessively sanguine to suppose that referring a dispute to a higher level will bring about a consensus unattainable at the lower level, but the commitment to attempt such resolutions is part of one's membership in an academic discipline. It is as it were the principle centripetal force counteracting the centrifugal tendencies of factions and "schools." The complaint in regard to Geertz's refusal to answer his critics is thus that it blocks the raising of these issues at a higher level. This is unfortunate, for the fundamental issue raised by the interpretivist/empiricist division is that of the orientations toward studying society as a system and as a lifeworld—the double perspective of modern social theory that Habermas articulates and attempts to reconcile in the second volume of *The Theory of Communicative Action.*

What conclusions can we extract from what these writers say about their disciplines, what they show in their own books, and what is said about them by reviewers? We can distinguish two major points, the first having to do with the relation of rhetorics to the purposes of disciplines, the second with the specific character of disciplinary arguments.

The question of what is the proper rhetoric for a discipline clearly is tied to the purpose of that discipline. If one wishes to hold that a discipline should produce public knowledge which reliably has stood the test of attempts to falsify it and which, as a whole, is progressive and cumulative, then the choices, attitudes, and sensibilities of individual scientists should not be given prominence in the writing of science. Having what one puts forth taken in this way is the source of great influence and prestige for natural scientists, and one is likely to have one's findings, if accepted, applied in ways that alter people's lives. Presenting and evaluating arguments in the empiricist repertoire, or as Text, would not seem a monstrous contradiction of form and content, or style and purpose. It is fairly widely accepted that this model of an academic discipline is problematic in the human or social sciences, however, for there observation is hermeneutic (and indeed doubly hermeneutic), and observer, observed, and audience are all subject to change, sometimes quite rapid and extensive, over time, making falsification, or even replication, and progressive refinement uncertain. Accepting this general point, social sciences have developed interpretivist programs which redefine *knowledge* as sympathetic understanding which should promote tolerance and even self-criticism in the audience. One might say this endeavor is progressive also, but ethically progressive. If intervention or application of this knowledge were to be made, it would at least be more humane and probably more effective than if it were not informed by this sympathetic understanding of the reasonableness of the other's actions given their horizon. Accordingly, interpretivists have developed a rhetoric that foregrounds the personal involvement of the writer, the interests that animate and the acts of selection and appeal that shape their writing, as well as the active role of the reader in grasping the meanings, all of which lead away from the writing as Text and back toward more commonsense and traditional notions of readership and authorship.

Suddenly one notices that McCloskey's view of economics is very hard to place on this simple grid. He pooh-poohs verificationism and prediction as goals for economics, being content, it would seem, with the "pure" activity of constructing and refining models of what does, or did, take place. This leaves him unable to account for the behavior of many economists who think they can predict with confidence the results of certain actions based on their knowledge. As an illustration of that confidence, Steven Rhoads points out that, given the statement, "a ceiling on rents reduces the quantity and quality of housing available," only two percent of the economists polled dissented.[24] (Edmondson, of course, can explain this as a fruit of rhetorical induction.) On the other side, his view is certainly not ethically progressive, and he would not be willing to tinker with the marketplace to the extent of introducing personal and political criteria for evaluating economic theories. "Success" in his view of economic discourse is neither referential accuracy (experimental verification or prediction) nor is it *verstehen*; it is "being cited," and he must accept the verdicts of the marketplace, though at times these verdicts may seem to him like hysterical stampedes from yesterday's to tomorrow's holy writs.

As we have seen, however, not all social scientists accept the interpretivist invitation to exchange knowledge for understanding, and consensus on the rhetorics proper for the disciplines cannot be expected without consensus on the purposes. The books we have examined are both descriptive of working practices and prescriptive about shedding certain postures and pretenses. They are both apologies for their disciplines (as they conceive them) and challenges to their opponents to answer specific criticisms of their own work and to field alternative accounts both of the knowledge to be gained from the discipline and the appropriate rhetoric for developing it. Perhaps that is enough to expect for one round in the academic dialectic.

Turning now to summarize what has been learned about the specific character of disciplinary arguments, we may begin with the most general and non-contentious. Academic discoursers may be seen as arguers seeking the reader's agreement rather than action, or, if this formulation emphasizes statements more than an interpretivist would like, we could rephrase as "seeks to get reader to see things the writer's way." Academic writing draws both on general lines of argument and proof (general topoi) and lines special to the discipline (and sometimes also to related disciplines). Thus Edmondson's descriptions of rhetorical induction and the actual-typical example in sociology apply *mutatis mutandis* to other disciplines as well, even, say, to literary criticism and rhetorical analysis, though not in the natural sciences. Most of the observations, which show the use of rhetoric in the discipline, concentrate on the most general proofs traditionally ranged under the heads ethos, pathos, and logos. We have already touched on the logoi as lines of argument which are especially well articulated by Edmondson for sociology in relation to the encyclopedia of general arguments (or warrants) of Perelman and Olbrechts-Tyteca. Comparative studies would be greatly advanced by comparable ones in other disciplines.

Considerations of ethos come into play as soon as we acknowledge that academic writing is not a perfect illustration of Text (with its explicit, autonomous reasonings). These books give numerous examples of the ways writers claim authority and solicit the reader's confidence in their professional judgment, commitment to right thinking values, reliability as selectors and interpreters of evidence, fair-mindedness, interest only in the truth, awareness of possible bias, and confidence that their approach is fruitful and their endeavor valuable. To a certain degree, the autonomy of the text can be saved if one thinks of ethos in terms of "implied author," that is, the author we infer assuming we knew nothing of her *hors de texte*. Geertz explicitly embraces this view of the authorial I in his analyses, and thus emphasizes the power of language, of writing, to constitute a self for its writer (and reader too). At what cost? At the cost of ignoring the writing as a historically situated act or treating it only lightly and incidentally—he does tell us how Malinowski happened to find himself with the leisure and opportunity to live among the Trobrianders, what sorts of military service Evans-Pritchard and Benedict were involved in, and so on, but his general tone is one of slight bemusement at the contingencies underlying great authorial acts. McCloskey's treatment contrasts very sharply: he gives details about the circumstances individuals found themselves in, the state of the field as they addressed it, and various bits of political ins-and-outs that crucially affected what they chose to do and how they were received, though it is also true that these factors are characteristically articulated in terms of the implicit roles of Knowing Subject and Implied Reader of the writing— i.e., "this writing allows us to see ourselves in this or that particularly flattering way." At what cost? At the cost, we have seen, of making it much harder to extract the effective principles of the "good" writing. McCloskey makes the case, perhaps more strongly than he means to, for close consideration of the particular historical situation in analyzing how a piece of writing (or the writing of a piece) works. His examples are all drawn from the recent history of economics, roughly the period during which he has been a "player," and it is clear that this kind of analysis depends heavily on an insider's immersion in the daily life of the institution. The reader will note that I am sufficiently convinced of the importance of the historical moment to have provided some indications of the scene in the disciplines when each of these studies came out, but I bump into the limits of my outsider's perspective at this point.

Insofar as it deals with readers, McCloskey is describing the appeal of pathos, which is broader than the painting of affecting scenes and includes all appeals to the reader's interests. The broadest appeal, which characterizes all academic writing, is to the reader's desire to understand some part of the world, though as we have seen, different kinds of understanding are offered. In particular, the interpretivists appeal to a desire to find the other rational and the other's world comprehensible, although different. In that sense, the reader colludes with the writer in reducing cases of apparent irrationality. Another interest one may engage is the desire to know the straight story, to know it like it is, which is generally dialectically produced in opposition to myths, received wisdom, or official pronouncements. Clearly our "rhetoric of" books draw deeply and often from this persuasive well. Also, they appeal to readers as potential writers, affirming that a writer's choices do make a difference; the reader can pick up a few tips from studying the cases. The lesson to be learned can be explicit and prescriptive, in McCloskey's case, or admonitory, as in Geertz's, or implicit, as in Edmondson's needling of the scientific register and telling citation of particularly awful metaphorical patches. But one can, as noted, imagine a world in which the way one wrote played at most a minor role in the success or acceptance of one's arguments, a world in which history and politics plus content were decisive, not prose style or textual strategies. People who take that view don't write "rhetorics of" or find them very convincing.

Finally, there is the matter of style as a means of persuading. Here I want to focus on the footing that writers establish with readers in the sense that I have developed that term in *Rhetoric as Social Imagination*, concentrating on the style of the writers we have examined as cases. McCloskey's style is distinctly polemical of the tough guy variety—very superior in that it is given to flat, categorical assertions, broad parodies of opposing views, and exaggeration, but it is also personal, solidary, and colloquial, emphasizing a broad range of common experience and values with any contemporary American reader, or at least academic reader, so that its superiority is not that of the specialist address-ing the layman, but of the smart and busy man of affairs who has no time to waste with jargon, pretension, or hair-splitting. It starts with the bottom line and it is willing to sacrifice some precision for energy, and not above promoting a weak argument with the same assurance and zeal as a strong one. By a curiously narrow stereotype, it is what one might call an unacademic footing, though it is certainly recognizable as one style of the academic "con-versation"—that of the knock-me-down arguer. Edmondson is in most respects an opposite—careful to assert no more than she can substantiate and always ready to qualify so as not to be misunderstood (more equal than superior); she does not demonstrate the breathtaking sweep of her erudition and "culture"—not for her the breadth of the Renaissance Man nor the heteroglossic range of McCloskey's voices down to pop culture and the colloquial, and she has no use for one of McCloskey's favorite devices, the argumentum ad vericundiam (*aka* appeal to the Biggies). She does not approach the reader as nearly as Mc-Closkey, maintaining a certain reserve, and her humor is dry and understated, eschewing ridicule. Consider for example the cool poise of "In this connection, it is interesting to find that authors of sociological works often give presence to features incompatible with the priorities stressed by the methodologies they claim to uphold" (p. 23). She is the careful scholar of the well-made, clearly articulated book, and she uses the word *standardly*, the unmistakable signature of having been there at philosophical Oxford. One of her very few passes at the polemical occurs when she links positivist/objectivist attitudes to "mas-culinism" and this is immediately flagged by a footnote that argues "genderism" is of course a more appropriate term. One recognizes that style of the academic conversation as well. Geertz's style, already discussed at some length, is a virtuoso blending of both, if such a thing be possible; it is possible, I think, only as a kind of alternation between categorical vehemence and an urge to concede some ground to objections even before a point is fully uttered, and between the sense of a professor speaking and a wordsmith honing epigrams. Clearly all of these writers explore alternatives to the self-effacing impersonality imposed, so they argue, by a scientistic Methodology (its empiricist repertoire), but the constraints of their argument and situation are not so strong as to impose another uniformity, a single footing for the now actively engaged knowing subject as both writer and reader.

V

DIALOGUES WITH THE DEAD
THE RHETORICS OF HISTORY

Compared to most of the disciplines we have considered, discussions of rhetoric in History constitute a venerable twenty-year tradition; the claim that the discourse of History is rhetorical rather than scientific would hardly constitute a bombshell or revelation. History, after all, has long been seen as poised somewhere between social science and literature: its favored mode of setting forth its knowledge is narrative, but the stories historians tell are about facts and are constrained by the documents, monuments, and artifacts of the past and evaluated in relation to the facts. For Gadamer (following Dilthey), History is the epitome of the humanities in contrast to the natural sciences, focusing as it does on particular acts and events rather than on general laws and principles. In addition, History has long cultivated methodological self-consciousness through historiography, and has been the object of philosophical scrutiny in the philosophy of history (though it is often noted that these two studies do not speak to each other, despite what appears to be a common interest in characterizing historical knowledge[1]). To be sure, History was not untouched by positivist canons of knowledge and developed its own horror of subjectivity, but its reflections are characterized by considerable sophistication in regard to the historian's acts of selection and shaping, and her dual commitment to order found and order made. Sooner or later in these discussions, mention is made of Ranke's goal of relating the past *wie es eigentlich gewesen*, but this goal is not generally held to commit the historian to positivist or correspondence theories of truth. Though there is something less than consensus on the precise characteristics of historical knowledge, general agreement on the purposes of History has prevailed for some time that it is not like natural science; rather, one is likely to come across such expressions of purpose as "giving voice to the dead" or even resurrecting them. Nonetheless, we will see a pattern of argument repeated in each of the three studies alleging the "literariness" or "rhetoricity" of good historical writing, studies otherwise quite dissimilar in theoretical frames and separated by time—namely, they all employ the rhetorical tactic of contrast, affirming the role of rhetoric in History in opposition to "science" or some other form of dead-headed naive subjugation to the facts. We will begin at the end of the 1960s with J. H. Hexter's writings on the rhetoric of history, which explicitly attack positivist and analytic accounts of language and knowledge, then turn to Hayden White's heavily discussed metahistorical writings, and conclude with Dominick LaCapra's recent *History and Criticism*, which still finds historians, both traditional and innovative, wanting in rhetorical sophistication.

1. The Rhetoric of History: J. H. Hexter

In 1968, the *International Encyclopedia of the Social Sciences* appeared with a thirty-page article on Historiography by J. H. Hexter, noted specialist in Tudor and Stuart history. Hexter subsequently included this piece with the title "The Rhetoric of History" in a volume of essays (*Doing History*, 1971); in addition, it proved to be the initial sketch for a three-hundred-page book, *The History Primer*, which also appeared in 1971.[2] I will draw upon both texts and the responses they received. My general sense of these responses is that Hexter was a bit ahead of his time. One reviewer in *History* said in 1975, "Professor Hexter has succumbed, I regret to say, to the use of the fashionable words 'rhetoric' (which normally means language), 'discourse' (which normally means language) and 'strategy' (procedure or method)."[3] Little did the reviewer, or Hexter, suspect how current these terms were about to become, and how convenient they would be to discuss some of the issues that Hexter tries to articulate!

As noted, Hexter's long piece and longer book are extended attempts to characterize the mode of knowing and the mode of writing of history. To this end, Hexter contrasts history to science, with "science" functioning as a kind of foil, and a variable foil at that, at times standing for a perhaps somewhat exaggerated "hard line" positivism, at times for quantified and mathematicized discourse, at other times for explanation by subsumption under general laws, and at times for Royal Society canons of exact, precise, nonfigurative, denotative terminology. Several philosophers found his rather casual, not to say cavalier, attitude toward the opponent vexing, arguing that Hexter inadvertently gives an example of the inadequacy of the historical mode of discoursing when it attempts to discuss philosophical issues. This response reflects the uneasy relations between historiography and philosophy of history mentioned above, but it should also be added that Hexter courted it with rather extended polemical attacks. To a considerable extent, Hexter's exasperation with the sciencemongers was characteristic of his generation of historians, many of whom, such as G. R. Elton (*The Practice of History*, Crowell, 1967), also sought to defend history's knowledge claims against arguments that only causal explanation from general laws could constitute knowledge. Setting aside Hexter's performance as a philosopher, let us sketch quickly the positive content of his "rhetoric of history."

Hexter argues that history differs sharply from science both in its knowledge and in its communicative task (hence "rhetoric" for him is not just arrangement and style, but includes the structures and strategies of argument as well). The kind of knowledge about the past that historians seek is essentially a branch of practical wisdom and draws heavily on diffuse, unmethodical experience both of common life and of the past. This position is very similar to that sketched by Louis Mink in asserting the autonomy of History as a discipline—Mink calls this special mode of knowing "synoptic judgment" and explicitly links it to the historian's phronesis. Hexter argues that the very goals of historical explanation are couched in the flexible, sliding terms of practical discourse. Historians seek, he says, "along with many other things, to enable their readers to follow the movement and to sense the tempo of events; to grasp and do justice to the motives and actions of men; to discern the imperatives that move men to action; and to distinguish those imperatives from the pseudo imperatives that have become mere exercises in pious ejaculation; to recognize the impact on the course of events of an accident, a catastrophe, or a bit of luck; and to be aware of what the participants in a struggle conceived the stakes to be" (RH, 372)— none of these being explanatory in a scientific sense, he notes, or communicable in a purely scientific rhetoric. Not only does the historian draw heavily on her phronesis in sizing up the record, she equally appeals to the practical wisdom— "commonsense" is Hexter's favorite term—of her readers. Accordingly, history does not compel us to accept innovative, counterintuitive models of the world— surprising discoveries—rather, it imparts to us "a sense of recognition achieved through renovation. By clearing away some confusing rubbish, a good historian enables us to see clearly what we already dimly sense might be there" (*Primer*, 51). Or, quoting the praise of "an acute and hard-nosed critic of historical writing": " 'Each point about it has just that air of obviousness which everyone can agree to, but which no previous writer seems to have attained' " (p. 50). ("What oft was thought. . . .") Hexter is quite explicit that the logical structure of historical discourse is that of the rhetorical enthymeme with its reliance on what is commonly believed. (This point is not quite as controversial as Hexter makes out; Carl Hempel, the arch-positivist and Hexter's original antagonist, argues that the general laws history makes use of are either drawn from other fields such as economics or "pre-scientific generalizations of everyday experience" [4]).

Here we can bring into play two themes from the early chapters: historical discourse, Hexter might have said, is not scientifically theorized, and it persuades in the way that Utterance does, rather than the way of Text. These statements are certainly consonant with his emphasis on historical understanding as something everyone engages in, and on History as the professionalization of an everyday activity. This professionalization, however, stops short of developing into an expert culture with its special terminology and ways of testing its knowledge. In short, Hexter really has argued that History is not a science, even in the very broad sense we have been using the term. Given the close association argued in chapter two of scientifically theorized discourse, Text, and the Culture of Critical Discourse, we may wonder what potential History, as Hexter conceives it, has to criticize and displace received wisdom. To be sure, her reliance on commonsense notwithstanding, the historian does develop a genuine experience of the other of history; her commonsense is transformed, Hexter argues, by its disciplined experience of the past through its documents, etc., and her task is to take the reader, with his narrow, ahistorical horizon, through her experiences to make the other of the past experienceable for him (*Primer*, p. 270). Here, one must say, Hexter stops; he does not explain how the professionalized commonsense of the historian can develop the critical force to dislodge or rebuke the mistaken "universals" of the reader's narrow horizon while still depending for assent so heavily on compatibility with other of the reader's received notions. Such force presumably would arise from the authority of the historian, which in part would be based on her having persuaded other professional historians on previous occasions. Otherwise, the historian is in the position of the ordinary arguer in everyday forums. Such apparently are the costs of Hexter's vigorous rescue of Clio from the embrace of "science."

Thus the historian's conception works with the loose, unmethodized, half-submerged savvy of practical wisdom, but one which is greatly enriched by the historian's experience, including her experience of the past, all combining into what Hexter calls the "second record" (the "alembic," Mink says, of her mind). In parallel fashion, the mode of communication is one that arises from and appeals to this sensibility in the reader; at some times more than others, it employs evocative, connotative, evaluative, figurative language. To some degree, this language is needed even to accomplish the goals of historical explanation. Moreover, Hexter argues, readers of history don't just want explanation when reading of a great event: "what they want is confrontation with the riches of the event itself, a sense of vicarious participation in a great happening, the satisfaction of understanding what those great moments were like . . ." (RH, 380). Here his key words become confrontation, participation, and accessibility, the last bearing the sense of Perelman and Olbrechts-Tyteca's "presence" and its classical antecedent *energia*. At this point his enthusiasm has brought him to the edge of literature, and he carefully retreats by emphasizing History's commitment to the facts of the surviving record; hence history is less universal than literature, which is committed to the depiction of only the most general truths about the nature and destiny of humanity.

On a somewhat more mundane level, Hexter offers a fairly extended discussion of why good historical prose is so difficult to write. This discussion touches many of the standard bases—prose is written, not spoken, lacking the expressive resources of tone and gesture, it is monologic, not dialogic, and so on—but viewed in relation to Utterance and Text, an unusual configuration emerges. Because he insists that the language of history is the common language, and the tasks it performs are those set in everyday life, his "common formal prose" is in fact not Text in Olson's sense; because it employs the categories and procedures of daily conversational head-scratching, it is written Utterance, brushed up in minor ways with a few terms of art from other disciplines (e.g., potato blight, international balance of payments) and a few terms with no good contemporary synonym (e.g., polis). It is nonetheless hard to *write* "common formal prose" that reads like conversation, to create, he points out, an illusion that one would never struggle with when trying to write scientific discourse. One knows, in the case of science, "he is going to have to learn a new language, master a new structure of discourse, and command a new rhetoric" (*Primer*, p. 60). The fact that he does not have to do this when learning to write history, according to Hexter, does not make history writing easier to learn to do. Thus History shares some of the problems that beset English composition courses that set the students the task of writing the familiar essay, another form that strives for the illusion of written Utterance. Hexter's argument suggests what some claim to know by experience, namely that teaching disciplinary discourse is *easier* than teaching students to write like Joan Didion or Lewis Thomas. We will address these questions directly in the next chapter.

Lest he be accused of mystification (and he was, anyway), Hexter offers some observations on what he calls the microrhetoric of history—the smaller acts of judgment that the historian is called upon to perform when he deploys footnotes, quotations, lists, and modalized speculations (so-and-so *must* have felt this, *may* have thought that). These remarks are among the shrewdest in his entire argument, and have recently been revisited by the philosopher of history W. H. Dray.[5] Still the mode of contrast with scientific use of these devices is maintained (to no advantage, Dray argues), but this finally does not detract from the subtlety of some of his observations, as for example on how lists cue the reader to tap into his implicit (shared) knowledge or not to, as the historian may desire. Thus a lightly annotated list like "Cardinal Ximenes, the pre-Reformation cardinal who reformed the church in Spain, and Girolamo Savonarola, the pre-Reformation monk who was burned at the stake for his reforming efforts in Florence, Luther, the first great figure of the Reformation . . ." is a cue *not* to tap into the implicit shared information; rather, it closes off further thought about the figures mentioned in a way that the simple unannotated list would not. One might link this effect, by the way, to the similar effect of spelling out the basis for a metaphor, as for example Bacon's famous lines from "Of Studies"—"Some books are to be tasted, others to be swallowed, and some few to be chewed and digested. That is, some books are to be read only in parts; other to be read, but not curiously; and some few to be read wholly, and with diligence and attention."

Though he gave himself vastly increased space to expound his theories in *The Primer*, Hexter did not really develop them, and to a considerable degree muddied them with personal anecdote, diatribe, and, as one reviewer said, "donnish humour." *The Primer* became, according to Dray, "curiously neglected." To some degree, the eccentricities of the book flourished, one supposes, because Hexter lacked a community of inquiry, one which has subsequently sprung into being. In any case, he does leave mysteries for others to explore further, chief among which are the mysterious operation of commonsense understanding as it draws upon its "second record" of experience and lore while pondering the matter of history and the largely unanalyzed rhetoric of presence in historical writing. Hexter would not have phrased the last point that way, of course, for despite his ear for certain new-fangled words such as "discourse," he had no premonition of the structuralist and post-structuralist waves that were about to wash many of his commonsense assumptions away. In History, the wave broke with the publication of Hayden White's *Metahistory*.

2. Possible Histories: Hayden White

In contrast to the reception of Hexter's book, the writings of Hayden White, especially his *Metahistory* and the articles collected in *The Tropics of Discourse*, virtually dominated historical reflection in the 1970s. His theory may fairly be said to have changed the game, disrupting the traditional boundaries and allocations of tasks and posing claims that virtually no one agreed with wholly, but which many wanted to analyze and "place" in various ways. White proclaimed the essential unity of history and the philosophy of history while rejecting most contemporary versions of the latter as the sterile debating of "essentially contested concepts." At the same time, he argued for the fundamental importance of concepts developed in literary criticism to understand the structures and possibilities of historical writing. Responses ranged from celebration to howls of "literary-critical imperialism" along with reaffirmations of distinctions and boundaries. I introduce White's theory for discussion with some reservations, for it is only marginally a rhetoric of History (via the theory of the master tropes); in fact, some refer to it, more accurately, as a poetics of history or historiography.[6] Nevertheless, it does take well-known positions on many of the basic issues, highlighting them and calling forth interesting counter-arguments as only an extreme position can.

Among the traditional questions discarded by White are those of truth and the proper purpose of History. Hexter finessed the question of disciplinary purpose by offering his own account as if it were the consensus of all historians. White observes that historians have differed and still do differ quite strongly as to the purposes—what he calls the formal arguments—of historical inquiry. Since, as we have seen, one can only assess the workings and values of a rhetoric relative to a disciplinary purpose, a chronic and irresolvable pluralism of sharply differing purposes would seem to paralyze the discussion of historical writing at the outset. White's strategy is to step outside (literally "meta-") these versions of history to outline a structure of possible purposes (four) and the relations of those purposes to their preferred shapes of narrative "emplotment" (Romance, Comedy, Tragedy, Satire), ideological stances (Anarchism, Conservatism, Radicalism, and Liberalism), and, above and beneath all, characteristic mode of figuration (Metaphor, Metonymy, Synecdoche, and Irony). These four sets of four generate a grid of possibilities and affiliations that can be used to analyze the writing of particular historians.

Where in all of this, one might ask, is White's own characterization of History as a discipline, or of the historical work as a kind of text? White's answer is

strongly formalist: "I will consider the historical work as what it most man-
ifestly is—that is to say, a verbal structure in the form of a narrative prose
discourse that purports to be a model, or icon, of past structures and processes
in the interest of *explaining what they were by representing* them" (*Metahistory*, p. 2). The formalist note is particularly marked in the phrase "structures and processes," as these give no priority to human acts and events, and
hence would include the matter of natural as well as human history, or indeed
geology, were one to represent it in narrative prose. Because history is a verbal
structure, its structural possibilities are given by the nature of language as a
medium of representation, which for White are the four master tropes. "These
tropes," he says, "permit the characterization of objects in different kinds of
indirect, or figurative, discourse. They are especially useful for understanding
the operations by which the contents of experience which resist description in
unambiguous prose representations can be prefiguratively grasped and prepared for conscious apprehension" (pp. 31, 34). For White, however, there are
no unambiguous prose representations: *all* language, even that of science, is
figurative, though science has stabilized on one standard figure—metonymy—
for its terminology, and so gives the impression of having a literal, denotative
language. Thus history, he insists throughout *Metahistory*, falls short of being a
science; it is a pre- or proto-science at best because it has not settled on a
specific mode of discourse, so that "historiography has remained prey to the
creation of mutually exclusive, though equally legitimate, interpretations of the
same set of historical events or the same segment of the historical process" (p.
428). As various critics have pointed out, there is something somewhat mythical
about this primary act of prefiguration performed upon the inchoate mass of
documents that apparently constitute the "raw data" of history. Documents
come already identified and shaped, and accompanied by a tradition of historical interpretation. But White's point is that *in principle* historical narrative
involves a figuration of the past, an act that is essentially poetic. The historical
account cannot be judged in terms of correspondence to the facts, as these too
are already prefigured by the master trope, or rather, accounts will all correspond more or less to the facts prefigured according to the trope that dominates
them, and hence truth cannot be assessed in absolute terms. For White, this
epistemological relativism is liberating, for it means that one is free to choose
the mode and trope on ethical and esthetic grounds.

This is clearly a strong textualist position, especially since it implies not just
that History is "all rhetoric," but that a great deal else is also. It has been called
idealist, but it is a linguistic idealism, in that the source of all structure is not
Mind but language, or at least language as it guides the mind of the historian.
Similarly, critics have seen deconstructionist or post-structuralist affinities in its
claim of the "impropriety" of all language, the equation of discourse with the
swerve of the trope. In relation to History, it sets up the historical text as an
autonomous construct which can be analyzed according to master trope,
formal argument, mode of emplotment, and ideological implication so that the

elective affinities between the levels and possible tensions in choice and execution can be discerned. It certainly provides a kind of explication of the imaginative work and power of the historian that Hexter asserted.

As charmed as some historians were at White's explanation of the shaping and ordering part of their work, they noted with various degrees of unease that the other commitment of their work, to finding and conveying true accounts of what happened, had been sacrificed. As Michael Ermarth put it in a genial review in *The American Historical Review*, "However falteringly or obliquely (that is, metaphorically), historical discourse concerns itself with real existence as well as formal coherence."[7] Eugene O. Golub more fiercely and extensively argued that in lopping off history's commitment to refer accurately to past events, White had undercut History as a discipline. The trouble begins, Golub says, with the classification of History as a proto-science, which depends on an unacknowledged positivism in its understanding of science. Golub disputes these claims and assumptions, arguing that historians do share a common purpose for their discipline—to give true accounts of what actually happened—and that they do frequently reach agreement about particular cases, just as occurs in courts of law, even though they may be of "contrasting temperaments, tastes, moral outlooks, and even ideologies."[8] Maurice Mandelbaum similarly argues that historians behave as though they are engaged in a disciplined inquiry: "Many historians self-consciously set out to show that some account given by a predecessor is mistaken and they attempt to produce data or arguments to establish their case. It is not that they are looking at the same segment of the past in a different way: they are contending that their predecessor misrepresented the process with which he claimed to be dealing."[9] Both Golub and Mandelbaum believe History has attained the status of an autonomous discipline which "has its own canons of method, knowledge, and proof: in word, it is a science" (Golub, p. 56)—though not a science in the positivist, objectivist sense. Thus do they attempt to restore the delicate position of History between natural science and literature.

Critics have also noted that White's strong formalist determination of content and mode for him generates an almost paradoxical freedom for the historian to choose a mode of figuration that seems wholesome and appealing to her (choosing, that is, on moral and aesthetic grounds). In particular, White offers *Metahistory* as a way of breaking the grip of the Ironic trope which he thinks dominates and undermines the contemporary historical consciousness, sapping it of vitality and self-confidence. By characterizing Irony as only one of the possible options, White wants to deprive it of its apparent inevitability and dominance, thus liberating historians from their own history. This, as Golub observes, is the siren song of Nietzsche, embracing a nihilistic relativism in the interest of freeing the energy and optimism to make it new, or at least different—an appeal which reached its peak sometime in the 1960s. And, as another critic points out, it also offers the appealing role to the historian of world-creating genius.[10] There are certainly many places in White's writings where his perspective produces contemptuous dismissal of the merely archival grubbing and quibbling in journal reviews that many take to be historical scholarship. To be sure, contempt for the drones is something of a standard feature of historiographic writings—an argument for joining the ranks of the enlightened—but rarely has the discussion been conducted so portentously for such high stakes. It is a heady rhetoric, and Dominick LaCapra, who articulates his position partly in opposition to White's, still wants to offer historians discursive power and freedom exceeding that of the good and careful scholar.

3. The Rhetoric of Sophistication: Dominick LaCapra

"Rhetoric and History," the lead chapter of Dominick LaCapra's *History and Criticism* (Cornell University Press, 1985), is very much in the tradition we have discussed; History is still located at the crossroads of literature and social science, and social science is still exerting a malign influence on it, reinforcing the working historian's naivete concerning the textuality of her sources and her problematic position as knowing and discoursing subject. The adversary is not scientism directly, but what LaCapra calls a " 'documentary' or 'objectivist' model of knowledge that is typically blind to its own rhetoric" (p. 17). LaCapra makes fun of the documentarist's piety of submission to the facts of the matter as reflecting an inadequate consciousness of its own rhetorical activity, though he too maintains that the historian must listen to the voices of the past and be prepared to be unsettled or disconcerted by them, for he wants to retain the authority of documentary backing, the resistance of the documentary record to the historian's "shaping imagination," that Hayden White too readily elided.

The core of LaCapra's attempt to raise his fellow historians' rhetorical consciousness is given as eight aspects of "rhetoric" in the instance of historical writing. These eight aspects function as canons of rhetorical sophistication and self-awareness. They are set forth by contrasting them with naive prevailing practice, sometimes polemically, but often with an accommodative, centrist weighing of values on both sides. In general, they are compiled out of Bakhtin's writings on dialogism as read through poststructuralist literary theory. Readers familiar with LaCapra's *Rethinking Intellectual History* will recognize several of these points discussed there as aspects of the textuality of historical documents. I will summarize these briefly, at the risk of simplifying to excess.

(1) History attempts a dialogue with the dead reconstructed from "textualized" remainders, and the historian's own voice is dialogized as she becomes involved in argument and polemic with other historians, her audience, her text, and even herself.

(2) the historian is trying to convince herself and her audience of some point with bearing on their present situation, but "the rhetorical dimension of historiography may rather serve to test current views by requiring the historian to listen attentively to possibly disconcerting 'voices' of the past and not simply project narcissistic or self-interested demands upon them" (p. 37; this is a prime example of centrist tactics: is it necessary, or even possible, entirely to escape the

latter, or just *simple* operations thereof? rhetoric *may* serve to *test* current views, but does it typically or always? if it does test common views, may some of them pass muster, or does *test* mean *contest*?)

(3) documents, as texts, are not mere symptoms of their times, but may stand in complex, critical, contestatory relations to them.

(4) "rhetoric exceeds not only documentary or referential but all utilitarian, workaday, and instrumental functions of language." By which he means to call attention to the element of celebration and epideictic in accounts of the past, an element that establishes some tension between the historian's language and "scientific criteria of meaning (such as univocal definition of terms)" (p. 39). This brings us close to Hexter's notions of participation but emphasizes more the public rather than the personal aspect of participation.

(5) "rhetoric engages the dialectic of recognition among speakers, of which certain forms of persuasion are only the monological variants." LaCapra here introduces the complex transferential relation of the historian to her subject (roughly, the tendency to replicate in her own work in displaced fashion certain aspects of the text under study), and urges the historian to reread "the so-called founding fathers with a sensitivity to those sides of their texts that have been obscured, misinterpreted, or underplayed, often because of the documentary or narrowly "scientific" grid through which they are perceived" (p. 40).

(6) History involves both sympathy and identification with the past and critical distance; "historiography is itself a tensely mixed mode of language use involving both documentary or 'scientific' knowledge and rhetoric in a broader and unavoidably problematic notions of cognition" (p. 41). (Combined with item 4, this does turn the struggle with documentarism into a struggle with scientism.)

(7) rhetorical consciousness places in question not only the "plain style" of antirhetoric ("a rhetoric unadorned by figures, unmoved by emotion, un-clouded by images, and universalistic in its conceptual or mathematical scope" (p. 42), but also the attempt to methodize or codify terminology and principles of usage (an oblique criticism of White's systematization of figuration in history).

(8) History must recognize its placement into the present contexts, especially the problematic relation of elite and popular culture as it generates readings and misreadings of the past. (This prepares the ground for his attack on Carlo Ginzberg.)

The constant prescriptions for the historian on all of these points are self-consciousness, self-criticism, and sophistication—qualities of mind that cannot be systematized, but can be invoked to criticize the works of other historians, which the rest of the book proceeds to do. For example, he criticizes Carlo Ginzberg's attempt to speak for a late medieval oral peasant culture as the real culture of the past, saying that his and other similar attempts at the true history of a period illustrate "a bizarre and vicious paradox whereby a vicarious relation to the oppressed of the past serves as a pretext for contemporary pretensions to dominance" (p. 69). Ginzberg's may be one of several attempts to valorize the naive of the past, but one might read backwards to say of LaCapra's canons that a certain contemporary notion of sophistication is being used to reinforce a different pretension to dominance, though there is of course nothing bizarre or paradoxical about a scholar claiming dominance on the basis of sophistication.

In a review of articles by White and books by LaCapra, Peter De Bolla raises in a very cagey, poststructuralist fashion the question of where LaCapra gets his notions of "reading" and "rhetoric." The source, he suggests, is literary theory, specifically deconstruction, and its introduction into historiography is a borrowing across disciplinary boundaries which is questionable insofar as deconstruction has not shown it can deal illuminatingly with historical texts and documents.[11] It is almost as if LaCapra is telling historians what they need to think and say if they are not to be sneered at by Theorists. To be sure, certain of his points would strike the traditionally minded historian as merely stating the well-established in the current jargon of literary theory, the whole trick being to know when and which texts to read "richly" as it were, when to take flight on the updrafts of uncanny rhetoric, and so on. Read in this way, "Rhetoric and History" is a reworking of standard questions about the relation of history to science and literature, the more recognizable as such because of its lambasting of unimaginative troglodytes and other witting and unwitting hankerers after plain style and the cool, rational, denotative language of Royal Society scientific prose. The service it performs for historians, then, would be to save the old wine from the rapidly deteriorating old wine bottles of imagination, intuition, intention, and commonsense.

As noted, in "Rhetoric and History," LaCapra restrains the impulse to free-swinging polemic ("bizarre and vicious paradox," etc.) as well as deconstructionist flag-waving, attempting a "reasonable" centrist rhetoric. His style is full of balanced, parallel "on the one hand/on the other's." For example, he writes strongly of the need for critical rationality in historical argument and especially self-critical rationality (p. 37), but also for releasing rhetorical power:

> The possibility that rhetoric may overwhelm familiar but fragile scientific procedures creates understandable anxiety, for if the recent past has taught us anything, it is that standard scientific procedures in evaluating evidence and testing hypotheses are all too easily jeopardized. Rhetorical power that rides roughshod over the demands of empirical accuracy and rigorous proof may at times be more objectionable than complacent business as usual. But, to be scientific, a discursive practice must recognize its own limits as well as the fact that those limits must sometimes be exceeded or even radically transformed. (p. 41)

Something for everybody here. Voicing the "anxiety" of the other side and endorsing it as "understandable" seems an exercise of what is sometimes called Rogerian rhetoric, which seeks to allay the spirit of contention by acknowledging the feelings and concerns of the other side. The next sentence, which appears to continue the "understanding" of the other side, however, has considerable spin on it which is apparent when one imagines a documentarist-scientist saying "rhetorical power riding roughshod etc. is *always* objectionable regardless of the complacency with which business as usual is conducted. And what is this 'at times' and 'sometimes' business? Who is going to decide when to break the rules, the rhetorician-historian-Übermensch?" Here LaCapra seems to be singing his own version of Nietzsche's song. And again, LaCapra has many lines depicting the decentering and dispersion of the self via dialogism into voices and parodies, but the remedies of sophistication, self-consciousness, and self-criticism seem squarely founded on the unified, self-directing consciousness of the historian. It may be that LaCapra's centrist rhetoric is finally quite appropriate, in that for all his attempts to bring historiography up to speed, he does not challenge some of the fundamental assumptions of historical writing. Like Bakhtin, one of his favorite authorities, LaCapra can be read two ways: moderately, in the fashion just indicated, or more radically, with sophistication, self-criticism, and self-awareness (where the self is a plurality of voices) becoming prime values and the essential focus of one's engagement with documents from and about the past, one's peculiar dialogue with the dead.

Regardless of its immediate source, the notion of transference in scholarly writing—that it reenacts in itself certain characteristics of the object of study—describes a force at work in a great deal of writing, not all of it confined to the humanities. I have experienced a repeated urge to cast this chapter in the form of a history of rhetorics of history, have ordered the sections chronologically and suggested they are stages in a tradition of reflection; further, I have suggested links to broader changes in reflections about language and rhetoric, and have even engaged in a little foreshadowing. Like a conscientious historian, I have not claimed that White was responding to Hexter (for which there is no evidence) and have claimed that LaCapra was responding to White (which I documented). All of these techniques create order in the fashion of narrative—the history of ideas, to be more exact—and it would be possible greatly to enhance all of them in detail and scope. But it would not contribute to the present purpose, which is to examine how historians reflect upon their rhetoric, especially in regard to similar reflections in other disciplines, though all disciplinary discourse is historical in that any contribution is offered in relation to what has been said, what is being said, and what ought to be said, both within the discipline itself and, depending on the discipline, on what is considered interesting, sound, and important in other branches of intellectual culture, not to mention society.

To return by way of summary to the near-constant in these discussions—the position of history between social science and literature—we may note that the division in the social sciences between interpretivists and those more given to generalization, model-building, comparison, and hypothesis-testing does not seem to generate comparable controversy in history, historians as a group being far more ready to affirm the role of the historian in selecting, ordering, evaluating, and interpreting its material from the past. Having affirmed their autonomy from the aims and methods of science, at least of the positivist-empiricist kind, they face the problem of explaining how what they produce is knowledge of a different kind. When they turn toward literature and literary criticism, they find aid and comfort in describing the surplus of meaning to be had from writing prose narrative, but not much help in grounding knowledge claims, which are highly marginal in most current literary theory. (That is one of the reasons claims that "it's all rhetoric" emanating from literary theory are not very *interesting*.) This is one way to understand the tensions underlying LaCapra's balanced sentences: he certainly does not say very much about truth or knowledge, but that could be either because he assumes it is pretty well taken care of in the standard procedures of the working historian (which only need to be augmented by greater sophistication) or because it is the process of becoming entangled self-consciously in a conversation with texts, impelled only by an ungrounded itch for figuring out what was really going on, that is of paramount interest and value, not the contribution of the product to public knowledge of the past. That, at least from the perspective of this study, is where it lies.

III

Implications

VI

CONVERSATION, DIALECTIC, AND THE QUESTION OF CLOSURE

> Scholarly discourse is in fact saturated in the kind of dialogic rhetoric that Bakhtin named "hidden polemic," when an utterance not only refers to a given topic, but engages with, or anticipates or seeks to discredit another actual or hypothetical speech act about the same topic. Our articles and monographs will make little sense to a reader who is outside the ongoing "conversation" to which they belong, and who is unable to identify the echoes of, allusions to, sly digs at, flattering appeals to, other writers on the same subjects. But scholarly discourse aspires to the condition of monologue inasmuch as it tries to say the last word on a given subject, to affirm its mastery over all previous words on that subject.
>
> —David Lodge[1]

> Insofar as deconstructionist theory has done away with our faith in *logos*, some ultimate Word, endless dialogue and dialectic will replace conclusiveness: the clearly stated enthymeme, the clincher sentence of the paragraph, the crisp summary conclusion. For better or for worse, a change not only in attitudes and epistemologies, but also in practices.
>
> The virtue of the text is heuristic, its potential for creating more textuality, commentary upon commentary: composition as an open-ended dialogue.
>
> —W. Ross Winterowd[2]

In many of its current academic uses, the term *discourse* is calculatedly vague and encompassing. It is the equivalent for pragmatics of *language*; like *language*, it is neutral as to speaking and writing, but it tries to avoid the

Implications

implications of abstract, underlying system associated (these days) with *language* in favor of emphasis on concrete, documentable practices of individuals and groups. Disciplinary discourse takes place within institutional settings and includes such spoken activities as laboratory and coffee room talk, formal conferences (panels, lectures, caucuses, talk in the book exhibits, at prearranged meals, on the program committee), talk in seminars, office hours, staff conferences, and so on. It includes such written manifestations as articles, books (and apprentice work: assigned papers, theses, and dissertations), reviews, referee's evaluations, bibliographies and handouts, and internal memoranda such as tenure, promotion, and employment recommendations. Although the written documents are almost always monologues, discourse is generally viewed as a doing together, and disciplinary discourse is defined by the topics and purposes of the discipline. Arjo Klamer's anecdote of economists dividing a pizza would not be an example of the discourse of economics, but of a kind of metaphorical shift of the language of that discourse into an unconventional domain. Similarly, applications of a subject via "consulting" are deemed marginal to the disciplinary pursuit and sometimes give rise to "applied" subdisciplines. Talk and writing are only disciplinary discourse when they serve the special collective purpose or reflect upon it. Scanning the activities listed here reminds us that a very sizable portion of disciplinary discourse is concerned not just with offering additions to the body of certified knowledge, but with certifying the things that are so offered and those that offer them—with forming and maintaining an evaluative consensus. Discourse so viewed is praxis and leans in the direction of the French sense of the term.

Latour and Woolgar's five-step ladder or scale of certitude is the core of one model of a disciplinary discourse, with statements ascending and descending the ladder as a result of scientists' toil much like angels. It is a deliberately external and inhuman model in that it would not occur to participants to describe their actions in those terms any more than price-conscious shoppers would describe their actions as maximizing economic efficiency. Rather, participants would employ a kind of folk vocabulary in describing their efforts as trying to show or prove something, or to convince people in the field that their idea is important, possibly even true. And they would, and do, describe what goes on as discussions, arguments, debates, conversations, conferrings, disputes, and so on. These terms all have their home base in spoken exchanges and often have a vaguely metaphorical aura when used to describe written work. In this chapter, we will put on the hat of the ethnographer or interpretive sociologist to examine the categories and images that people, and especially scholars, use to symbolize their own endeavor. We imagine a somewhat schematic exchange:

—What exactly is academic discourse?
—It is a somewhat specialized version of X.

We want to focus on "X" and how it is specialized.

A few minutes' rooting around in a desk dictionary heightens one's awareness of how rich and abundant are the terms for "X," how subtle the nuances and potential discriminations are. Certain of the basic verbs, such as *prove, demonstrate,* and *show,* involve the accomplishment of a perlocutionary aim: they pair, that is, with verbs like *argue, cite,* and *discuss,* which name activities that typically function as means for accomplishing the proof, etc. It is these latter words for discursive activity that primarily concern us.

A preliminary sense of the traits that partition this segment of the lexical field of modern English can be gathered from a comparison of the entries and "synonym notes" for the words *converse, discuss,* and *argue* (and derived nouns), since these words are heavily used by scholars to describe what they are doing and have been foregrounded by the recent flowering (or outbreak) of discursive self-consciousness. They are to be sure common words for everyday exchanges and are more socially than individually oriented: they are symmetric predicates (Jones discussed the matter with Brown. / Jones and Brown discussed the matter, etc.) taking complements with *with*; it is not surprising that when Habermas chooses a term for the activity that enacts communicative (as opposed to cognitive-instrumental) rationality, it is *argumentation.*

The aspect of mutuality appears for *converse/ation* in the dictionaries' definition as "exchange of thoughts or feelings"; the term "informal" also often appears, partly as a contrast to *discuss/ion.* The lexicographers' consensus here would seem to support the decision of conversational analysts to take what they sometimes call "casual" conversation or "chat" as the basic, unmarked case, though it is already an idealized one insofar as many analysts further stipulate that this case assumes equal speaking rights for all participants (that is, rights to the floor, to set and change topics, to initiate and terminate their participation) and that there is no mutually agreed-upon agenda or business to be done. Casual conversation is considered a for-itself, noninstrumental activity with its own satisfactions, good at most for presenting oneself as a clever or decent member of the community, assessing the other in these terms, and establishing a basis of mutual goodwill. Thus committee meetings, staff conferences, job interviews, service exchanges, news interviews, and conferences with the principal are not casual conversations, though bits of casual conversation may occur before or after the business is done, or as interludes. From this perspective, it is a little odd to speak of disciplinary discourse as conversation; conversation, in various social milieus, can be considered something of a social skill, one that is quite distinct from skill in academic or other institutionalized discourse. More crucially for our purposes, because casual conversation has no agenda, it lacks any internal tendency toward resolution or closure. Because it isn't going anywhere, it is impossible to say when it has arrived at its goal.

Discussion and argument differ from conversation in being more organized by a common goal, namely that of "an effort to reach agreement, to ascertain truth, or to convince" (*American Heritage Dictionary*). Dictionaries distinguish between discussing and arguing in somewhat differing terms, but they generally agree that arguing is yet more organized than discussion in assuming a division of opinion over the point at issue (a division pro and contra) and the systematic presentation of arguments and evidence supporting one side by each party. Discussion does not assume the topic has been formulated as a controversial issue, and those who prefer it to arguing usually do so because of the openminded, noncontentious treatment of the topic by participants. Perelman and Olbrechts-Tyteca discuss the distinction by contrasting the terms *discussion* and *debate* (or rather, their French cognates), linking them to the ancient ones heuristic/eristic. Rather surprisingly, since eristic has heavily negative connotations in English ("characterized by disputatious often subtle and specious reasoning"—*Webster's Seventh New Collegiate*), they say in its favor that "debate" may be the most efficient way to get the best reasons pro and contra on the table. So characterized, arguing is the direct descendant of the Ancients' *dialectic.*

If arguing is an effort to reach agreement, etc., then the producing of reasons and counter-reasons must somehow bring that about—through, presumably, an agreement to accede to the argument with the best support and a common understanding of what constitute good reasons (this is one of the chief functions of methodology or what Kuhn calls disciplinary matrix). The dictionaries, however, do not specify who does the agreeing. Two models suggest themselves: one is the Anglo-Saxon adversarial legal pleading, where the arguer pro is not attempting to persuade the arguer contra but rather a judge and/or jury who are committed to impartiality (this is one way of thinking of the role of qualified, ratified members of the disciplinary community and what Stephen Toulmin calls "the objective standpoint of rational judgment"[3]); in the other model, there is no judge, and the party to be convinced is indeed the one arguing the contrary side. In this case, a rather high level of skill in alternating between partial and impartial stances is assumed, and it is probably this model that is in people's minds when they prefer discussion as the mode more likely to produce consensus. Argument, to them, polarizes, forcing people to commit themselves to stances they must also be prepared to modify or abandon. However, academic argument often attempts to slip between these two models, arguing against a position that is not quite held by anyone. As Douglas Park notes, this technique is commonly used to set up an academic argument: "Often, especially in scholarly writing, an article will carefully define a public attitude or state of knowledge in the way that best creates an exigence for the argument to follow. And generally readers tolerate these fictions as long as they are not too obviously contrived or too much at odds with the real state of affairs as the readers perceive it."[4] Excesses and other unskillfulness in portraying the opposing position have a variety of bad names: in one variety, the position contra is so simplified and exaggerated that it is a straw man; if the position is one that might have been held in the past, but is now not held by anyone, it is a dead horse; if it is portrayed as ludicrous, preposterous, monstrous, absurd, dehumanizing, contradictory, sexist, bourgeois, nihilistic, subversive, revisionist, or what have you, then the techniques are those of *argumentum ad invidium* and *per consequentiam*—polemical scaring off of anyone who even flirts with the position. Academics experience much uneasiness with these techniques when they become too overt; the tenet of Text that limits response to what is explicitly said attempts to curb some of these off-the-page tours and appeals, but they are still quite common in academic writing, if only because they endow academic arguments with vital consequences. They are shady, but they keep the blood pulsing and the presses rolling.

Thus, although argument and discussion share an orientation toward resolving or settling an issue (and differ mainly in the procedures they follow), the exact means by which this resolution is achieved remain somewhat mysterious in the commonsense understanding. Indeed, Daniel O'Keefe maintains that the relevant everyday sense of *argument* is only "interaction in which extended overt disagreement between the interactants occurs."[5] That is, argument may be oriented toward resolution and agreement, but it does not necessarily produce them.

Conversation, discussion, argument—these then are some of the commonsense terms in which discourses can be understood. And indeed, two of them have been elaborated and applied in recent books that repay some examination. Argument, Michael Billig maintains in *Arguing and Thinking: A Rhetorical Approach to Social Psychology*, is the fundamental process that modern social psychology struggles, fairly unsuccessfully, to grasp. Conversation, Richard Rorty argues in *Philosophy and the Mirror of Nature* and other writings, is the proper model for philosophic discourse. These two disciplines are central to the study of rationality and rhetoric: as Billig points out, social psychology, under the rubrics of self-presentation and attitude change (among others), deals with the phenomena rhetoric has been studying for two millennia; similarly, as Rorty says, philosophy has traditionally claimed for itself the role of the *dominatrix disciplinarum,* and has been the place where the discourses of particular disciplines have been compared and reflected upon, a kind of logic of logics and methodology of methodologies, or, essentially, a theory of knowledge-producing discourses. Both books pursue their cases to the point of paradox: they are strong, sustained arguments for the irresolvability of arguments and the inconclusiveness of disciplinary discourse. The implications of their arguments are thus quite in line with the tendency of textualist or poststructuralist thinking noted in the second epigraph, and this tendency is of a piece with the one that we set out initially to resist. Having surveyed what is at issue in representing academic discourse one way or another, we will finally take up what is said, and should be said, about it in textbooks of college writing.

1. Thinking as Arguing: Michael Billig

Arguing and Thinking: A Rhetorical Approach to Social Psychology is the third book by Michael Billig in a decade. It is unlike any of the "rhetorics of" considered so far, as it is not a rhetorical analysis of social psychology as a scientific discipline; rather, the "rhetorical approach" is to the domain of human behavior studied by social psychology: how people think and affect the thinking (or attitudes) of others. Billig points out that rhetoric and social psychology share the same central concerns: self-presentation, labeling and categorization, attitude change, and in general "the nature of the soul." "In fact," he says, "it could be suggested that modern social psychology has set itself the task of translating into actuality Plato's dream of a complete science of persuasion."[6] However, Billig argues, social psychology is crippled by metaphors of social life that gloss over argument and argumentativeness, namely social life as a play (role-playing) and as a game (following rules). These give pictures of harmonious, well-ordered performance which conceal the struggle backstage and on the sidelines. Instead, Billig wants to view social life as intensely, intrinsically argumentative, and uses the image of man the arguer that is central to the rhetorical tradition to criticize major parts of theory and practice in social psychology.

Billig is too savvy a writer to think that he can displace the ruling metaphors in a discipline simply by pointing out the way things really are. He doesn't claim any epistemological privilege for his stance, characterizing it only as that of an antiquarian psychologist—one who likes to direct his researcher's gaze on the work of the Greek and Roman rhetoricians, on the Talmud and Midrashim, and on Boswell's *Life*. From this tour, he collects a counter-image of man the arguer, expounding on Protagoras' claim that there are always two sides to a question (or, to every side of a question—logos—there are opposing anti-logoi), Quintilian's Principle of Uncertainty ("we can never capture the infinite variety of human affairs in a finite system of psychological laws"), and the spirit of contradiction that drives people to find the anti-logoi and to struggle to have the last word, which he thinks is far deeper and more pervasive than the attempt to reach agreement. (So Galileo is once again the model in a different way—*e pur si muove.*) The antiquarian recovery of the old vision of man provides a vantage point from which to criticize the standard treatment of a variety of topics in social psychology: the cognitive science image of thinking as problem solving, categorization (and particularization), attitudes and attitude change (and cognitive dissonance). It is clear that social psychology as an academic discipline does not escape this ceaseless play of stance and counterstance, and that Billig's own book illustrates argumentativeness at work right at home in social psychology itself. And thus there is some criticism of the rhetoric of social psychology after all, especially of its programmatic and textbook claims to replace the muddled, tangled, contradictory lore of traditional thinking (and commonsense) with the progressive enlightenment of empirical science. Thus Billig presses hard the paradox of academic psychology which by argument hopes to establish some findings and laws as beyond argument, as off the scale of contestable statements (into Type 5 "statements" à la Latour and Woolgar), safely lodged in the domain of fact, or even tacit knowledge (the psychologist's commonsense). That would be the ultimate bootstrapping maneuver to achieve self-transcendence, and it would not be unlike one of the ways that dialectic was viewed in the tradition, especially in Platonic theory, though hardly in practice. This contradiction has been noted before, but Billig amplifies it with animation and urbane, if one-sided, wit.

Billig distinguishes between the rhetoric of form and the rhetoric of content (invention, or constructing arguments) and the bulk of the book is devoted to the latter, making sure and thoughtful use of Perelman and Olbrechts-Tyteca's discussion of the types and strategies of nontechnical argument. He is thus led into the area of commonsense reasoning, where he makes some observations which are very useful for the project at hand. He notes that commonsense has a dual aspect: on the one hand, it is taken as the implicit knowledge and values on which members of a community agree; it is by appeal to it that arguments are persuasive and agreement achieved. On the other hand, as articulated in proverbial maxims, it is so fluid and flexible and context bound that it can embrace maxims that, out of context, are contradictory ("out of sight, out of mind" / "absence makes the heart grow fonder").[7] His antiquarian search discovers a list of forty-seven such maxims arranged antithetically and attached as a "Promptuary" to Bacon's *The Dignity and Advancement of Learning*. His reading of modern social psychology texts, however, turns up the promise to discover order and precision in the application of maxims through controlled experimentation. This, he argues, is an utterly hopeless endeavor for two reasons. The first is that Quintilian's Law means that there is an infinity of situations in which contrary proverbs may be applicable, and thus an infinity of experiments would be required to sort out the conditions of their application. Second, whether or not a maxim has been inconsistently applied in a situation is itself a matter of negotiation and opinion, and so social psychologists would end up arguing over the interpretation of their experiments, as they have in the past. It is impossible, therefore, to systematize commonsense reasoning or to develop a scientific theory of its application.[8]

There are nonetheless observations that can be made about the workings of commonsense reasoning or arguing, and Billig collects some interesting notes about the process of arguing against commonsense, which is of course one of the principal situations where scientific theorizing is praised. He begins the discussion by tracing some of the vicissitudes of assumptions concerning racial superiority and purity, which were uncritically shared by educated Europeans a century ago and now are not only discredited but not discussable (taboo). (The *attitudes*, however, die harder, he notes, and still manifest themselves by attaching to other common and unquestionable values such as equality of treatment). In general, he argues, citing Perelman and Olbrechts-Tyteca, a challenge to a received majority view from a minority is enough to deprive the view of self-evidence and to trigger attempts to theorize it by majority thinkers. The consequences of this tendency, though, are not as unequivocally wholesome as one might suppose. Given the interminability of argument, communities may justifiably want certain values and facts to stand effectively beyond question. He cites a recent effort by an antisemitic minority to place the historical reality of the Holocaust in question. One can see reasons why such an effort ought not to be taken seriously, or even ought to be effectively suppressed, but a rigorous civil libertarian would trust to the power of reasoned debate to put the challenge to rest. One such anti-Holocaust pamphlet did recently appear with a preface by Noam Chomsky defending the writer's right to argue his case, though Chomsky hastened to add when criticized "Personally, I believe the gas chambers existed" (cited from Billig, p. 221). Billig notes that inadvertently, as it were, Chomsky has admitted the disputability of what most regard as fact and concludes that we face a fundamental social dilemma, "in which the value for free argumentation tugs in a contrary direction to that of other values" (p. 222). Here we might say the commitments of scientific theorizing and the norms of Habermas's discourse appear profoundly impractical, given the needs of communities to make choices and take actions. Of course, Habermas never maintained that *discourse* was a practical mode of doing business, but only a mode that participants can shift into when their cooperative endeavor becomes troubled. Billig suggests that it may be quite proper to refuse to engage in debate with certain parties, not because you know ahead of time that you will fail to reach an understanding with them, but because the very act of treating their statements as discussible may concede too much. It is quite remarkable that he who so strongly advocates contrary and unconventional questioning as the very life of the mind should press his own position to the point where limits are visible. It is no coincidence that this discussion, as well as others in the book, is haunted by reminders of the final solution the Athenians found for the problem Socratic dialectic posed. One might draw one of two conclusions from Billig's argument here: the first, less radical one is the by now familiar point that academic discourse cannot expect its norms and practices to be honored and adopted in deliberations on public issues and public policies; the second, more radical one is that academic discussions are never completely isolated from social and political implications, and it is naive at best, or irresponsible at worst, to act as if they were.

Billig may well be right that argument is always situated in ways that assume some commonsense, and too that it is not always oriented toward reaching understanding or consensus. This view of argument does not directly dispute Habermas's claim that reaching understanding is the inner telos of human speech, but it does require that something be added to the spirit of contention to yield consensus. Thus there arises a problem of accounting for consensus like that noted by Harry Collins for the relativist–social constructionist view of scientific discourse, namely, since any number of interpretations and accounts are possible, how is it that scientists manage to select one to agree on? What, as he puts it, "is the mechanism of the closure of debate?"[9] Billig does not raise this problem, for he is not at all concerned to evaluate, much less defend, social psychology's claim to knowledge. We have on the one hand the scientistic confidence in precise, controlled experiments and, debunking it, the endless dialectic of Protagoras and Quintilian. It is therefore hard to know how he would treat claims that scientific discourse is nonetheless different in the rapidity and completeness with which it forms consensus, the grounds of its consensus, or the progressiveness of its claims. Protagoras may have been a genius, and the genius of Billig's book, but he was a Sophist who promoted one of the earlier blindness/insight arguments that have often been felt to undermine all knowledge claims, even relative ones (e.g., my insight is better than yours, my blindness less costly). As Herbert Simons notes in a review, Billig's "Protagorean relativism" places his own authority in question too.[10]

So strongly and sweepingly does Billig argue his theses that he draws little or no distinction between social psychology and everyday analysis and explanation of actions. If there are special qualities of social psychology as a disciplinary discourse—apart from the language of objective science which he derides—they are not identified. In this he aligns himself with a growing number of social theorists who argue that sociology (and social psychology) is merely an elaboration of commonsense reasoning about actions and motives. Its overall aim (to explain people's actions) and its basic concepts (intention, motivation, and belief) are basically the same as those guiding everyday discussion of behavior.[11] On this conception, social psychology and sociology are at most extensions of commonsense understanding and continually fall back into it by a natural process of assimilation.[12] At this point we have arrived at what we earlier called Garfinkel's legacy: if indeed, the social scientist must enter the commonsense world of his subjects' understanding to reconstruct its rationality from within, what is the role of scientific theorizing in sociology? Actually, proponents of nondistinctness do offer some differentiating traits: for Philip Pettit, a reflexive awareness of social agents as acting so as to maintain face, for example, is a motive a social scientist would characteristically impute but is rarely voiced in accounts given by the agents themselves. Roy Wallis and Steve Bruce explicitly address this question and give three criteria differentiating sociological from commonsense accounts by actors: (1) "Actors are primarily concerned with living and not explaining," (2) "Actors' explanations typically arrive at a point of satisfaction earlier," and (3) "Actors are preoccupied primarily with the personal rather than the general. Sociologists seek, through systematic comparison, to explore typical patterns, to form general accounts, and thus to achieve some explanatory economy" (p. 104). To a considerable degree, these criteria reinscribe the traits of scientific theorizing, though noticeably as matters of degree not reflecting any sharp difference in the *aim* of the discourse. It seems clear that without a clear and distinct different aim (such as Jack Bilmes argues for), the discourse of social psychology slides very easily into popular account-giving in terms of dispositions, motives, and intentions, to which, proverbially, there is no end. There is no claim to special public knowledge and no problem finding the mechanism of closure. Thus social psychology, which scientistically set out to extract the theory embedded in all the rhetorical lore, is swallowed up by its antiquarianly restored forebear, its vaunted reflexivity a ponderous spelling out of the *amour propre* maxims of La Rochefoucauld—not, to be sure, the most common of commonsense, but hardly new knowledge either.

On Billig's vision of discourse as arguing, then, all claims are potentially topics for argument, including those argued yesterday. Not only does this view fail to account for the delimitation of the arguable said to be characteristic of the academic disciplines, but it also fails to account for the settling of issues in other discursive domains. Several reviewers, sensing a kind of radical autonomy given to the play of argumentation, have suggested that Billig ignores the relation of argumentation to power: the ways forums, agendas, and ratified participants are defined,[13] or the way forces external to a discourse may both permit and limit it.[14] It is all very well to point out, as Billig does in his account of Chomsky's preface, that some ungrounded, possibly naive assumptions are being made about the force or power of reasoned argument to settle issues, but at various times and circumstances, certain arguments are held to be cogent and to prevail, whether by judicial, legislative, administrative, or other "expert" fiat, and it is that process of settling or resolving issues, not just the closure of debate, that remains outside the scope of Billig's vision. As we shall see, it also eludes the vision of discourse as conversation developed by Richard Rorty.

2. Richard Rorty and the Conversation of Mankind

The image of disciplinary discourse as conversation so prevalent these days is to a large extent the work of one writer, the philosopher Richard Rorty. His book *Philosophy and the Mirror of Nature* (1979) and collection of articles *The Consequences of Pragmatism* (1982) have been very widely reviewed, cited, argued over, and above all, influential in promoting a certain conception of philosophy in which the notion of philosophy as conversation figures prominently. Rorty's writings are not philosophy, or even the rhetoric of philosophy, but metaphilosophy—philosophical reflections and arguments about what philosophy should be and do. Rorty describes a fundamental opposition between systematic and edifying endeavors in philosophy, an opposition so deep and pervasive that there is no common ground on which to conduct an argument between the two conceptions. His purpose is not to reconcile the opposites but to advance the edifying view as the superior one. The two views contrast in what they call it, how they do it, and what they do it for:

> systematic philosophy
> —does epistemology
> —using arguments
> —to conduct inquiry
> vs.
> edifying philosophy
> —does hermeneutics
> —using satires, parodies, and aphorisms
> —to avoid the ruts and blinders of inquiry.

The systematic endeavor assumes that for any philosophic question that may arise, sufficient agreement can be found to arrive at a reasoned consensus; edifying philosophy denies this, and by that very denial falsifies the basic systematic assumption. The systematists could reply either that the edifiers were not really philosophers, and therefore their claims do not have to be accommodated by philosophy, or that the edifier's very act of presenting his argument implies more basis for agreement than he is willing to acknowledge. The first line of argument has in fact been frequently used by analytic philosophers to deal with such figures as Nietzsche, Heidegger, and Derrida. If you admit them into the club, as Rorty does, then the club will never be the same. Rorty chooses to promote the edifying conception as the better choice and model for a new kind of philosophizing, or, rather, a new kind of job for philosophers to do. Rorty's own writings employ edifying strategies, seeking to displace one foundational metaphor (philosophy as a mirror of nature) with another (philosophy as a proliferating kudzu vine).[15] Rorty conceives of edifying philosophy (and his own writings) as therapy for the urge to establish the truth much as the analytic philosophers offered therapy against "metaphysics." In fact, however, Rorty does not just use satires, parodies, and aphorisms to displace systematic endeavors; he also uses arguments of the types that traditionally bear weight even among the systematically inclined, writing histories of problems, analyzing particular positions as responses to the problems, drawing distinctions, and so on. The resulting very complicated mix presents different faces to different reviewers. Some say, for example, that *Philosophy and the Mirror of Nature* is scarcely argued at all and then loosely and fallaciously; others say that it is packed with interesting arguments which they proceed to restate and either endorse or argue against. The books do indeed raise many issues and have excited much argument; here we must concentrate on Rorty's claims about philosophic discourse itself, and especially on the notion of conversation as an alternative to argument.

Philosophic discourse has always been different from the other disciplines, and Rorty, for all his end-of-philosophy flourishes, is out to find another basis for the difference. In a perhaps somewhat tongue-in-cheek parenthesis, he gives up on philosophy as *regina scientiarum* but claims it is still *dominatrix disciplinarum*,[16] and, recast as hermeneutics, it still retains a position outside of and between (though presumably no longer *above*) the disciplines:

> Hermeneutics sees the relations between various discourses as those of strands in a possible conversation, a conversation which presupposes no disciplinary matrix which unites the speakers, but where the hope of agreement is never lost so long as the conversation lasts. This hope is not a hope for the discovery of antecedently existing common ground, but *simply* hope for agreement, or, at least, exciting and fruitful disagreement. Epistemology sees the hope of agreement as a token of the existence of common ground which, perhaps unbeknown to the speakers, unites them in a common rationality. For hermeneutics, to be rational is to be willing to refrain from epistemology—from thinking that there is a special set of terms in which all contributions to be conversation should be put—and to be willing to pick up the jargon of the interlocutor rather than translating it into one's own. . . . For epistemology, conversation is implicit inquiry. For hermeneutics, inquiry is routine conversation. Epistemology views the participants as united in what Oakeshott calls an *universitas*—a group united by mutual interest in achieving a common end. Hermeneutics views them as united in what

> he calls a *societas*—persons whose paths through life have fallen together, united
> by civility rather than by a common goal, much less by a common ground.
> (*Mirror*, p. 318)

The "conversation" imagined here is that of cross-disciplinary talk, or talk of
the big picture; Rorty does not deny that disciplines are *universitates* pursuing
mutually agreed upon inquiries and conducting arguments that do arrive at
conclusions, given the previously established and accepted contexts, but of
course that possibility of consensus runs out at the borders of the discipline.
"Normal discourse is that which is conducted within an agreed-upon set of
conventions about what counts as a relevant contribution, what counts as
answering a question, what counts as having a good argument for that answer
or a good criticism of it" (*PMN*, p. 320). Thus the doing of normal science, or
any normal discourse, cannot be a model for philosophy, and philosophy
cannot be a normal discipline. "The product of abnormal discourse can be
anything from nonsense to intellectual revolution, and there is no discipline
which describes it, any more than there is a discipline devoted to the study of
the unpredictable, or of 'creativity' " (p. 320). In "Idealism and Textualism" he
suggests literary criticism as a model for a properly abnormal discipline which
manages to carry on without "an encompassing critical vocabulary" and without argumentation (*Consequences*, p. 142). Indeed, part of the mission of
philosophy should be to call attention to the limited scope of normal disciplinary inquiry. "One way to see edifying philosophy *as* the love of wisdom is to see
it as the attempt to prevent conversation from degenerating into inquiry, into a
research program. Edifying philosophers can never end philosophy, but they
can help prevent it from attaining the secure path of a science" (*PMN*, p. 372).
And what edifying work can do for philosophy, philosophy can do for "the
conversation" generally.

Rorty offers a number of images of the new role of the philosopher in relation
to other discourses. One is that of the "informed dilettante, the polypragmatic,
Socratic intermediary between discourses. In his salon, so to speak, hermetic
thinkers are charmed out of their self-enclosed practices. Disagreements between disciplines and discourses are compromised or transcended in the course
of the conversation" (*PMN*, p. 317). Another is that of kibitzers listening in on
the philosophical self-reflections of the disciplines and contributing their
schooled awareness of the kinds of arguments people make when they phi-
losophize (p. 393). (This last conception, minus the cute image, sounds very like
an extremely common argument in any defense of "doing theory.") He models a
complex of virtuous attitudes: the ability to listen and "decenter," and thus
dialogically to enter the lifeworld of the other; a passion for the openness and
endlessness of the conversation; an orientation toward a sense of wonder; and a
sense of the provisionality and limitations of any practice however successful
("The danger which edifying discourse tries to avert is that some given vocabulary, some way in which people might come to think of themselves, will deceive
them into thinking that from now on all discourse could be, or should be,

normal discourse. The resulting freezing-over of culture would be, in the eyes of edifying philosophers, the dehumanization of human beings" [p. 377]). Thus the edifying role appeals to many of the cardinal virtues of liberal humanism and Rorty loses no opportunity for contrasting it to the narrow, rigid, exclusive, elitist, arrogant stance of the Kantians/epistemologists/ systematic constructors/ normals. How can one argue with that, or rather, how can one *argue* with that?

Many reviewers, though skeptical, do not argue, remarking mainly on limitations of the book's assumptions and design. Some have questioned Rorty's fairly uncritical extension of Kuhn's model of scientific change (is normal discourse really as normal as Rorty says it is? how "incommensurable" are the disciplines?). Others have noted that some of the stages of the argument are not proven and in fact scarcely argued for, as for example that Rorty has not really *proved* that normal inquiry is bad for you and ought to be given up. Jonathan Lieberson points out that Rorty only says that another view of philosophy is possible.[17] Thus his argument is rather like that of the social constructionists of chapter three; he denaturalizes or ironizes the epistemological conception of philosophy ("the cultural overseer who knows everyone's common ground—the Platonic philosopher-king who knows what everybody else is really doing whether *they* know it or not," p. 317) but cannot ground his own conception as superior, "grounding" being a move in the other guy's game. At the same time, Rorty is a fairly utopian ironist, or at least buoyant about the salutary effect of an Olympian stance, to use Gusfield's terms. And reviewers have observed that Rorty hasn't demonstrated that edifying philosophy is good for you,[18] and further, that "broadening oneself" is presumably the value of all the liberal arts, not just philosophy.[19] Alexander Nehamas points out that Rorty's whole historical and political account of the rise and fall of the systematic program is conducted under intellectualist assumptions and is not a "genealogy" in a Foucaultian sense that would inquire into the ideological and political ramifications of the entire Enlightenment program, of which epistemology is only a part, though a key part.[20] There are indeed strong affinities of temperament and design between Rorty and McCloskey (who cites Rorty frequently): epistemology is like McCloskey's Methodology in being dead, dispensable, and well-gotten-rid-of, so that scholars can go on about their proper business with less pretentiousness. And Rorty's proposal is open to a similar objection. Robert Hollinger suggests that the language of science, knowledge, and truth is taken seriously in our society, and if philosophy aspires to effective social and political critique, it might think twice about renouncing such language in favor of tolerant conversation: Rorty would rather have *The New York Review of Books* as the model of scholarly exchange than *Science*, but "*The* fact that liberal intellectuals favor the *New York Review of Books* over *Science* means little in a culture dominated by the Military-Industrial-Scientific establishment."[21]

Certain reviewers, however, have attempted to argue with the sketch of the philosopher's new role. Leon Pompa asks "what is the topic of cross-disciplinary conversations?" Conversations have topics, and if there is a topic which participants select that transcends the subject-matter of each discipline, then this topic would seem to fall within "the traditional conception of philosophizing as critical reflection on the various activities in which we engage, in order to arrive at some understanding of how they are conducted, what they involve, how they differ from one another, and what we should expect of them."[22] This objection poses more difficulties for Rorty's charming dilettante role than for the kibitzer, since the latter could at least function as a repository of previous reflections on this subject, and could save the disciplinary thinker the effort of reinventing the wheel and the trouble of embracing certain recognized follies, though he would presumably refuse the role of arbiter. But the rights and responsibilities of kibitzers are by no means clear, and their contributions are frequently unwelcome. Rorty may indeed be thinking of something like "consultant," who at least is invited to offer his opinions, though the question of who is in charge is still up for grabs. If the philosopher doesn't speak for the big picture as the curator of the "conversation of mankind" as it were, or is a curator with no interest in orderly system, why should he be invited, beyond his ability to contribute increasingly antiquarian observations of the form "back when we did Epistemology, people used terms like yours and were thought to have gotten into trouble"? Pompa's point is that cross-disciplinary conversation presupposes some common ground and general, shared interest, and this presupposed ground undercuts Rorty's argument that the possibility of reasoned consensus runs out at the borders of disciplines. Philosophers may choose not to function as specialists on this more general level of reflection, but they cannot declare a priori that reasoned consensus is beyond reach.

Robert Schwartz also questions the role of the edifying philosopher, this time in relation to disciplinary reflection. It is not clear, he says, what the edifier could contribute except perhaps a critical distance that committed practitioners of a discipline might lack. But, he notes, "this sort of distancing oneself from one's work, attempting to appreciate the force of criticism, and striking balances or compromises with competing theories would seem to be the hallmark of objective open-minded inquiry in general."[23] Schwartz suggests that the philosopher's outsider perspective is hardly irreplaceable for the discipline and places him in danger of being merely a shallow critic. This is of course not an argument against philosophers offering to perform the kibitzer/dilettante role, only a question as to its plausibility or probable outcome.

As noted earlier, reviewers have differed on how to take Rorty's writing—as normal philosophic argument? as abnormal "conversation"? One reviewer, Anthony Palmer, complains about Rorty's technique of polemical caricature of the bad guys and the reader's lack of opportunity, customary in a seminar or symposium, to ask "Did Ryle or Davidson or Whitehead actually say that?"[24] However, he concedes, "In conversation, of course, such a question would be out of place." If *Philosophy and the Mirror of Nature* is an example of it, this "new conversation" will sacrifice some of the precision and fairness of academic dialectic. Thus he finds these conversational liberties more irritating than edifying. Harry Ruja also complains that "rigorous argument" is sacrificed to conversation.[25] Similarly, Raimond Gaita complains of the many false dichotomies offered the reader, the tendency of conversation to become merely bad argument, and even the rudeness of not really engaging the "partner" in a conversation: "One cannot treat one's 'partner' in a conversation as a medical exhibit and still retain him as a partner in *conversation*."[26] These complaints boil down to the objection that Rorty does not cast his claims in the standard form of the scholarly dialectic so that they may be scrutinized critically.

A more sympathetic analysis of Rorty's technique is given by Richard Bernstein, who ascribes features of what might be called loose argumentation to the "rhetorical subtext" by which Rorty deliberately avoids offering a new systematic position: "His deliberate use of such vague distinctions as the 'normal' and the 'abnormal,' the 'familiar' and the 'unfamiliar' [attacked by one reviewer as a bad argument], or even between 'systematic' and 'edifying' philosophy are rhetorical devices designed to cure us of the expectation that philosophy must be 'constructive,' must be conceived of as a form of inquiry that provides us with foundations."[27] "Still," Bernstein continues, "one wants to know, Where does Rorty really stand?" Rorty is aware we will ask such questions, but "Every time we think we can really pin him down, he nimbly dances to another place and introduces a new set of distinctions." These are much the same terms that textualists use to defend Derrida against Searle.[28] Bernstein also notes certain ironic endorsements of surprising positions which he calls "crypto-positivism" (and which have bothered some reviewers). Similarly, though Bernstein does not mention it, Rorty uses the extremely standard line of philosophical argument based on tracing the history or heritage of philosophical issues and distinctions, but he does not pursue it with the thoroughness and care philosophers might expect. Some reviewers (Richard J. Donovan, Raimond Gaita[29]) have complained of this, but others (Robert Schwartz, Victoria Choy[30]) suspect Rorty does not intend to be taken too seriously on this point. Irony and a nose for fun are powerful recuperative devices, and Bernstein does eventually extract a liberal commitment to extending the franchise for conversation and dialogue without limit as a basis for "community," an ethical position like the one Bernstein derives from Gadamer and Habermas and which he strongly endorses. There is, however, a very considerable difference between Habermas's critical stance and this remark of Rorty's: "On my view, we should be more willing than we are to celebrate bourgeois capitalist society as the best polity actualized so far, while regretting that it is irrelevant to most of the problems of most of the population of the planet" (*CP*, p. 210n16, cited in Nehamas, p. 412).

We have traced enough of Rorty's argument (or program) and the responses to see that it strongly parallels the discussion in the social studies of science over the same period. Thus some of the reviewers' questions about the kibitzer role seem of a piece with the dialectic of the stranger and stance of the outsider discussed in chapter three. The parallel extends further, in that the sociologist who offers an account with no truth claims attached—or even disabled—is very like the edifying philosopher who has gotten over the pursuit of truth. Such a sociologist stands in much the same relation to her or his more scientifically inclined colleagues as the edifier does toward the systematists. The edifier is also clearly related to the interpretive sociologist (vis-à-vis the empiricist) in the task of facilitating understanding between discrete worlds with a scaled down claim of superior understanding. All of these stances recommend themselves in terms of their modesty and their openness to the integrity and difference of the other's perspective, and all of them characterize themselves as mavericks in relation to the prevailing purposes and logics of their disciplines. The edifying philosopher appears to be in a slightly different position, however, insofar as what he dissents from is not a particular pattern of argument or proof, but argument itself, or so a philosopher might say. Rorty does not provide an easy target in this regard, however, for he does employ quite standard philosophical arguments as well as transgressive ones, combat by metaphor, parody, polemic, irony, exaggeration, and an exuberant proliferation of voices and perspectives which he doesn't quite endorse ("Here is one picture . . ." "For the textualist . . ."). That is, if Rorty's writings are to be taken as a model for the new, edifying conversation, it does not appear to be utterly distinct from traditional philosophic argument, which thus still provides a repertoire of moves within the expanded conversation of the discipline. If Rorty had exclusively transgressed or frontally attacked the discursive norms of the discipline, he would have been received with far greater rage and censure than he has. If, as Alexander Nehamas suggests, it is perhaps impossible while doing philosophy to change the topic of philosophy, so too it is perhaps harder than Rorty suggests to get outside of it.

Conversation, for Rorty, is thus the preferred alternative to argument, and it is important to see in what ways it is. For Rorty, conversation is not opposed to dialectic, since he speaks approvingly of "the Socratic conversation," which is certainly organized into the pursuit of stances pro and contra. The crucial attribute of conversation, for Rorty, is that it is an end in itself; it is not an attempt "to reach conclusions or to convince," or, as Rorty puts it, to "succeed," any more than making baskets is the purpose of basketball, which "mistakes an essential moment in the course of an activity for the end of the activity."[31] Presumably what Rorty has in mind is that the true aim of basketball is to have a game of basketball. This interpretation jibes with his concluding comments that the new program would not feel like a fight in which something is eternally gained for the universe—the attitude he associates with Plato (though he is quoting William James) and opposes to that of Socrates. But here the game metaphor seems to sidestep conflict and contention much as Billig notes in social psychology and in addition the fact that a game of basketball does produce a winner and that making baskets is a means to that end (and sometimes not the best means, in the case of a deliberate slowdown to run out the clock). Or does Rorty mean to allow for local episodes of argument without their being taken up in a larger structure of arguing and winning? One of the principal traits of the "conversation" metaphor for philosophy is that it is not oriented toward settling matters—that's not why one has a conversation. Instead, Rorty offers a vision of an endless, inconclusive series of exchanges which is curiously like Billig's unending argument, though arrived at from the opposite direction. That is, Billig's spirit of contention striving always to have the last word (a striving, to adapt Hobbes, that ceases only with death) overruns all closure or resolution just as Rorty's open, peaceable dialogues avoid identifying and settling the point at issue. One should, however, read these lines on playing the game in the light of the passage cited earlier from *PMN* which links the conversation to the hope for agreement, "or at least fruitful disagreement." Such a conversation might well be said to be oriented toward agreement and even to anticipate disagreement; there would be little, then, to distinguish it from argument, and one could paraphrase von Clausewitz that for Rorty, conversation is a continuation of argument with an admixture of other means.

Why then does Rorty insist on conversation as if it were vitally different from argument? As we have seen, argument, for Rorty, seems to presuppose the existence of "antecedently existing common ground," though, more strictly speaking, it is not argument but "rationally grounded consensus" that seems to involve grounds, so that the philosopher could seize upon any such agreement and use it as proof that such grounds must have existed "antecedently." Rorty wants to block this ascent, and to treat agreement as something that just might happen without being an argument for anyone's conception of shared reason (or paradigm, or normalizing framework of assumptions). But if agreements are subject to critical evaluation (as even Rorty's "fruitful" disagreements suggests), then one can ask for some account of how good reasons come to be identified. At this point, it is useful to set commonsense terminology aside and consider the discussion of these points in argumentation theory.

Joseph Wenzel, Brant Burleson, and Jürgen Habermas distinguish three perspectives on argumentation: the rhetorical, the dialectical, and the logical, and it is the dialectical that is of concern here.[32] Dialectic is concerned with the procedures of argumentation, especially with argumentation pro and contra as a means of submitting claims to critical scrutiny. As such, it values explicitness and candor in the articulation of positions, the bracketing of other, potentially persuasive considerations, the freedom of participants to express their views fully "without fear or favor," and the agreement to accede to the position supported by the best reasons. As such, it is what Habermas described as *diskurs* and very close to Gouldner's Culture of Critical Discourse. On this view, reasons are judged best not on "antecedent" grounds but in terms of the degree to which they advance the common purpose of the participants, which may be in turn be scrutinized on the levels of meta-theory and self-reflection. Obviously, dialectic, on such a conception, is not the equivalent of common-sense argument, and is at most the distant descendant of Socratic dialectic as outlined in the *Gorgias*, dramatized by Plato, and discussed by Billig. It would be tempting to describe it as an institutionalization and specialization of ordinary argument, but Habermas emphasizes rather its normative force—it is a code which guides discourse in the disciplines, but is at best imperfectly realized in them; it provides a basis for criticizing previous agreements (the prevailing consensus), but it cannot guarantee that any agreement perfectly instantiates it, for participants may be subject to limitations and influences which have not been explicitly brought out and of which they are unaware. Agreements produced by dialectic are always provisional and would provide little evidence for shared (or universal) foundational beliefs.

This does not mean, however, that dialectic would be endless in quite the sense contemplated by Billig, Winterowd, or Rorty. Dialectic is the mode, at least ideally, of disciplinary discourse, but insofar as disciplinary discourse is oriented toward reaching understanding, its adoption of dialectic is instrumental. This view, as much as Rorty's, does mean that there is no special role for philosophy in adjudicating or settling disputes; philosophy would no longer be the arbiter of good reasons; that role would be left to the arguers and other qualified participants in the particular argument. Thus part of the traditional role of philosophy would be taken over by theory in the various disciplines (Habermas describes most of his own work as "social theory," not philosophy); another part would remain in the interpretive role bridging the disciplinary discourse and everyday understanding. Thus, in a rather surprising fashion, Habermas's theory of communicative rationality and action ends up dissolving the traditional roles of philosophy that Rorty objects to; to say that rationality inheres in the norms and practices of disciplinary dialectic (as well as elsewhere) is to free these discourses from any external regulation or court of appeal. The principles that guide them are sufficiently straightforward that scholars seem to grasp them without special schooling in logic; when they are obscured, they can be brought to the fore via shifts to the meta-levels. They are conversation-like in this self-regulation, but they are oriented toward earning and granting the privilege of the last, or latest, word.

3. Teaching Academic Discourse

In recent years, a number of people have argued that what should be taught in required college writing courses is academic discourse—a proposal that on the face of it seems staggeringly simple, straightforward, and all but self-evident. In relation to the history of college "composition," however, the proposal is anything but self-evident; rather, it seems conservative, even reactionary: one thinks of mini-lit-crit assignments like "Stephen Crane's Color Symbolism" or "The Theme of Obsession in 'The Rocking Horse Winner' " (title corrected by teacher to "Obsession in 'The Rocking Horse Winner' "). After all, even the standard course organized around the "modes" assigned papers describing a process, arguing a public issue, and so on—papers unlikely to see the light of day in any academic journal but ones that rehearsed tasks conceivably more like those the students might be given in the "world of work" or later life. It reflects a certain amount of courage even to argue for academic discourse as the goal of a college writing course, but it reflects more than courage: it reflects as well invigorated, albeit diverse, understandings of "academic discourse." The reader at this point hardly needs to be reminded that academic discourse is an enterprise that can be understood in rather different ways, but it is useful to see how different the images of academic discourse are in these pedagogical programs. Here three such programmatic articles will be reviewed: Elaine Maimon's (mentioned in the Introduction), Patricia Bizzell's, and David Bartholomae's. All of these proposals regard the academic world as a discourse community (with various subcommunities) and view the writing course (or courses) as a means of initiation into that community. The rules and principles to be inculcated are accordingly general and fundamental, though some emphasis is given to the learning of the discourses of different disciplines. The general program is very well stated by David Bartholomae in the opening to his article, "Inventing the University": "Every time a student sits down to write for us, he has to invent the university for the occasion—invent the university, that is, or a branch of it, like history or anthropology or economics or English. The student has to learn to speak our language, to speak as we do, to try on the peculiar ways of knowing, selecting, evaluating, reporting, concluding, and arguing that define the discourse of our community. or perhaps I should say the *various* discourses of our community. . . . "[33] None of these writers would question the truth or propriety of this, but they differ on what the core of academic discourse is and on why it is an appropriate and valuable thing to teach.

In "Maps and Genres: Exploring Connections in the Arts and Sciences," Elaine Maimon argues that it furthers the aims and values of liberal education to teach the conventions of writing in different disciplines; it promotes the "intellectual mobility" characteristic of educated people (p. 116) and enables them to engage in Rortian conversations with members of other disciplines— which she calls "dialectic," but which lacks any oppositional structure. As noted in the Introduction, she regards disciplinary discourses as constituted by readily abstractable conventions, some of form (the lab report, the use of passive voice, etc.) and some of behavior ("the ritual of formal acknowledgement"). Majors in one discipline will learn respect for the verbal traditions of other disciplines, and, having mastered the conventions of a discipline, they may innovatively break them in a spirit of verbal play or creativity (p. 112).

Maimon's essay reflects I think the almost inevitable tendency of the term *convention* to trivialize the concept of discourse, whether academic or disciplinary. There are of course forms and procedures that can be imitated (or flouted) in the writing of any discipline, but one can certainly imitate those without coming anywhere close to engaging in the discourse. A student who addressed a subject in such a way would only be a beginning-level initiate in David Bartholomae's scheme of development.

The concern that the student not be taught "blind conformity to a set of arbitrary conventions tacitly understood by colleagues in other fields" (p. 112) that led Maimon to her encouragement of creative, playful rule breaking is far more central to Patricia Bizzell's discussion in "College Composition: Initiation into the Academic Discourse Community."[34] Writing done in college courses is generally done for the instructor, who, as far as the student is concerned, sets the topic, makes the rules, and assigns a grade. Nonetheless, what is sought from the student is not passive, docile imitation and obedience—the more or less willing production of alienated labor—but the joining in and adopting of the discourse as a means of enriching and extending the student's own integrity. Thus she censures the writers of one textbook (Janice Lauer, Gene Montagu, Andrea Lunsford, and Janet Emig) for characterizing one type of research paper as follows: "Research writing sometimes assumes a *pseudo-persuasive aim* (authors' emphasis) when the minimum expectations of the professors are that you will retrieve information familiar to them and organize it in a familiar pattern so that you will persuade them that you understand the subject as they and others like them understand it."[35] Bizzell objects that this description, which is accurate enough, implies that there is something fake about this initiatory exercise, and misses the chance to explain what it means that the information and pattern are familiar to the teacher and "others like them"; instead (and this is my extension of Bizzell) they endorse a kind of easy, unexamined "us/them" split with perhaps some hints of jejune cynicism. Somewhat later in the essay, she cites a contrasting description of argument in the history research paper in another writing across the curriculum textbook by Elaine Maimon, Gerald L. Belcher, Gail W. Hearn, Barbara F. Nodine, and Finbarr W. O'Connor:

> In a history class you are obligated to back up your interpretation with the kind of evidence that historians will accept. They will not accept as a decisive answer, for example, what Charles II said about his own foreign policy. But historians may disagree on what the answer is, not because it is a mere matter of taste but because the range of facts to be considered in forging an answer is so great. Nor is a disagreement among historians on the subject just a matter of knowledge, of one knowing more about the period than another. The facts known equally to both historians may be open to several equally plausible interpretations. In such a case, there are certainly answers that are plainly wrong—inconsistent with the facts—but several answers that are *reasonable*, worthy of belief.[36]

Bizzell praises this passage for demystifying academic discourse; in this case, it suggests to students on what grounds they can have things to say—how they can enter the discourse of historians at least so far as to be able to show that they understand the subject as historians do. The passage makes clear to them what is arguable (and hence important) and how it is argued: the discourse of history is argument in which evidence and the interpretation of evidence are crucial but do not issue in one right answer.

Bizzell criticizes Lauer et al. at another point as well for failing to convey to the student the special norms and procedures of academic discourse. The situation they raise has to do with writing for a instructor who has expressed strong opinions on a controversial issue. The student writing on that issue does not need to be told whether and how much to agree or disagree with the instructor—how to successfully manipulate him or her—rather, "What he and his teacher need is a conventional system of inquiry that temporarily suspends personalities without suppressing or manipulating them. Such a system exists in the conventions of discourse that constitute intellectual work in the academic community" (p. 201). Here the phrase "conventions of discourse" cuts deeper than matters of format and use of the passive voice; the "conventions" in question are those of the ethos of science and of Text, especially that of impersonality, conceived to function this time not to protect scholars and their work from personal attack, but to protect students from a sense of pressure to subordinate themselves to their professors' wills, to maneuver their way around them, or to engage in quixotic acts of self-assertion. For students properly to understand their instructors as their "audience," then, they must understand them as acting in a particular institutional role, one which defines and limits the grounds on which they may evaluate their students (at least insofar as they are students). Bizzell quotes with approval the lines of Maimon et al.: "It is not sufficient to imagine your instructor as your audience; you must go further and imagine your instructor playing a particular role—representative of scholars in a discipline or representative of people who hold the view opposing the one you are arguing" (p. 202). This instruction does not merely replace the instructor as helpful, sympathetic friend with the instructor as adversary; rather, the concept is of the instructor as partner in the academic dialectic, subjecting the writing to scrutiny for the quality of its evidence and reasoning. Actual instructors, of course, may fall short of enacting this role, and it is not amiss for someone helping a student in a writing center to point out that her argument is well constructed and supported, but is one her particular instructor is not favorably disposed to (if such is known to be the case). But she should still be told the grounds on which her paper is properly judged and on which, if necessary, she can appeal.

David Bartholomae is also concerned with initiation or transitional writing and writing assignments, and he too objects to writing assignments which dodge the instructor as audience by stipulating audiences for student papers ("Describe baseball to an Eskimo"), since if students are to learn academic discourse, they will have to learn to insert themselves into our community by addressing us. On his view, students usually come to the university "able to enter into a conventional discourse and speak, not as themselves, but through the voice of the community" (p. 156)—able, that is, to invoke the commonplaces and assume the common purposes of everyday discourse. "The university, however, is the place where 'common' wisdom is only of negative value—it is something to work against. The movement toward a more specialized discourse begins (or, perhaps, best begins) both when a student can define a position of privilege, a position that sets him against a 'common' discourse, and when he or she can work self-consciously, critically, against not only the 'common' code but his or her own" (p. 156). This opposition of the academic and the everyday evokes the Schütz-Garfinkel types of theorizing and Olson's Utterance/Text as well. Taken as defining the movement into academic discourse, it introduces an unmistakable note of opposition, of struggle and resistance between life orientations; it forces into view antagonistic codes of what is interesting and what points can be made. As Bartholomae emphasizes in the latter part of his quote, however, full initiation into the academic discourse is reflected not just by the supplanting of one discourse by another, but by the ability to argue within the academic code and with oneself. As he says somewhat later, "At an advanced stage, I would place students who establish their authority as *writers*; they claim their authority, not by simply claiming that they are skiers or that they have done something creative, but by placing themselves both within and against a discourse, or within and against competing discourses, and working self-consciously to claim an interpretive project of their own, one that grants them the privilege to speak" (p. 158). Here one might well hear echoes of Gouldner's culture of critical discourse. Bartholomae illustrates these traits and stages in relation to freshman placement essays at the University of Pittsburgh, but he fully acknowledges that they constitute his own statement of values and sense of skilled academic writing. This process of initiation is not entirely incompatible with learning certain formulas, standard moves, and a new set of commonplaces; in fact, he even gives his own version of the universal English paper generator passed on to him by one of his teachers: "While most readers of ———— have said ————, a close and careful reading shows that ————." (The "close and careful reading" tag is somewhat antiquated, though perhaps still more serviceable than theorists would like to think.) There is thus nothing particularly inward or mysterious about this claiming of authority and placing oneself in a discourse. Bartholomae demystifies academic discourse by emphasizing that the authority of a disciplinary author is not a position of wisdom above argument but an orientation toward argument within the set of topics, texts, and techniques that constitute the discipline. The advanced initiate argues with other texts, received accounts, her own initial thoughts, proverbial wisdom, and other bits of discourse lying about and in so doing escapes the struggle and alternation between a relatively powerless, ignorant, and naive "we" and a superior, sophisticated, learned "they" who not only know all the answers, but write all the questions. The advanced student has learned, as Billig might say, that in academic discourse there are no right answers, only good arguments, and that the writer's task is not to vanquish or silence opposing arguments or to attain the unshakable conviction of the closed mind, but to handle opposing arguments in a way that establishes his own fair-mindedness—just as their teachers do.

There is nonetheless a distinct current of "colonialism" running in Bartholomae's essay: the student acquires membership not just in "another" culture, but one which is contemptuous of everyday commonplaces and attitudes applied to academic problems, and Bartholomae reminds us that in such situations, the natives experience "loss, violence, and compromise" as they accommodate to the ways of the colonials. He does not attempt to justify the privilege and authority that mastery of disciplinary discourse confers within the (admittedly small) world of the university; he merely affirms that it is so, and that mastering it is expected and rewarded when we respond to and grade student writing. Bartholomae pulls up short of making the strongest case for academic discourse, the case which this study has been slowly building, namely, that however ponderous and oblique some of its procedures may be, academic writing does embody ideals of non-coercive cooperation, that it marks out a space in which ideas can be impartially entertained, rigorously scrutinized, and openly evaluated on public grounds—that it is, in short, not only privileged and authoritative, but good and in some sense deserving of its privilege and authority. *That* is the view of academic discourse that we ought to hold before us, and *that* is the goal that should guide the teaching of academic writing.

Bartholomae's essay has itself become the object of dialectic scrutiny and critique by a number of scholars, notably Joe Harris and Kurt Spellmeyer.[37] Harris queries Bartholomae's use of the term "community" and his notion of undergraduate education as "induction" into the academic community—the process, that is, in which "they," who start out so unlike "us," become more like us. As this study has amply shown, academic discourse is a very general term, and includes the making of claims to expert, authoritative knowledge in areas disputed by other disciplines and by contending approaches even within the discipline. True, academic discourse also includes textbooks, which report the currently agreed-upon basics of the subject, but to take textbooks as the epitome of academic discourse, as Olson sometimes does, presents a seriously one-sided and limited view; it leads to equating community with consensus, as Harris notes, but academic discourse can at least as well be viewed as a peculiarly disciplined dissensus like that characterizing other deliberative bodies such as Congress or courts of law. From the perspectives of newly enrolled freshman and their instructors, the differences of "they" and "we" seem palpable and gross, with academic discourse displaying several singular attributes:

—it is oriented toward updating and extending the "state of the art" through incrementation of knowledge and improvement of technique; it thus assumes that the existing state of the art is always incomplete and in some sense wrong; and it holds open to questioning the very methods and assumptions that have hitherto proven relatively successful.

—it is oriented toward publication, not toward personal reflection and meaning-making; it is critical of, and attempts to go beyond, received opinion ("platitudes," "stereotypes").

—it limits its techniques of advocacy and critique to public and disciplinary grounds.

These attributes are not discipline-specific, though a thorough grounding in and critical perspective on the state of the art in any particular discipline requires years of study beyond the undergraduate ones, and hence the notion of undergraduate writing courses initiating students into "our" discourse can only be a very general and schematic one. Undergraduate majors do not write papers contributing to knowledge, but remain on the margin, as much observers as participants. One of the great, gaping holes in current academic self-understanding is any positive model of the undergraduate as knowing or learning subject; we tend simply to think of undergraduates as beginners or proto-graduate students, and undergraduate teaching as some sort of professional recruiting (when it is not generalized consciousness raising or horizon-broadening). The ideal of liberal culture discussed by James Berlin in relation to writing instruction in this century seems pretty well exhausted, and none of the alternatives discussed by Berlin (skills for life, preparation for democratic citizenship, expressivist self-exploration) have filled in the gap.[38] We can *describe* the undergraduate years as a time during which students with the broad aims of participating in public and professional life encounter some of the monuments and some of the techniques of intellectual endeavor; what is unclear is what impact this encounter is supposed to have on the students.

How sinister, oppressive, or alienating this encounter seems depends on how closed, monolithic, and uncritical academic discourse seems. For Kurt Spellmeyer, who equates academic discourse with discipline-specific writing, it is deeply alienating. He finds urging students to support their convictions with arguments and evidence that others will accept to amount to "the admonition to suppress feelings and beliefs for the sake of public approval," which, he argues, "encourages an attitude of calculating alienation, the antithesis of Herbert Marcuse's notion of 'praxis in the "realm of freedom,"' praxis that does not require submission to 'an "alien" objectivity'" (Spellmeyer, p. 267). Spellmeyer's equating of "going beyond feelings or internal conviction" with "suppression" is clearly polemical, as is his equating of disciplinary discourse with "impersonal, an automatic knowledge" which is uncritical and which supports a "narrow vocationalism." This conception has much in common with Robert Hariman's discussed in chapter two, and leads Spellmeyer to advocate the "transgressive" personal essay as the antidote for dreary, passionless, pompous, pseudo-or proto-disciplinary writing.

Spellmeyer cites a student paper turned in, he says, in an "entry level" sociology course to show the unappealing results of inculcating the convention of impersonality. I will cite the first two paragraphs of it from Spellmeyer's article:

> The modern world in which we live is a complex and fast-moving one. Modern societies are plagued by reoccurring, extensive social problems. Although there exist many serious problems, the one which demands immediate examination and resolution is that of suicide among youths. Children are taking their own lives with an alarming frequency. Whatever the reasons may be for these tragedies, an emphasis must be placed upon preventing them rather than analyzing them after they have occurred.
>
> In this work, *Suicide: A Study in Sociology*, Emile Durkheim studies the various causes associated with suicide. He categorizes the different types of suicide into four basic groups: egoistic, anomic, altruistic, and fatalistic. All four of these classifications can be applied to the growing problem of youth suicide in society. . . . (p. 271)

Spellmeyer says of this: "Superficially, this passage is the work of an advanced student-writer, insofar as it closely approximates the ideal of systematic, impersonal, 'academic' discourse" (p. 271). It's a little hard to mistake these paragraphs for even superficially good academic writing, or even "academic" writing (unless Spellmeyer's shudder quotes are essentially question-begging), since the prose is redundant, infelicitously phrased, and ignorant (reoccurring). On a slightly deeper level, it fails to pose a problem of any urgency or interest, personal or academic, and it proceeds to concentrate on exactly what it has attempted to dismiss (causes of suicide). Spellmeyer argues that the passage is bad because it is deeply as well as stylistically impersonal: "despite this apparent sophistication, the discussion strikes me as ultimately unsuccessful because its impersonality is not simply a rhetorical posture, but evidence of a pervasive absence of commitment" (p. 271). Commitment, or investment—yes, one could put it that way, but I wonder whether the source of the problem is the teacher telling the student that his personal experience is irrelevant, and whether the solution is to urge the student "to bring himself into the conversation, possibly in a preliminary 'working paper' on the destructive forces in his life and the lives of his friends" (pp. 274–75). Spellmeyer's use of the "conversation" metaphor here suggests that he wants a sense of face-to-face encounter in which "the discussion" would loosen up and get down to the things that matter personally. What a curious turn of phrase it is, to refer to a discussion as "ultimately unsuccessful." Pointless maybe, or unsatisfying, but unsuccessful?

Clearly the paper is sorry business reeking of twenty-year-old Engfish and meriting at best the plodder's C. It is so typical of papers submitted in college that one must suspect that some deep quirk in the system is generating them. Spellmeyer does not cite the assignment that triggered this paper, a fairly serious omission in that writing teachers have come to recognize that a huge amount of cuing goes on in assignment giving—which does not mean that students already understand the cues. From what Spellmeyer and the paper say, one can imagine an assignment such as "How does Durkheim's theory of suicide help us to understand the alarming incidence of teenage suicide today? What suggestions might Durkheim make about how to stem this tide?" Thus the assignment would be an instance of the general "Describe/Apply/Assess a Concept" type (with the "Assess" part muted). Such assignments aim to develop the student's basic ability to establish referential links between theory and the world as otherwise known, which might or might not include the world as personally experienced ("Have you or someone you've known ever considered or attempted suicide? How might Durkheim's theory of suicide help to understand that experience?"—an assignment in Phenomenological Sociology 410). The assignment leads the student toward making some such links or connections (note that the assignment subtly presupposes that such links do exist—the "relevance," that is, of Durkheim's theory is assumed). The student who makes some links (or some standard links—not any link will do) will pass, though the instructor is looking for some novelty or originality that would indicate a talent for the subject.

It is fairly easy to guess the assignment for this paper, for it is an old standby of Introductory Sociology. Can you imagine reading, say, even just thirty papers a year on "Durkheim's Theory of Suicide" for twenty years? Of course, no one does; Readers do it, and it's important to keep changing Readers, because the papers don't change. I'm not suggesting the paper is a commodity which can be purchased; this paper is so common as to have negligible cash market value. Rather, it can be found in the files of many dormitories and Greek affiliates. As technology advances, these files become computerized, which creates new possibilities in diffused textuality. If the instructor, influenced by Spellmeyer, insists on some references to personal experience, these can readily be intercalated between paragraphs of the standard text. Minor changes of focus and emphasis can be made in the introduction to adjust to trickier phrasings of The Question. These variations point to inadequacies in our concept of plagiarism, since in many cases the author of the first draft is not known, and the original is not protected by publication or copyright. This is alienation, all right, but it is the result of perceived indifference on both sides, of "priorities," as they say. It is unlikely to be remedied by a change in theory or assignment as long as the material conditions of instruction remain the same.

The by-now-proverbial saying that we don't teach writing, we just assign it means in this case that the instructor is asking the student to make certain moves of categorization and analysis characteristic of sociological discourse without (apparently) pointing that out, or pointing out for that matter what "discuss" means in an academic paper. In addition, the instructor probably did not compare the academic, sociological discussion of Durkheim or suicide to other kinds of discourse that deal with the subject. That really is a bit much to expect of someone lecturing to the 180 students of Soc 101. But it does suggest the usefulness of a course that would foreground not "academic discourse" as such but academic rhetoric—its construction of reasonableness and authority, its differences from prevailing popular rhetorics, and its implied audience. Such a course or courses should analyze the way academic rhetoric symbolizes experience—its foundational and habitual tropes—so that certain assumptions appear self-evident, others problematic and requiring solutions, and yet others are invisible. It should discuss the play of other voices in academic writing, its "hidden polemic," including but not limited to those explicitly cited and ranged on a spectrum from mortal antagonism and opposition to unqualified endorsement. But it should not do this in a spirit of textualist superiority, not to debunk, not to destabilize only, for such moves are powerfully attractive to bright undergraduates, who will mistake them for the full array of skills for critical analysis and evaluation; other, more practical undergraduates are less impressed, noting that the daily business of the disciplines does seem to be conducted by serious-minded people despite their putative naivete. And we should discuss the critical and emancipatory roots and aspirations of academic rhetoric, its attempts and successes at lifting the public understanding out of bigotry, narrow-mindedness, dogmatism, and the unthinking perpetuation of "tradition." Academic rhetoric must apply the principle of critique to itself, not glossing over the way it can be used for power and social control, but it can adequately do so with acts less dramatic than seppuku. Academic rhetoric can be studied without producing scandal, cynicism, or guffaws.

In addition to discussing academic rhetoric in relation to the discourse of the disciplines we should examine its operation in policy deliberation and social control through "expertise." The deliberation of an educated public should be enriched by the skill of its participants in using, in critically drawing upon, the discourses of knowledge. One might well focus on the uses and limitations of the popular news and opinion media, and of popularized knowledge such as that offered in *Psychology Today*; popularization itself could be a central issue for a writing course. Thinking in this way of the role of writing instruction in undergraduates' lives, namely as the study of the uses of knowledge, puts rhetoric/writing back at the center of a liberal arts education, not in terms of epistemic privilege, but as a kind of clearinghouse. The student should be able to see, at least in principle, how the expert discourses produce knowledge that may be of service to life's purposes. Lacking such a sense of usableness, the student is left humbly contemplating the vast impenetrable edifice of the academic arcane.

CONCLUSION
A CONTENTION OF RHETORICS

In the theory of argument, rhetoric, dialectic, and logic are distinguished as perspectives on argumentation focusing respectively on the process, procedure, and product of argument. Rhetoric, as the study of process, directs its attention to speakers, hearers, purposes, occasions, as they affect attempts to persuade. Dialectic, as the study of the procedure, focuses on the argumentation pro and contra, the rules for the scrutiny of evidence and argument, opportunities for rebuttal, restatement, and clarification; it is normatively idealized as *diskurs* in Habermas's theory—the mode which secures communicative rationality. Logic, finally, treats the product of argument in terms of the validity of the arguments. So defined, these subjects range over all sorts of discourses insofar as they are argumentation, and provide a framework for analyzing academic argument, or even the argumentation of particular disciplines. Within this scheme, rhetoric ceases to pair with any single antagonist (reason, demonstration, etc.); as a perspective on argumentation, it involves, among other things, the rules and means of selecting qualified (or ratified, or certified, or authoritative) participants and the deployment of various devices to enhance persuasiveness. Thus one may describe particular modes or styles of discourse as rhetorics, speaking, for example (as we have), of the rhetoric of objectivity or the rhetoric of self-awareness. And it is in fact just in these terms that we can best describe the change, or struggle, or crisis of academic writing in the last decade or so—not, that is, in terms of logic (or proof) giving way to rhetoric (or persuasion), but of the rhetoric of impersonal objectivity being challenged by the rhetoric of reflexive self-awareness.

As previous chapters have shown, the rhetoric of objectivity has been the dominant mode across the disciplines. This rhetoric shields disciplinary discourse from suspicions of personal bias and the partiality arising from subjectivity, especially that arising, as used to be said, from the passions. The discourses produced are regarded as autonomous texts and are not to be criticized as the work of their authors, nor should the authors appeal to the particular desires, preferences, antipathies, and inclinations of the audience. Similarly, this rhetoric insulates the discourse from appeals to authority or conflicts with prevailing ideology—the "pure" discourse of the disciplines can pursue its aim of knowledge without regard for prevailing social interests. This rhetoric, which so restricts the range of its appeals as to be called "anti-rhetoric," has also proven powerful for the advisory roles that disciplines are often invited to perform. Academic specialists in the posture of disinterest are above the fray, and their testimony is valued precisely because it is untainted by the interest that usually animates contending parties and points of view in practical disputes. Indeed, experts often experience discomfort at the desire for clarity and certainty expressed in deliberative forums, feeling that they are called upon to conspire in denying the conditionality of their expert knowledge, its underdetermination by the facts, and its dependence on arguable assumptions. That is, academics are accustomed to fielding arguments and positions that are moments in the process of academic dialectic, rather than those that constitute received wisdom, and when the focus shifts to this process, rather than to the products that eventually find their way into textbooks, impersonality and disinterest give way to contentious arguing pro and contra.

Thus texts, viewed as moments in a dialectic, are clearly not self-demonstrating, authenticating, or grounding. They are offerings—submissions, as we say— that are evaluated and selected through processes of scrutiny, challenge, debate and critique. As Gouldner emphasizes, these processes lead to the questioning of assumptions and the rolling-back of the horizon of the taken-for-granted. This is the homeground of methodical doubt and hostility to commonsense reasoning for its untheorized categories and for its indifference to subtleties and refinements with no immediate, apparent use. Insofar as the academic disciplines are aware of themselves as a culture, it is a culture that guards itself against the complacency of commonsense reasoning and received opinion, even opinion within the discipline. To be sure, it has been widely recognized that the canons of scrutiny and evaluation cannot be applied as impersonal algorithms; acts of professional judgment are required, though they are to operate under the guidance of norms of fairness and must be conveyed in terms that conform to those norms. None of these requirements, of course, can *guarantee* that a reviewer's report is not a "strategic" manipulation of the code for motives of personal prejudice, malice, or *parti pris.*

There is perhaps nothing inherent in the academic dialectic that requires scholars to apply this scrutiny to their own work, except a desire to forestall criticism, but this impulse itself may be sufficient to account for much qualification and argumentation in disciplinary writing. Academics are expected to be self-critical, and to give some evidence of it in their writing. If, however, as Joseph Wenzel suggests, dialectic (especially of the institutionalized, public kind) inevitably characterizes its participants as self-conscious advocates, and if, as he also claims, the ultimate virtue of dialectic is candor in the disclosure of claims and reasons, then it is easy to see how academic discourse would place high value on candor with respect to the writer's relation to her discourse. In recent decades the value placed on the expression of critical self-awareness has risen sharply, especially awareness directed at the very founding assumptions of the discourse itself. Paralleling the rise of hermeneutic and textual theories of knowledge in the human sciences has been the rise of the rhetoric of self-awareness.

Contending Rhetorics

Linked to the rhetoric of objectivity has been the epistemology of correspondence—the view that a claim or hypothesis is to be evaluated in terms of its accuracy as a representation of the way things are in the world. As philosophers have emphasized that "the way things are in the world" is not directly, immediately accessible, but itself the product of acts of selection, foregrounding, and symbolization (which are acts performed by some *body*), the process of evaluating claims takes on the aspect of a social and political struggle between competing views of the world in its various aspects: reality, even the natural world, is not "there" yielding to and sometimes mysteriously resisting our attempts to model "her"; rather, reality is constructed by the essentially social processes of inquiry, scrutiny, acceptance and rejection. All scholars are interested parties, whether they acknowledge it or not, and social constructionist epistemologies link up with rhetorics that aspire to enhance authority and credibility by calling attention to their subjective and social filiations and affiliations.

One of the greater ironies to emerge from this study, however, is that this rhetoric of self-awareness, which begins with emphasizing the sociality of discourse, ends up viewing writing as the act of individuals. Gusfield, McCloskey, Geertz each in their ways foreground the power of a writer's prose, her rhetorical and strategic skill, in establishing authority and credibility. This is a very traditional view of authorship, bordering on romantic theories of genius; it is reflected, too, in their responses to scholarly writing in terms of essentially personal qualities of the writers—the writers' sensitivity, awareness and candor about the complexity and limitations of their stances, fair-mindedness, social commitments, and values, their intelligence, intensity, and imaginative penetration that constitutes actually "being there." This is heady stuff, treating scholars as if they were all Foucault's "founders of discursivity," or Kuhn's paradigm-initiating "exemplars." What this view tends to minimize is the degree to which scholars are constituted as authors by the disciplinary discourse: as laymen, however gifted, they would have no place to read and send their work, no one to publish it, review it, read it, or cite it and argue with it. The works and views they must refer to, the very issues they can address, are "given" by the state of the disciplinary discussion at the time. True, these things are not fixed and enumerable prior to the act of writing in most cases, but would-be authors must nonetheless define discursive niches within the current field of possibilities offered by the discipline to insert themselves in. "This book fills a hitherto unsuspected need"—yes, but the need, once claimed, must be apparent. Further, scholars who attempt to shift fields, or even sub-fields, quickly discover that their authorship does not transfer to the new field, though it may assist, a little, in gaining them entry.

Thus, while the rhetoric of objectivity may seem hostile to language, calling merely for windowpane prose, the ruthless narrowing of the range of rhetorical appeals, and the modest profile of the professional scholar, we ought to be somewhat skeptical of a view that suggests disciplinary discourse is now open as never before to innovation and experiment, eagerly awaiting original acts of authorial ingenuity. In writing this book, I have struck my own balance between these modes of authority and appeal as I attempt to bring readers with certain interests and concerns through a process of inquiry and reflection to the affirmation of certain values—a small, practical synthesis, as it were, not a grand one, in this contention of rhetorics. Other writers will do the same.

NOTES

Introduction

1. James Clifford, "Introduction: Partial Truths" in James Clifford and George E. Marcus, eds., *Writing Culture: The Poetics and Politics of Ethnography* (Berkeley: University of California Press, 1986).

2. Terry Eagleton, *Literary Theory* (New York: Oxford University Press, 1982), pp. 205–207.

3. Jürgen Habermas, "On Leveling the Genre Distinction between Philosophy and Literature," in *The Philosophical Discourse of Modernity*, trans. Frederick Lawrence (Cambridge, Mass.: MIT Press, 1987), p. 190.

4. Michael Ryan, *Marxism and Deconstruction* (Baltimore, Md.: Johns Hopkins University Press, 1982), pp. 115–16.

5. Elaine P. Maimon, "Maps and Genres: Exploring Connections in the Arts and Sciences," in Winifred Bryan Horner, ed., *Composition and Literature: Bridging the Gap* (Chicago: University of Chicago Press, 1983), pp. 110–25.

6. Charles Bazerman, "What Written Knowledge Does: Three Examples of Academic Discourse," *Philosophy of the Social Sciences* 11 (1981): 361–87; Susan Peck MacDonald, "Problem Definition in Academic Writing," *College English* 49 (1987): 315–31; see also "Comment and Response," *CE* 50 (1988): 212–20.

7. See for example Charles Bazerman, "Codifying the Social Scientific Style: The APA *Publication Manual* as a Behaviorist Rhetoric," in John S. Nelson, Allan Megill, and Donald N. McCloskey, eds., *The Rhetoric of the Human Sciences* (Madison: University of Wisconsin Press, 1987), pp. 125–44. This is reprinted in his *Shaping Written Knowledge* (Madison: University of Wisconsin Press, 1988), all of which repays examination.

8. John S. Nelson, "Seven Rhetorics of Inquiry: A Provocation," in Nelson et al., pp. 407–36.

9. Walter Benn Michaels, "Against Formalism: Chickens and Rocks," in Leonard Michaels and Christopher Ricks, eds., *The State of the Language* (Berkeley and Los Angeles: University of California Press, 1980), pp. 410–20.

10. These issues are discussed at some length in relation to the rhetoric of advice writing in my *Rhetoric as Social Action: Explorations in the Interpersonal Function of Language* (Bloomington: Indiana University Press, 1986).

11. Michael C. Leff, "Modern Sophistic and the Unity of Rhetoric," in Nelson et al., pp. 19–37. Kenneth Burke cites Richard McKeon's review of the medieval definition of rhetoric stemming from Cassiodorus as "the science of speaking well in civil questions"—*Rhetoric of Motives* (Berkeley and Los Angeles: University of California Press, 1969), p. 101.

12. Michael Calvin McGee and John R. Lyne, "What Are Nice Folks Like You Doing in a Place Like This?" in Nelson et al., pp. 381–406.

13. Richard A. Cherwitz and James W. Hikins, *Communication and Knowledge: An Investigation in Rhetorical Epistemology* (Columbia, S.C.: University of South Carolina Press, 1986), p. 62.

14. Burke, *Motives*, p. 41 (et passim).

15. C. H. Knoblauch, "Modern Rhetorical Theory and Its Future Directions," in Ben

W. McClelland and Timothy R. Donovan, eds., *Perspectives on Research and Scholarship in Composition* (New York: Modern Language Association, 1985), p. 29.

1. Reason, Rationality, and Rhetoric

1. See for example the discussion in Martin Hollis, *The Cunning of Reason* (Cambridge: Cambridge University Press, 1987). For the status of the *homo economicus* axiom in microeconomics, see below, chapter 4, section 1.

2. See R. Nisbet and T. Wilson, "Telling More Than We Can Know: Verbal Reports on Mental Processes," *Psychological Review* 84 (1977): 231–59.

3. Chaim Perelman, *The New Rhetoric and the Humanities* (Dordrecht: Reidel, 1979), pp. 35, 124.

4. Cited from Alfred Schütz, "The Problem of Rationality in the Social World," *Economica* 10 (1943): 130.

5. See David Lewis, *Convention* (Cambridge, Mass.: Harvard University Press, 1969); Edna Ullmann-Margolit, *The Emergence of Norms* (Oxford: Clarendon Press, 1977); Trevor Pateman, "David Lewis's Theory of Convention and the Social Life of Language," *Journal of Pragmatics* 6 (1982): 135–57.

6. H. Paul Grice, "Logic and Conversation," in Peter Cole and Jerry Morgan, eds., *Syntax and Semantics, Vol. III: Speech Acts* (New York: Academic Press, 1975), pp. 41–58.

7. Asa Kasher, "Gricean Implicature Revisited," *Philosophica* 29 (1982): 25–44.

8. See for example Elinor Ochs Keenan, "The Universality of Conversational Implicature," *Language in Society* 5 (1976): 67–80; Jack Bilmes, "Misinformation and Ambiguity in Verbal Interaction: A Northern Thai Example," *International Journal of the Sociology of Language* 5 (1975): 63–75.

9. Mary Louise Pratt, "The Ideology of Speech Act Theory," *Centrum* new series 1 (1981): 5–18; reprinted as "Ideology and Speech Act Theory" and somewhat modified in *Poetics Today* 7 (1986): 59–72; so also on the narrowness of Grice's concept of conversation Ferenc Kiefer, "What Do Conversational Maxims Explain?" *Linguisticae Investigationes* 3 (1979): 57–74. Another problem with Grice's theory is, I believe, that speakers have other interests that may conflict with their general interest in maintaining conversation as an efficient means of doing business, such as controlling the interpretation and use that others make of what they say; it is almost as if "conversation" for Grice corresponds to Habermas's mode of *dialogue* in which the practical purpose of the talk exchange is temporarily suspended. Of which more below.

10. Michael Mulkay, *Science and the Sociology of Knowledge* (London: George Allen & Unwin, 1979).

11. Mulkay, *Science*, pp. 94–95; Gernod Boehme, "Cognitive Norms, Knowledge-Interests and the Constitution of the Scientific Object: A Case Study in the Functioning of Rules for Experimentation," in Everett Mendelsohn, Peter Weingart, and Richard Whitley, eds., *The Social Production of Scientific Knowledge* (Dordrecht: Reidel, 1977), pp. 129–42.

12. "Certified knowledge" is Robert Merton's term in *The Sociology of Science* (Chicago: University of Chicago Press, 1973); and see J. M. Ziman, *Public Knowledge* (Cambridge: Cambridge University Press, 1968).

13. Michael Polanyi, "The Republic of Science," *Minerva* 1 (1962): 54–73; reprinted in *Knowing and Being*, ed. Marjorie Grene (Chicago: University of Chicago Press, 1969), pp. 49–72.

14. Polanyi's theory of adsorption of gases, the subject of his dissertation in Physical Chemistry in 1916, was denounced by Einstein and Fritz Haber as implausible and discredited for many years, so completely that he felt he could not teach it in his own classes, though he believed it to be correct (as it eventually was recognized to be). See

"The Potential Theory of Adsorption," *Science* 141 (1963): 1010–13; reprinted in *Knowing and Being*, pp. 87–96.

15. The precise modus operandi of the elites, and their use of rules of method and evaluation, is discussed in more detail in Derek L. Phillips, *Wittgenstein and Scientific Knowledge* (London: Macmillan, 1977), especially chapter 7, "The Demarcation Problem in Science."

16. See W. Newton-Smith, *The Rationality of Science* (London and Boston: Routledge & Kegan Paul, 1981); also Larry Laudan, *Progress and Its Problems* (Berkeley: University of California Press, 1977) and *Science and Values: The Aims of Science and Their Role in Scientific Debate* (Berkeley: University of California Press, 1984), Rom Harré, *Varieties of Realism* (Oxford and New York: Blackwell, 1986); Mary Hesse, *Revolution and Reconstruction in the Philosophy of Science* (Bloomington: Indiana University Press, 1980); Joseph C. Pitt and Marcello Pera, eds., *Rational Changes in Science* (Boston Studies in the Philosophy of Science 98) (Dordrecht: Reidel, 1987).

17. Schütz, "The Problem of Rationality in the Social World," pp. 130–49; Harold Garfinkel, *Studies in Ethnomethodology* (Englewood Cliffs, N.J.: Prentice Hall, 1967).

18. Alfred Schütz, "Common-sense and Scientific Interpretation of Human Action," *Philosophy and Phenomenological Research* 14 (1953): 1–37.

19. Jürgen Habermas, *The Theory of Communicative Action, Vol. I, Reason and the Rationalization of Society*, trans. Thomas McCarthy (Boston: Beacon Press, 1984), pp. 120–36. Hereafter *TCA*, Vol. I.

20. Joseph Gusfield, *The Culture of Public Problems: Drinking-Driving and the Symbolic Order* (Chicago: University of Chicago Press, 1981).

21. Michael Calvin McGee and John R. Lyne, "What Are Nice Folks Like You Doing in a Place Like This?" in John S. Nelson, Allan Megill, and Donald N. McCloskey, eds., *The Rhetoric of the Human Sciences* (Madison: University of Wisconsin Press, 1987), pp. 393–94.

22. See for example R. Gordon Shepherd, "Selectivity of Sources: Reporting the Marijuana Controversy," *Journal of Communication* 31 (1981): 128–37; Brian L. Campbell, "Uncertainty as Symbolic Action in Disputes Among Experts," *Social Studies of Science* 15 (1985): 429–53; Christopher Hamlin, "Scientific Method and Expert Witnessing: Victorian Perspectives on a Modern Problem," *Social Studies of Science* 16 (1986): 485–513; Sheila S. Basanoff, "Contested Boundaries in Policy Related Science," *Social Studies of Science* 17 (1987): 195–230. See also the study of the attempts of economists to apply their expertise to the management of the British National Health Service by Michael Mulkay, Trevor Pinch, and Malcolm Ashmore, "Colonizing the Mind: Dilemmas in the Application of Social Science," *Social Studies of Science* 17 (1987): 231–56.

23. A useful guide to Gadamer's discussion of phronesis is in David Couzens Hoy, *The Critical Circle* (Berkeley: University of California Press, 1978); see also Joel Weinsheimer, *Gadamer's Hermeneutic* (New Haven, Conn.: Yale University Press, 1985). Weinsheimer follows Gadamer in referring to phronesis as "commonsense."

24. All citations of the *Nichomachean Ethics* from the translation of W. D. Ross.

25. Chaim Perelman, "Reflections on Practical Reason" (*The New Rhetoric and the Humanities*, pp. 124–33); Richard Sorabji, "Aristotle on the Role of Intellect in Virtue," in Amelie Oksenberg Rorty, ed., *Essays on Aristotle's Ethics* (Berkeley: University of California Press, 1980), pp. 201–20; David Wiggins, "Deliberation and Practical Reason," in Rorty, pp. 221–40.

26. See for example the portrait sketched by Bertrand Russell and cited by Perelman from Brand Blanchard in Perelman's "The Rational and the Reasonable" in *The New Rhetoric and the Humanities*, p. 118.

27. Georgia Warnke, *Gadamer: Hermeneutics, Tradition, and Reason*, (Stanford, Calif.: Stanford University Press, 1987), p. 162.

28. Jürgen Habermas, "What Is Universal Pragmatics?" in *Communication and the Evolution of Society*, trans. Thomas McCarthy (Boston: Beacon Press, 1978), pp. 1–68.

29. Donald N. McCloskey, *The Rhetoric of Economics* (Madison: University of Wisconsin Press, 1985), pp. 24–28; Michael Oakeshott, "The Voice of Poetry in the Conversation of Mankind," in *Rationalism and Politics* (London: Methuen, 1962); Richard Rorty, *Philosophy and the Mirror of Nature* (Princeton, N.J.: Princeton University Press, 1979).

30. Jonathan Culler, "Communicative Competence and Normative Force," *New German Critique* 35 (1985): 133–44.

31. Jürgen Habermas, *Theorie des kommunikativen Handelns, Band I, Handlungsrationalität und gesellschaftliche Rationalisierung* (Frankfurt am Main: Suhrkamp Verlag, 1981); *TCA*, Vol. I, p. 10.

32. Robert Hollinger, "Practical Reason and Hermeneutics," *Philosophy and Rhetoric* 18 (1985): 113–21.

33. Hubert Dreyfus and Paul Rabinow, "What Is Maturity? Habermas and Foucault on 'What Is Enlightenment?' " in David Couzens Hoy, ed., *Foucault: A Critical Reader* (London: Basil Blackwell, 1986), pp. 109–22.

34. See David Ingram, *Habermas and the Dialectic of Reason* (New Haven, Conn.: Yale University Press, 1987), pp. 202–203n38.

35. Such is the conclusion of Allen Wood in "Habermas's Defense of Rationalism," *New German Critique* 35 (1985): 145–64.

36. Michael Ryan, *Marxism and Deconstruction* (Baltimore, Md.: Johns Hopkins University Press, 1983), p. 113; see also Ingram, *Habermas and the Dialectic of Reason*, pp. 238–39n11.

37. Jürgen Habermas, "Dialectical Materialism," cited from Richard Bernstein's introduction to his collection of essays *Habermas and Modernity* (Cambridge, Mass.: MIT Press, 1985), p. 21.

38. On this and several points, Habermas's view closely resembles Wayne Booth's in *Modern Dogma and the Rhetoric of Assent* (South Bend, Ind.: Notre Dame University Press, 1974).

39. See for example Hollinger ("Practical Reason and Hermeneutics"), and Ingram (*Habermas and the Dialectic of Reason*).

40. Gadamer, "On the Scope and Function of Hermeneutical Reflection," D. Linge, trans. and ed., *Philosophical Hermeneutics* (Berkeley: University of California Press, 1976), pp. 18–43; see also Joel Weinsheimer, *Gadamer's Hermeneutics* (New Haven, Conn.: Yale University Press, 1985), pp. 170–71.

41. David Ingram, "The Possibility of a Communication Ethic Reconsidered: Habermas, Gadamer, and Bourdieu on Discourse," *Man and World* 15 (1982): 156.

42. Chaim Perelman and Lucie Olbrechts-Tyteca, *The New Rhetoric* (South Bend, Ind.: University of Notre Dame Press, 1969), p. 117.

2. Impersonality and Its Discontents

1. William Labov, *Sociolinguistic Patterns* (Philadelphia: University of Pennsylvania Press, 1972), p. 120.

2. See Michel Foucault, *Archaeology of Knowledge*, trans. A. M. Sheridan Smith (New York, Pantheon Books, 1972).

3. A plea to restore the "grapholect" as the norm of classroom speaking can be found in E. D. Hirsch, Jr.'s *The Philosophy of Composition* (Chicago: University of Chicago Press, 1977).

4. David R. Olson, "From Utterance to Text: The Bias of Language in Speech and Writing," *Harvard Educational Review* 47 (1977): 257–81; "Oral and Written Language and the Cognitive Processes of Children," *Journal of Communication* 27: 3 (1977): 10–26; Jerome S. Bruner and David R. Olson, "Symbols and Texts as Tools of

Intellect," *Interchange* 8.4 (1977–78): 1–15; David R. Olson, "Writing: The Divorce of the Author from the Text," in Barry M. Kroll and Roberta J. Vann, eds., *Exploring Speaking-Writing Relationships* (Urbana, Ill.: NCTE, 1981), pp. 99–110; David R. Olson and Nancy Torrence, "Learning to Meet the Requirements of Written Text: Language Development in the School Years," in C. H. Frederiksen and J. F. Dominic, eds., *Writing: The Nature, Development, and Teaching of Written Communication* (Hillsdale, N.J.: Lawrence Erlbaum, 1981): pp. 235–55.

5. Angela Hildyard and David Olson, "Literacy and the Specialization of Language: Some Aspects of the Comprehension and Thought Processes of Literate and Non-literate Children and Adults," cited from Brian V. Street, *Literacy in Theory and Practice* (Cambridge: Cambridge University Press, 1984), p. 20. The article was to appear in Neil Warren, ed., *Studies in Cross-Cultural Psychology*, Vol. II (London: Academic Press, 1977–80).

6. Carmen Luke, Suzanne De Castell, and Allan Luke argue that it is in fact the institutional context of *use* rather than the intrinsic anonymous quality of textbooks that gives them this authority ("Beyond Criticism: The Authority of the School Text," *Curriculum Inquiry* 13.2 (1983): 111–27); Olson replies that the relation of Text conventions and social relations is parallel and interactive, not one-way determining, as they suggest (same issue, pp. 129–30). I am indebted to Avon Crismore for calling the Luke et al. article to my attention.

7. Basil Bernstein, "Social Class, Language and Socialization," in Piers Paolo Giglioli, ed., *Language and Social Context* (Harmondsworth: Penguin Books, 1972), pp. 157–78.

8. Martin Nystrand, Anne Doyle, and Margaret Himley, "A Critical Examination of the Doctrine of Autonomous Texts," in Martin Nystrand, ed., *The Structure of Written Communication* (New York, Academic Press, 1985), pp. 81–107.

9. Jack Goody and Ian Watt, "The Consequences of Literacy," in J. Goody, ed., *Literacy in Traditional Societies* (Cambridge: Cambridge University Press, 1963); Eric Havelock, *Prologue to Greek Literacy* (Toronto: OISE Press, 1976); H. Innis, *The Bias of Communication* (Toronto: University of Toronto Press, 1951); Marshall McLuhan, *The Gutenberg Galaxy* (Toronto: University of Toronto Press, 1962); Walter J. Ong, *The Presence of the Word,* (New Haven, Conn.: Yale University Press, 1967); Milman Parry, "The Making of Homeric Verse," in A. Parry, ed., *The Collected Papers of Milman Parry* (Oxford: Clarendon Press, 1971).

10. David R. Olson, "On the Language and Authority of Textbooks," *Journal of Communications* 30.1 (1980): 193.

11. Alvin W. Gouldner, *The Dialectic of Ideology and Technology: The Origins, Grammar, and Future of Ideology* (New York: Seabury Press, 1976), p. 43.

12. Cited from Gouldner, *Ideology*, p. 48.

13. Alvin W. Gouldner, *The Future of Intellectuals and the Rise of the New Class* (New York: Seabury Press, 1979), p. 28.

14. Michael Billig, Susan Condor, Derek Edwards, Mike Gane, David Middleton, and Alan Radley argue in *Ideological Dilemmas* (London, Newbury Park, Beverly Hills, New Dehli: Sage Publications, 1988) that even commonsense thinking in the developed democracies is trickled down Enlightenment social theory.

15. Robert Hariman, "The Rhetoric of Inquiry and the Professional Scholar," in Herbert W. Simons, ed., *Rhetoric in the Human Sciences* (London, Newbury Park, New Dehli: Sage Publications, 1989), pp. 211–32.

16. Jacob Bronowski, *Science and Human Values* (New York: Harper, 1956), p. 75.

17. These papers are collected in *The Sociology of Science* (Chicago: University of Chicago Press, 1973), from which they are cited in the text.

18. Thomas Gieryn, "Boundary Work and the Demarcation of Science from Non-Science," *American Sociological Review* 48 (1983): 781–95.

19. Robert Merton, *Science, Technology, and Society in Seventeenth-Century England* (Bruges, Belgium: Saint Catherine Press, 1938).

20. Marlon Blissett, *Politics in Science* (Boston: Little, Brown, 1972).

21. Michel Foucault, "What Is an Author?" in *Language, Counter-Memory, Practice* (Ithaca, N.Y.: Cornell University Press, 1977), pp. 113–38.

22. See *New York Times Book Review*, Sunday, October 11, 1987, pp. 39, 68. Gay's book was published by Yale University Press, 1987.

23. Barry Barnes and R.G.A. Dolby, "The Scientific Ethos: A Deviant Viewpoint," *European Journal of Sociology* 2 (1970): 3–25.

24. Rom Harré, *Varieties of Realism* (Oxford: Oxford University Press, 1986), pp. 85–95.

25. Karin Knorr-Cetina, *The Manufacture of Knowledge* (Oxford: Pergamon Press, 1981), pp. 7–8; Derek Phillips, "Epistemology and the Sociology of Knowledge: The Contribution of Mannheim, Mills, and Merton," *Theory and Society* 1 (1974): 59–88.

26. Ian I. Mitroff, *The Subjective Side of Science* (New York and Amsterdam: Elsevier, 1974); also "Norms and Counter-Norms in a Select Group of the Apollo Moon Scientists: A Case Study in the Ambivalence of Scientists," *American Sociological Review* 39 (1974): 579–95; Nigel Gilbert and Michael Mulkay, *Opening Pandora's Box: A Sociological Analysis of Scientists' Discourse* (Cambridge: Cambridge University Press, 1983); Bruno Latour and Steven Woolgar, *Laboratory Life: The Social Construction of Scientific Facts* (Beverly Hills and London: Sage Publications, 1979); H. N. Collins, "Son of Seven Sexes: The Social Destruction of a Physical Phenomenon," *Social Studies of Science* 11 (1981): 33–62; also "The Replication of Experiments in Physics," in Barry Barnes and David Edge, eds., *Science in Context: Readings in the Sociology of Science* (Cambridge, Mass.: MIT Press, 1982), pp. 94–116.

27. H. M. Collins and T. J. Pinch, "The Construction of the Paranormal: Nothing Unscientific Is Happening," in Roy Wallis, ed., *On the Margins of Science: The Social Construction of Rejected Knowledge* Sociological Review Monograph 27 ([Keele, Eng.]: University of Keele, 1979), pp. 237–70.

28. David Travis, "On the Construction of Creativity: The 'Memory Transfer' Phenomenon and the Importance of Being Earnest," in Karin Knorr, Roger Krohn, and Richard Whitley, eds., *The Social Process of Scientific Investigation* (Dordrecht: Reidel, 1981), pp. 165–96.

29. J. M. Ziman, *Public Knowledge* (Cambridge: Cambridge University Press, 1968).

30. Harry N. Collins and Trevor Pinch, *Frames of Meaning: The Social Construction of Extraordinary Science* (London: Routledge & Kegan Paul, 1982), pp. 154–67.

31. Warren O. Hagstrom, *The Scientific Community* (New York: Basic Books, 1965), pp. 279–81.

32. Bertrand Russell, *The Impact of Science on Society* (London: Allen & Unwin, 1952), p. 110; cited from Michael Polanyi, "The Potential Theory of Adsorption," *Science* 141 (1963): 1013, with strong dissent.

33. M. D. King, "Reason, Tradition, and the Progressiveness of Science," *History and Theory* 10 (1971): 3–32.

34. So Michael Mulkay: "the sociological notion of 'universalism' presupposes that technical criteria are generally available in science, in such a way that firm, impersonal judgments can be made with respect to most knowledge-claims and, thereby, with respect to the rewards and facilities which scientists deserve." *Science and the Sociology of Knowledge* (London: George Allen & Unwin, 1979), p. 65.

35. It should perhaps be noted that scientific articles and proposals are often *not* refereed anonymously, and that scientists seek personal knowledge and contact with colleagues and competitors as well as the most authoritative people in their field. They may not know who's out there reading them very exactly when they begin to publish their work, but they try to find out as much as they can as soon as possible. See also on this point Karin Knorr-Cetina, *The Manufacture of Knowledge* (Oxford: Pergamon,

1981), pp. 7–8, 28n28; Michael Mulkay calls attention to the work of Zuckerman and Merton on the greater weight and consideration given to papers by known scientists; see Mulkay, "Some Aspects of Cultural Growth in the Natural Sciences," *Social Research* 36 (1969): 22–52.

36. A. C. Cournand and Harriet Zuckerman, "The Code of Science: Analysis and Some Reflections on Its Failure," *Studium Generale* 23 (1971): 950.

37. This appears as the core of canon 2 of Text as set forth in my *Constructing Texts: Toward a Theory of Composition and Style* (Bloomington: Indiana University Press, 1981): "Text expects writers to produce novel, even counterintuitive, facts and viewpoints; cogency and assent are based on logical consistency and evidence; writer and reader enact membership in an imagined community of inquiring minds"—p. 28.

38. Michael Lynch, *Art and Artifact in Laboratory Science* (London: Routledge & Kegan Paul, 1985), p. 272.

39. Bruno Latour and Françoise Bastide, "Writing Science— Fact and Fiction: The Analysis of the Process of Reality Construction Through the Application of Socio-Semiotic Methods to Scientific Texts," in Michel Callon, John Law, and Arie Rip, eds., *Mapping the Dynamics of Science and Technology: Sociology of Science in the Real World* (London: Macmillan, 1986), pp. 51–66.

40. Roger Krohn, "Scientific Ideology and Scientific Process: The Natural History of a Conceptual Shift," in Everett Mendelsohn, Peter Weingart, and Richard Whitley, eds., *The Social Production of Scientific Knowledge* (Dordrecht: Reidel, 1977), pp. 69–102; Harriet Zuckerman, "Deviant Behavior and Social Control in Science," in Edward Sagarin, ed., *Deviance and Social Change* (Beverly Hills: Sage Publications, 1977), pp. 87–138.

41. Another way of squaring the discrepancies outlined above has been to argue that the Mertonian norms were at one time taken to govern all of a scientist's activities with a kind of ivory tower innocence and purity that has been heavily eroded by the forces of Big Science, a product of the vast increase in the numbers of scientists since World War II, the bureaucratization of their activities brought on by funding from central sources, and the marshalling of those activities in the interest of various social objectives, foremost among which is National Defense. Hence emerges an ever-widening gap between the increasingly stylized and antiquated ethos of science—the persona of the scientist—as sketched by Merton and the realities of self-promotion and hustling, political maneuvering and machination. Historians of science, however, can produce many examples suggesting that the Golden Age of science is hard to locate at any time in the past.

42. Lawrence J. Prelli, "The Rhetorical Construction of Scientific Ethos," in Simons, *Rhetoric in the Human Sciences*, pp. 48–68.

3. Irony and Reflexivity

1. Richard Rorty, *The Consequences of Pragmatism* (Minneapolis: University of Minnesota Press, 1982), p. 140.

2. Charles Bazerman, *Shaping Written Knowledge* (Madison: University of Wisconsin Press, 1988), p. 295.

3. P. McHugh, "On the Failure of Positivism," cited from Jürgen Habermas, *TCA*, Vol. I, 126.

4. B. Gillespie, D. Eva, and R. Johnston, "Carcinogenic Risk Assessment in the United States and Great Britain: The Case of Aldrin/Dieldrin," *Social Studies of Science* 9 (1979): 265–301.

5. Jürgen Habermas, "The Problem of Understanding Meaning in the Social Sciences," *TCA*, Vol. I, 102–41.

6. Rev. of *Culture* by James D. Orcutt, *Sociology and Social Research* 67 (1982): 100–101.

7. Joseph Gusfield, "The Literary Rhetoric of Science: Comedy and Pathos in

Drinking-Driver Research," *American Sociological Review* 41 (1976): 16–34; Michael Overington, "A Critical Celebration of Gusfield's 'The Literary Rhetoric of Science,'" *American Sociological Review* 42 (1977): 170–73; cited in John O'Neill, "The Literary Production of Natural and Social Science Inquiry: Issues and Applications in the Social Organization of Science," *Canadian Journal of Sociology* 6 (1982): 105–19; Michael E. Lynch, "Technical Work and Critical Inquiry: Investigations in a Scientific Laboratory," *Social Studies of Science* 12 (1982): 499–533; Michael Mulkay, "What Is the Ultimate Question? Some Remarks in Defense of the Analysis of Scientific Discourse," *Social Studies of Science* 12 (1982): 309–19.

8. Ross Homel, "Young Men in the Arms of the Law: An Australian Perspective on Policing and Punishing the Drinking Driver," *Accident Analysis and Prevention* 15 (1983): 499–512; Helena Z. Lopata, "Social Construction of Social Problems Over Time," *Social Problems* 31 (1984): 249–72; William B. Bankston, Quentin A. L. Jenkins, Cheryl Thayer-Doyle, and Carol Y. Thompson, "Fear of the Drunk Driver: Analysis of an Emergent Social Problem," *Deviant Behavior* 7 (1986): 107–20; Lonn Lanza-Kaduce and Donna M. Bishop, "Legal Fictions and Criminology: The Jurisprudence of Drunk Driving," *Journal of Criminal Law and Criminology* 77 (1986): 358–77; Mark Peyrot, "Cycles of Social Problem Development: The Case of Drug Abuse," *Sociological Quarterly* 25 (1984): 83–96; Nachman Ben-Yehuda, "The Sociology of Moral Panics: Toward a New Synthesis," *Sociological Quarterly* 27 (1986): 495–513.

9. Steve Woolgar and Dorothy Pawluch, "Ontological Gerrymandering: The Anatomy of Social Problems Explanations," *Social Problems* 32 (1985): 214–47.

10. I have discussed this convention in "My Words of An Other," *College English* 50 (1988): 63–73. Social theorists are not the only ones vulnerable to an outbreak of these marks; philosophers, literary theorists, generally anyone who writes about accounts of the real are prone to them. So Michael McCanles scolds Allan Megill for his use of them around the words *ordinary, normal, reality,* and *extant* in his book *Prophets of Extremity: Nietzsche, Heidegger, Foucault, Derrida* (Berkeley: University of California Press, 1985): "On the one hand, Megill would appear to condemn these thinkers in the name of an 'ordinary' philosophical realism that, on the other hand, he can only relegate to the equivocal limbo of quotation marks"—rev. of Megill, *Poetics Today* 8 (1987): 202.

11. Lawrence E. Hazelrigg, "Is There a Choice Between 'Constructivism' and 'Objectivism'?" *Social Problems* 33 (1986): 1–13.

12. In a review of my *Rhetoric as Social Imagination*, Roger D. Sell lists numerous examples where I privilege (gerrymander) my own account as simply the way things are. Some of these examples are disputable, and most could be fixed up by adding quotation marks, but he tellingly cites a point at which I dismiss John Simon's view of good usage as "a simplification of adult life: for once we do not need to remind ourselves of our own limitations, or rein in our aggressive contempt for others with different values" (*RSI*, p. 79). As in the passage from Gusfield, it is the academic intellectual's characterization of what adult life is that speaks. There are plenty of adults who would not take humility and tolerance as essential to adult life. See Roger D. Sell, rev. of *RSI*, *Journal of Pragmatics* 12 (1988): 117–23.

13. Bonnie Steinbock, "Drunk Driving," *Philosophy and Public Affairs* 14 (1985): 293.

14. Julian Waller, "Identification of Problem-Drinking among Drunken Drivers," *JAMA* 200 (1967): 124–30.

15. Stephen Pfohl, "Toward a Sociological Deconstruction of Social Problems," *Social Problems* 32 (1985): 228–32; Gayatri Spivak, Introduction to Jacques Derrida, *Of Grammatology* (Baltimore, Md.: Johns Hopkins University Press, 1974).

16. William L. Tam, "The Symbolic Interactionist 'I' as Ironist: Toward Alternative Worlds," *Symbolic Interaction* 7 (1984): 175–89.

17. Rev. of *Culture* by Robert Reiner, *British Journal of Sociology* 34 (1983): 273–74.

18. See for example the articles in David Couzens Hoy, ed., *Foucault: A Critical Reader* (Oxford and New York: Basil Blackwell, 1986).

19. Rev. of *Culture* by Barry Schwartz in *American Review of Sociology* 88 (1982): 599–602.

20. Karin D. Knorr-Cetina makes almost exactly the same move of placing the Schütz/Garfinkel distinction in question (along with the Mertonian norms, which she argues are very similar to the four or five traits special to scientific theorizing) and then arguing in her account of her laboratory study that "there are no rationalities unique to laboratory action." See *The Manufacture of Knowledge: An Essay on the Constructivist and Contextual Nature of Science* (Oxford: Pergamon Press, 1981), pp. 21–22.

21. J. Paul Peter and Jerry C. Olson, "Is Science Marketing?" *Journal of Marketing* 47 (1983): 111–25; David Rudd, "The Intimidating Bastion of Scientific Knowledge: A Way to Breach the Ramparts," *Studies in Higher Education* 9 (1984): 113–21.

22. Nicholas Tilley, "The Logic of Laboratory Life" (rev. of Latour and Woolgar) *Sociology* 15 (1981): 117–26.

23. Michael Lynch, "Technical Work and Critical Inquiry: Investigations in a Scientific Laboratory," *Social Studies of Science* 12 (1982): 499–533.

24. Alfred Schütz, "The Stranger: An Essay in Social Psychology," *American Journal of Sociology* 49 (1944): 499–507.

25. Renato Rosaldo, "Where Objectivity Lies: The Rhetoric of Anthropology," in John S. Nelson, Allan Megill, and Donald N. McCloskey, eds., *The Rhetoric of the Human Sciences* (Madison: University of Wisconsin Press, 1987), pp. 87–110.

26. Michael Lynch, *Art and Artifact in Laboratory Science* (Routledge & Kegan Paul, 1985).

27. Paul Tibbetts and Patricia Johnson, "The Discourse and *Praxis* Models in Recent Reconstructions of Scientific Knowledge Generation," *Social Studies of Science* 15 (1985): 739–49.

28. Steve Woolgar, "On the Alleged Distinction Between Discourse and *Praxis*," *Social Studies of Science* 16 (1986): 309–17.

29. Richard D. Whitley, "From the Sociology of Scientific Communities to the Study of Scientists' Negotiations and Beyond," *Social Science Information* 22 4/5 (1983): 681–720.

30. Steve Woolgar, "Laboratory Studies: A Comment on the State of the Art," *Social Studies of Science* 12 (1982): 487.

31. Woolgar thus argues that "selective relativism" (in the sense of Woolgar and Pawluch) is being applied even in the "strong programme" of sociology of science.

32. N. C. Mullins, rev. of *Laboratory Life* in *Science, Technology, and Human Values* 30 (1980): 55.

33. Michael Mulkay, "The Scientist Talks Back: A One-Act Play, with a Moral, about Replication in Science and Reflexivity in Sociology," *Social Studies of Science* 14 (1984): 265–82.

34. Harry N. Collins, "An Empirical Relativist Programme in the Sociology of Scientific Knowledge," in Karin Knorr-Cetina and Michael Mulkay, eds., *Science Observed* (Beverly Hills and London: Sage Publications, 1983), pp. 85–115; see also Harry N. Collins and Trevor Pinch, *Frames of Meaning: The Social Construction of Extraordinary Science* (London: Routledge & Kegan Paul, 1982).

35. Ellsworth R. Fuhrman and Kay Oehler, "Discourse Analysis and Reflexivity," *Social Studies of Science* 16 (1986): 301–302.

36. Martin Hollis, "The Social Destruction of Reality," in Martin Hollis and Steven Lukes, eds., *Rationality and Relativism* (Oxford: Blackwell, 1982), pp. 67–86.

37. Graham Wilson, "Make Me Reflexive—But Not Yet: Strategies for Managing

Essential Reflexivity in Ethnographic Discourse," *Journal of Anthropological Research* 43 (1987): 29–41.

38. Steve Woolgar, ed., *Knowledge and Reflexivity* (London: Sage Publications, 1988), p. 168.

39. Steve Woolgar, "Laboratory Studies: A Comment on the State of the Art," *Social Studies of Science* 12 (1982): 488.

40. Steven Shapin, "Talking History: Reflections on Discourse Analysis," *Isis* 75 (1984): 125–28.

41. Jonathan Potter, "Discourse Analysis and the Turn of the Reflexive Screw: A Response to Fuhrman and Oehler," *Social Studies of Science* 17 (1987): 171–77.

42. Fuhrman and Oehler, "DA and Reflexivity," p. 297. This problem is well known in reader response theory, particularly in relation to Wolfgang Iser's theory of consistency building and rebuilding.

43. Steve Woolgar, "Irony in the Social Study of Science," in Knorr-Cetina and Mulkay, *Science Observed*, pp. 263–64n5.

44. *Ketmen* is a wonderful term of Czeslaw Milosz's for the double-mindedness and dual-voicedness developed in countries under tyrannical repression. It is the cultivation of two simultaneous accounts of everything, one which is according to party line and public reality, the other for personal use only among trusted friends.

45. Natural attitude is Melvin Pollner's term. See *Mundane Reasoning* (Cambridge: Cambridge University Press, 1987).

4. Arguments and Appeals

1. Donald N. McCloskey, "The Rhetoric of Economics," *Journal of Economic Literature* 21 (1983): 481–517; *The Rhetoric of Economics* (Madison: University of Wisconsin Press, 1985); Rev. of *Rhetoric of Economics* by Adrian Winnett, *Journal of Economic Psychology* 8 (1987): 109.

2. Bruce J. Caldwell and A. W. Coats, "The Rhetoric of Economists: A Comment on McCloskey," *Journal of Economic Literature* 22 (1984): 575–78; revs. by Joel Mokyr, *Historical Methods* 20 (1987): 126–28; by F. H. Hahn, *Journal of Economic Literature* 25 (1987): 101–104; and by Michael S. McPherson, *Journal of Economic History* 47 (1987): 596–98.

3. Rev. by J. A. Kregel, *Economic Journal* 97 (1987): 278–80.

4. The Rhetoric of Economics," p. 512; *The Rhetoric of Economics*, p. 46.

5. See for example David Edge, "Quantitative Measures of Communication in Science: A Critical Review," *History of Science* 17 (1979): 102–34.

6. Arjo Klamer, "As if Economists and Their Subject Were Rational," in John S. Nelson, Allan Megill, and Donald N. McCloskey, eds., *The Rhetoric of the Human Sciences* (Madison: University of Wisconsin Press, 1987): 163–83.

7. Milton Friedman, "The Methodology of Positive Economics," cited in Klamer, "As if," p. 173.

8. Rev. by Arjo Klamer, *Quarterly Journal of Speech* 72 (1986): 469–72.

9. Jonathan Potter, "Discourse Analysis and the Turn of the Reflexive Screw: A Response to Fuhrman and Oehler," *Social Studies of Science* 17 (1987): 173.

10. Unfortunately for the articulation of these points, Edmondson engages in a running battle with Alfred Schütz; her readings and citations of his essays are uniformly hostile and dismissive, though Schütz read through Garfinkel as we have done might have helped rather than hindered her argument.

11. Chaim Perelman, "The Rational and the Reasonable," in Theodore Geraets, ed., *Rationality Today* (Ottawa: University of Ottawa Press, 1979), p. 215.

12. Joachim Matthes, rev. of *Rhetoric in Sociology, American Journal of Sociology* 92 (1986): 771–73.

13. George E. Marcus, "Contemporary Problems of Ethnography in the Modern

World System," in Clifford and Marcus, eds., *Writing Culture: The Poetics and Politics of Ethnography* (Berkeley, Los Angeles, and London: University of California Press, 1986), pp. 165–93.

14. Arjo Klamer questions the image of harmony McCloskey projects (rev. of McCloskey, p. 471).

15. Clifford Geertz, *Works and Lives: The Anthropologist as Author* (Stanford, Calif.: Stanford University Press, 1988), p. 141.

16. See for example George E. Marcus and Michael M. J. Fischer, *Anthropology as Cultural Critique* (Chicago: University of Chicago Press, 1986), p. x. Dan Sperber, *On Anthropological Knowledge* (Cambridge: Cambridge University Press, 1985), agrees, though he distinguishes between ethnography, which is the interpretive stuff, and anthropology, which aspires to general, nontrivial hypotheses about the variability of human cultures—a science of culture. This distinction is roughly that of description vs. explanation.

17. Clifford Geertz, "Blurred Genres: The Refiguration of Social Thought," *American Scholar* 49 (1980): 165–79.

18. Rev. of *Works and Lives* by Richard A. Shweder, *New York Times Book Review*, Feb. 28, 1988, p. 13.

19. Paul Shankman, "The Thick and the Thin: On the Interpretive Theoretical Program of Clifford Geertz," *Current Anthropology* 25 (1984): 261–70; Shankman's article is followed by fifteen responses by other anthropologists and a response by Shankman; Geertz, as is apparently his custom, declined to reply.

20. James Clifford, cited in Geertz, p. 133.

21. *Local Knowledge,* 1983, cited in Shankman, p. 278.

22. Jürgen Habermas, "Theories of Truth," cited in Brant R. Burleson, "On the Foundations of Rationality: Toulmin, Habermas, and the *a priori* of Reason," *Journal of the American Forensic Society* 16 (1979): 112–27.

23. Stephen Toulmin, *Human Understanding* (Cambridge: Cambridge University Press, 1972).

24. Steven E. Rhoads, rev. of McCloskey, *American Political Science Review* 81 (1987): 338–39.

5. Dialogues with the Dead

1. See for example the remarks by Louis O. Mink, "The Autonomy of Historical Understanding," *History and Theory* 5 (1966): 24–28, and, considerably later, Hans Gellner, "White's Linguistic Humanism," *History and Theory* Beiheft 19 (1980): 9–11.

2. J. H. Hexter, "Historiography" in *International Encyclopedia of the Social Sciences* (New York: Macmillan, 1968); *Doing History* (Bloomington: Indiana University Press, 1971); *The History Primer* (New York: Basic Books, 1971).

3. Denys Hay, rev. of *Primer* and *Doing History* in *History* 60 (1975): 81.

4. Carl Hempel, "The Function of General Laws in History," *Journal of Philosophy* 39 (1942): 47.

5. W. H. Dray, "J. H. Hexter and the Microrhetoric of History," *Clio* 15 (1986): 259–75.

6. Frederic Jameson, "Figural Relativism, or The Poetics of Historiography," rev. of *Metahistory, Diacritics* 6 (1976): 2–9; Dominick LaCapra, "A Poetics of Historiography: Hayden White's *Tropics of Discourse,*" *Modern Language Notes* 93 (1978), reprinted in *Rethinking Intellectual History* (Ithaca, N.Y.: Cornell University Press, 1983).

7. Michael Ermarth, rev. of *Metahistory* in *American Historical Review* 80 (1975): 961–63.

8. Eugene O. Golub, "The Irony of Nihilism," *History and Theory* Beiheft 19 (1980): 62.

9. Maurice Mandelbaum, "The Presuppositions of *Metahistory,*" *History and Theory* Beiheft 19 (1980): 51.

10. David Carroll, "On Tropology: The Forms of History," Response, rev. of *Metahistory, Diacritics* 6 (1976): 58–64.

11. Peter De Bolla, rev. of articles by White, books by Dominick LaCapra, in *Diacritics* 16 (1986): 49–58.

6. Conversation, Dialectic, and the Question of Closure

1. David Lodge, "After Bakhtin," in Nigel Fabb, Derek Attridge, Alan Durant, and Colin MacCabe, eds., *The Linguistics of Writing: Arguments Between Language and Literature* (New York: Methuen, 1987), pp. 95–96.

2. W. Ross Winterowd, "Post-Structuralism and Composition," *Pre/text* 4 (1983): 86–87.

3. Stephen Toulmin, *Human Understanding* (Cambridge: Cambridge University Press, 1972).

4. Douglas Park, "The Meanings of 'Audience' " *College English* 44 (1982): 253.

5. Daniel J. O'Keefe, "The Concepts of Argument and Arguing," in J. Robert Cox and Charles Arthur Willard, eds., *Advances in Argumentation Theory and Research* (Carbondale: Southern Illinois University Press, 1982), p. 9.

6. Michael Billig, *Arguing and Thinking: A Rhetorical Approach to Social Psychology* (Cambridge: Cambridge University Press, 1987).

7. Clifford Geertz touches on this property of commonsense understanding as well in "Common Sense as a Cultural System," in *Local Knowledge* (New York: Basic Books, 1983), pp. 73–93. He calls it "immethodicalness" (p. 90), one of the five "quasi-qualities" of commonsense. The others are naturalness, practicalness, thinness, and accessibleness. J. H. Hexter, defending commonsense as not seriously contradictory, gives the oft-cited pair "Look before you leap" and "He who hesitates is lost." See *The History Primer*, p. 270.

8. Here too Geertz agrees, saying that commonsense cannot be characterized cross-culturally in terms of its content, its logical structure, or its substantive conclusions, but only by evoking its "generally recognized tone and temper" (*Local Knowledge*, p. 92).

9. Harry N. Collins, "An Empirical Relativist Programme in the Sociology of Scientific Knowledge," in Karin D. Knorr-Cetina and Michael Mulkay, eds., *Science Observed: Perspectives on the Social Study of Science* (London: Sage Publications, 1983), pp. 85–114.

10. Herbert W. Simons, rev. of Billig in *Quarterly Journal of Speech* 74 (1988): 262–64.

11. See for example Roy Wallis and Steve Bruce, "Accounting for Action: Defending the Common Sense Heresy," *Sociology* 17 (1983): 97–111; Jack Bilmes chides them for seeming "a little coy" in claiming a "heretical" or marginal status for their widely held views—*Discourse and Behavior* (New York: Plenum, 1986), p. 188.

12. Philip Pettit, "Rational Man Theory," in Christopher Hookway and Philip Pettit, eds., *Action and Interpretation: Studies in the Philosophy of the Social Sciences* (Cambridge: Cambridge University Press, 1978), pp. 43–64.

13. See Greg Myers, "Persuasion, Power, and the Conversational Model" (rev. of Billig, Nelson et al., and Brian Vickers, *In Defense of Rhetoric*), *Economy and Society* 18 (1989): 231.

14. Stephen Reicher, rev. of Billig, *British Journal of Social Psychology* 27 (1988): 283–88.

15. For readers unfamiliar with the kudzu vine, it is essential to know that it is an extremely vigorous leguminous vine introduced into the USA from Japan as a groundcover. In the Southern states, it has escaped cultivation and poses a greater threat to Western civilization than Honda and Nissan combined; for gardeners, it resembles

the common bindweed *(Convolvulus)* the way a boa constrictor resembles a garden snake.

16. Richard Rorty, "Philosophy as a Kind of Writing: An Essay on Derrida," in *Consequences of Pragmatism*, p. 106; *Philosophy and the Mirror of Nature*, p. 320.

17. Jonathan Lieberson, rev. of *PMN, Philosophy of Science* 47 (1980): 657–59.

18. David R. Hiley, rev. of *PMN, International Philosophical Quarterly* 20 (1980): 363–66.

19. Alvin I. Goldman, rev. of *PMN, The Philosophical Review* 90 (1981): 424–29.

20. Alexander Nehamas, "Can We Ever Quite Change the Subject?: Richard Rorty on Science, Literature, Culture, and the Future of Philosophy," *Boundary Two* 10 (1982): 395–413.

21. Robert Hollinger, rev. of *PMN, Journal of Value Inquiry* 16 (1982): 162.

22. Leon Pompa, rev. of *PMN, Inquiry* 24 (1981): 359–73.

23. Robert Schwartz, rev. of *PMN, Journal of Philosophy* 80 (1983): 51–67.

24. Anthony Palmer, rev. of *PMN, Mind* 92 (1983): 446–48.

25. Harry Ruja, rev. of *PMN, Philosophy and Phenomenological Research* 42 (1981): 299–300.

26. Raimond Gaita, rev. of *PMN, Philosophy* 56 (1981): 427–29.

27. Richard J. Bernstein, *Beyond Objectivism and Relativism* (Philadelphia: University of Pennsylvania Press, 1983), p. 202. For a more extended examination of Rorty's mode of "arguing," see Bernstein, "Philosophy in the Conversation of Mankind," *Review of Metaphysics* 33 (1980): 745–76.

28. Compare Rorty's own argument that Derrida is not a philosopher of language, though he does have a constructive "bad side"—"Philosophy as a Kind of Writing: An Essay on Derrida," *CP*, pp. 90–109.

29. Richard J. Donovan, rev. of *PMN, Man and World* 14 (1981): 349–53.

30. Victoria Choy, rev. of *PMN, Synthèse* 52 (1982): 515–41.

31. Richard Rorty, "Pragmatism, Relativism, Irrationalism," in *Consequences*, p. 172.

32. Joseph W. Wenzel, "Jürgen Habermas and the Dialectical Perspective on Argumentation," *Journal of the American Forensic Association* 16 (1979): 83–94; Brant R. Burleson, "On the Foundations of Rationality: Toulmin, Habermas, and the *a priori* of Reason," *JAFA* 16 (1979): 112–27; Joseph W. Wenzel, "Perspectives on Argument," Malcolm Sillars, ed., *Proceedings of the First SCA/AFA Conference on Argumentation* (SCA, 1980); Jürgen Habermas, *TCA*, Vol. I, pp. 25–26.

33. David Bartholomae, "Inventing the University," in Mike Rose, ed., *When a Writer Can't Write* (New York: Guilford Press, 1985), pp. 134–65.

34. Patricia Bizzell, "College Composition: Initiation into the Academic Discourse Community," *Curriculum Inquiry* 12 (1982): 191–207.

35. Janice M. Lauer, Gene Montagu, Andrea Lunsford, and Janet Emig, *Four Worlds of Writing* (New York: Harper & Row, 1981); cited from Bizzell, p. 109.

36. Elaine Maimon, Gerald L. Belcher, Gail W. Hearn, Barbara F. Nodine, and Finbarr W. O'Connor, *Writing in the Arts and Sciences* (Cambridge, Mass.: Winthrop, 1981); cited in Bizzell, p. 203.

37. Joe Harris, "The Idea of Community in the Study of Writing," *College Composition and Communication* 40 (1989): 11–22; Kurt Spellmeyer, "A Common Ground: The Essay in the Academy," *College English* 51 (1989): 262–76.

38. James A. Berlin, *Rhetoric and Reality: Writing Instruction in American Colleges, 1900–1985* (Carbondale: Southern Illinois University Press, 1987).

INDEX

Maimon, Elaine 3, 147
Maimon et al. 148
Mandelbaum, Maurice 120
Marcus, George 102
Marshall, John C. 55
Matthes, Joachim 102
McCloskey, Donald 31, 89ff., 141
McGee, Michael Calvin and John R. Lyne 10, 28, 97
McHugh, Peter 67
McPherson, Michael 91
Merton, Robert 38, 53ff.
metaphors 97, 134
methodology 24, 90ff.
Michaels, Walter Benn 8
Mink, Louis 115
Mitroff, Ian 61
Mulkay, Michael 24, 59, 79

Nehamas, Alexander 141, 144
Nelson, John S. 7
Newton-Smith, W. H. 21f.
Nietzsche, Friederick 72, 124, 139
Nystrand, Martin et al. 46

O'Keefe, Daniel 133
Olson, David 28, 44ff., 61, 97, 151
ontological gerrymandering 70
outsider (stranger) 11, 66, 68, 76, 88, 111, 142f.

Palmer, Anthony 142
Park, Douglas 132
Parsons, Talcott 22, 26, 54
Pateman, Trevor 23
Perelman, Chaim 21, 29, 101
Perelman, Chaim and Lucie Olbrechts- Tyteca 10, 12, 38, 89, 96, 110, 132, 135
Pettit, Philip 137
Pfohl, Stephen 72
Phillips, Derek 55
phronesis 21, 29, 29, 37, 100, 115
Plato 145
Polanyi, Michael 25, 91
Pompa, Leon 141
Potter, Jonathan 83, 99
Pratt, Mary Louise 23
Prelli, Lawrence 60f.

presence 38, 44, 97, 116
Protagoras 134

Quintilian's Law 134f.

repertoires 81, 109
rhetorical induction 98, 110
Rhoads, Steven 109
Rorty, Richard 65, 73, 138ff.
Rosaldo, Renato 77
Ruja, Harry 142
Russell, Bertrand 58
Ryan, Michael 3, 35

Schütz, Alfred 8, 26ff., 50, 149
Schwartz, Barry 74
Schwartz, Robert 142
Shankman, Paul 105f., 108
Shapin, Steven 83
Simons, Herbert 137
Sorabji, Richard 29
Spellmeyer, Kurt 151ff.
Spivak, Gayatri 72
Szasz, Thomas 56f.

Tam, William 70, 73
Text 28, 44ff., 51, 109, 115f., 132, 149
Tibbetts, Paul and Patricia Johnson 77
Tilley, Nicholas 76
Toulmin, Stephen 108
Travis, David 56

Wallis, Roy and Steve Bruce 137
Warnke, Georgia 30
Weber, Max 36
Wenzel, Joseph 145, 157
White, Hayden 118ff.
White, James Boyd 13
Whitley, Richard 78
Wiggins, David 29
Wilson, Graham 80
Winnett, Adrian 94
Winterowd, W. Ross 129
Woolgar, Steve 79, 84
Woolgar, Steve and Dorothy Pawluch 70f.

Ziman, J. M. 25, 56f.
Zuckerman, Harriet 60f.

GEORGE L. DILLON is Professor of English at the University of Washington. He has published books on semantics, literary language, composition theory, and the rhetoric of advice writing. He is author of *Constructing Texts: Elements of a Theory of Composition and Style, Language Processing and the Reading of Literature: Toward a Model of Comprehension,* and *Rhetoric as Social Imagination: Explorations in the Interpersonal Function of Language.*

DATE DUE

GAYLORD

PRINTED IN U.S.A.